Oliver Wendell Holmes

Oliver Wendell Holmes was one of the most influential figures in American law. As a Supreme Court justice, he wrote foundational opinions about such important constitutional issues as freedom of speech and the limits of state regulatory power. As a scholar and Massachusetts High Court judge, he helped to reshape the common law for the modern industrial era. And yet, despite the many accounts of his career, Holmes himself remains an enigma. This book is the first to explore the nineteenth-century New England influences so crucial to the formation of his character. Inspired by Ralph Waldo Emerson's Transcendentalism, Holmes belonged to a group of men who formulated a philosophy known as American pragmatism that stood as an alternative to English empiricism and German rationalism.

This innovative study places Holmes within the Transcendentalist, pragmatist tradition and thereby unlocks his unique identity and contribution to American law. Wells's nuanced analysis will appeal to legal scholars, historians, philosophers, and general readers alike.

Catharine Pierce Wells is a professor of law at Boston College Law School. Wells has published more than thirty articles, with a focus in the fields of tort law and American jurisprudence.

Cambridge Historical Studies in American Law and Society

Recognizing legal history's growing importance and influence, the goal of this series is to chart legal history's continuing development by publishing innovative scholarship across the discipline's broadening range of perspectives and subjects. It encourages empirically creative works that take legal history into unexplored subject areas, or that fundamentally revise our thinking about familiar topics; it also encourages methodologically innovative works that bring new disciplinary perspectives and techniques to the historical analysis of legal subjects.

Series Editor

Christopher Tomlins, *University of California, Berkeley*

Previously Published in the Series

William Kuby, *Conjugal Misconduct: Defying Marriage Law in the Twentieth-Century United States*

Justin Desautels-Stein, *The Jurisprudence of Style: A Structuralist History of American Pragmatism and Liberal Legal Thought*

Angela Fernandez, *Pierson v. Post, the Hunt for the Fox: Law and Professionalization in American Legal Culture*

Rebecca E. Zietlow, *The Forgotten Emancipator: James Mitchell Ashley and the Ideological Origins of Reconstruction*

Robert Daniel Rubin, *Judicial Review and American Conservatism: Christianity, Public Education, and the Federal Courts in the Reagan Era*

Matthew Crow, *Thomas Jefferson, Legal History, and the Art of Recollection*

Oren Bracha, *Owning Ideas: The Intellectual Origins of American Intellectual Property, 1790–1909*

Anne Twitty, *Before Dred Scott: Slavery and Legal Culture in the American Confluence, 1787–1857*

Leia Castañeda Anastacio, *The Foundations of the Modern Philippine State: Imperial Rule and the American Constitutional Tradition in the Philippine Islands, 1898–1935*

Robert Deal, *The Law of the Whale Hunt: Dispute Resolution, Property Law, and American Whalers, 1780–1880*

Sandra F. Vanburkleo, *Gender Remade: Citizenship, Suffrage, and Public Power in the New Northwest, 1879–1912*

Reuel Schiller, *Forging Rivals: Race, Class, Law, and the Collapse of Postwar Liberalism*

Ely Aaronson, *From Slave Abuse to Hate Crime: The Criminalization of Racial Violence in American History*

Stuart Chinn, *Recalibrating Reform: The Limits of Political Change*

Oliver Wendell Holmes

A Willing Servant to an Unknown God

CATHARINE PIERCE WELLS

Boston College

CAMBRIDGE
UNIVERSITY PRESS

CAMBRIDGE
UNIVERSITY PRESS

University Printing House, Cambridge CB2 8BS, United Kingdom

One Liberty Plaza, 20th Floor, New York, NY 10006, USA

477 Williamstown Road, Port Melbourne, VIC 3207, Australia

314–321, 3rd Floor, Plot 3, Splendor Forum, Jasola District Centre,
New Delhi – 110025, India

79 Anson Road, #06–04/06, Singapore 079906

Cambridge University Press is part of the University of Cambridge.

It furthers the University's mission by disseminating knowledge in the pursuit of
education, learning, and research at the highest international levels of excellence.

www.cambridge.org
Information on this title: www.cambridge.org/9781108475952
DOI: 10.1017/9781108686839

First published 2020

Printed in the United Kingdom by TJ International Ltd, Padstow Cornwall

A catalogue record for this publication is available from the British Library.

Library of Congress Cataloging-in-Publication Data
NAMES: Wells, Catharine Pierce, author.
TITLE: Oliver Wendell Holmes : a willing servant to an unknown God / Catharine
Pierce Wells, Boston College, Massachusetts.
DESCRIPTION: Cambridge, United Kingdom ; New York, NY, USA : Cambridge
University Press, 2020. I Series: Cambridge Historical Studies in American Law and
Society I Includes index.
IDENTIFIERS: LCCN 2019027922 (print) I LCCN 2019027923 (ebook) I ISBN
9781108475952 (hardback) I ISBN 9781108686839 (epub)
SUBJECTS: LCSH: Holmes, Oliver Wendell, Jr., 1841–1935 – Philosophy. I
Pragmatism.
CLASSIFICATION: LCC KF8745.H6 W45 2020 (print) I LCC KF8745.H6 (ebook) I DDC
347.73/2634 [B] – dc23
LC record available at https://lccn.loc.gov/2019027922
LC ebook record available at https://lccn.loc.gov/2019027923

ISBN 978-1-108-47595-2 Hardback

For Ruth Anna Putnam
Teacher and Friend

Contents

Acknowledgments

Many people have helped in the preparation of this book, and I am grateful to them all. Special thanks are due to people who read and commented on earlier drafts. So, thank you to Jim Repetti, Frank Garcia, Thomas Healy, Stephanie Wildman, and Michael Tobriner. Three readers were patient enough to read many iterations, and I owe them a deep debt of gratitude: Leslie Espinoza Garvey, Carole O'Blenes, and Marion Fremont-Smith. My current research assistant, Phillip Popkin, has played a vital role in cite checking and assembling the manuscript. Finally, I am especially grateful to Dean Vincent Rougeau and Boston College Law School for giving me release time to work on the project.

Parts of Chapters 2 and 3 were previously published in the *Journal of Supreme Court History*. These parts are included here with its permission.

The pictures that appear between Part 1 and Part 2 are courtesy of the Massachusetts Historical Society and are reproduced with their permission.

Introduction

Born and bred on Beacon Hill during the height of the American Renaissance, Oliver Wendell Holmes was one of the most interesting men of his era. At twenty, he enlisted in the Union Army, where he survived three serious wounds and a nearly fatal bout of dysentery. Returning home, he began a legal career that spanned seventy years and included service as a practicing lawyer, a legal scholar, and a law professor. He spent fifty years on the bench, moving from the Massachusetts Supreme Judicial Court to the Supreme Court of the United States. Since his death in 1935, his legacy has been the subject of hundreds of books and scholarly papers. Many of these offer important insights, but, taken as a whole, they convey an image of Holmes that is more like a Rorschach inkblot than a real man of flesh and blood. In this book, I try to recreate the man by exploring the historical circumstances that formed him and his own unique response to those circumstances.

It is no exaggeration to say that Holmes is the preeminent voice of American law. There are many reasons for this. First, there was the longevity of his career. Second, there was the fact that his tenure on the bench was extremely well timed. When he served on the Massachusetts court, it was a leader in reshaping the common law to meet the needs of the industrial age; and when he arrived at the US Supreme Court, it was the beginning of the Progressive Era when new forms of regulation posed challenges of interpretation and constitutional adjudication. Nor was his influence simply the result of his judicial opinions. He also wrote two of the classics of American jurisprudence. In *The Common Law* (1881), Holmes traced the development of the common law from ancient times to the present day. In doing so, he made a distinctive statement about the nature of law. His second contribution to legal theory – "The Path of the Law" (1898) – was in the form of a speech to Boston University law students. The speech is notable both for its analysis of law and for the wise counsel it has given to generations of law students.

But Holmes is not just known for his professional accomplishments – his private life has been a subject of continuing interest. He came from an illustrious family – his father was famous, both as a poet (a friend of Longfellow and Emerson with whom he founded the *Atlantic Monthly*) and as a medical educator (he was one of the moving spirits behind Harvard Medical School, serving on its faculty and then as its dean). Holmes, the son, received public notice as a hero of the Civil War. Later, when he served on the Supreme Court, he was well known for his quotable opinions and his striking appearance. He was exceptionally tall, stood very straight, had thick white hair, and sported a military mustache. He was an imposing figure who captured the public imagination as he became the subject of countless books, a general release motion picture, and even a Broadway show. By the time of his death, he had achieved a measure of fame greater than most presidents.

For Holmes, the price of celebrity has been high. Celebrities are not just people who are famous; they are the shared images of our public life. Since his death, Holmes's persona has survived many such incarnations. At first, he was the "Yankee from Olympus," standing for the triumph of old-fashioned American values over the creeping mediocrity of the industrial age. Dozens of books sang his praises, portraying him as a seasoned jurist who represented the law's ability to be both flexible and fair.

All this changed, however, with the Second World War. After the war, there were some who thought that Holmes's pragmatism was tainted, finding it incompatible with the high ideals they had fought to defend. And the Cold War provoked a similar reaction. American values faced off in an ideological struggle with godless communism, and, in this context, Holmes's blunt skepticism seemed like an embarrassment.

With the end of the Cold War, one might have expected that Holmes's reputation would be restored, but a third image emerged. Influenced by the American misadventure in Vietnam, a new set of scholars found Holmes's love of war pathological and unacceptable. Like their 1950s counterparts, these writers believed that Holmes was a poor – even dangerous – role model. They thought that he, like so many war veterans, had been psychologically damaged by military service. They painted him as cold and distant; they argued that he was handicapped as a judge due to his inability to empathize with others. But not everyone agreed. Holmes still has many admirers who think of him as a fitting ideal for American law.

What, then, is Holmes's story and why have so many found it compelling? To tell Holmes's story is not an easy task. Amidst all the controversy, it is hard to find the man of flesh and blood whose real life became the repository for so much ambivalence. Holmes was a private person. Like many New Englanders, he was reticent to speak about what was most personal to him. He would occasionally – and somewhat coyly – hint at it. Sometimes, we can hear it when he talks about the Civil War – hence, we have "The Soldier's Faith" and other intensely personal speeches. But the heart of his philosophy – the part that involved "great questions of right and wrong" and "the relations of man to God" – remained unexpressed. Thus, we cannot understand Holmes simply by reading his words. To understand the words, we must try to understand the man who spoke them.

For this reason, this book is divided into two parts. In Part I, I explore Holmes's early life and influences. In Part II, I consider his intellectual development and his mature writings, including some of his legal opinions. The conclusion I reach is that Holmes's personal philosophy rested on three main pillars. The first was pragmatism. Pragmatism fueled his intellectual humility, reminding him that there is no privileged access to the truth. The second pillar was his commitment to empirical science. Holmes believed in the scientific method, and had an enduring interest in applying it to the study of law. The third pillar came from Emerson, whose Transcendentalism inspired him to live what Emerson had described as a life that was "secretly beautiful."[1]

This project has been complicated by the fact that even a superficial reading of Holmes's words suggests two very different attitudes that underlie his work. On one hand, Holmes was reductionist – law is reduced to power, knowledge to belief, etc. Note, for example, the way in which he debunks the concept of natural law:

The jurists who believe in natural law seem to me to be in that naïve state of mind that accepts what has been familiar ... as something that must be accepted by all men everywhere.[2]

Rejecting this, Holmes identifies law with the power to punish, finding the foundation of law in the fact that his fellow citizens "tell me that I must

---

[1] Ralph Waldo Emerson, *The Young American* (Feb. 7, 1844).
[2] Oliver Wendell Holmes Jr., *Natural Law*, 32 Harvard Law Review 40, 41 (1918).

do and abstain from doing various things or they will put the screws to me." The clear implication is that Holmes believes that law is a way of decision-making that is shaped by instinct and custom, and that its power is enhanced by the seeming inevitably of thinking as we always do. Thus, Holmes's reductionism leads him to equate law with power, and the demand for justice with the very same instinct that makes "a dog fight for its bone."

On the other hand, Holmes had a speculative reach that seemed to find hidden meanings, glimmers, and echoes of the divine in every aspect of human experience. It is not incidental that he would sometimes refer to the Universe (with a capital U) or Law (with a capital L). Note, for example, how he closes *The Path of the Law* with the suggestion that law is a path to mystical insight:

The remoter and more general aspects of the law are those which give it universal interest. It is through them that you not only become a great master in your calling, but connect your subject with the universe and catch an echo of the infinite, a glimpse of its unfathomable process, a hint of the universal law.[3]

Does this suggestion return him to the realm of natural law? And if so, we are left to wonder: Where is the dog? Where is the bone?

This duality was no mere ambivalence about law. In fact, we see something similar when he talks about truth and the meaning of experience. For example, here is the reductionist account:

When I say that a thing is true, I mean that I cannot help believing it. I am stating an experience as to which there is no choice. But as there are many things that I cannot help doing that the universe can, I do not venture to assume that my inabilities in the way of thought are inabilities of the universe. I therefore define the truth as the system of my limitations and leave absolute truth for those who are better equipped.[4]

And here is Holmes, the mystic, suggesting truth rises from life in the same way that a mist rises from a swamp.

Life is a roar of bargain and battle, but in the very heart of it there rises a mystic spiritual tone that gives meaning to the whole. It transmutes the dull details into romance. It reminds us that our only but wholly adequate significance is as parts of the unimaginable whole. It suggests that even while we think that we are egotists we are living to ends outside ourselves.

---

[3] Oliver Wendell Holmes Jr., *The Path of the Law*, 10 Harvard Law Review 457, 478 (1897).
[4] Oliver Wendell Holmes Jr., *Ideals and Doubts*, 10 Illinois Law Review 1, 2 (1915).

Can Holmes be both a mystic and a skeptic? If he can learn the secrets of life by listening to a "mystical spiritual tone," then why is he so skeptical about man's ability to know "absolute truth"?

This duality presents a special problem for understanding Holmes. Was Holmes just pontificating with no particular desire to be consistent? If not, which voice should we credit as serious? Or, in the alternative, how can these voices be reconciled? The answers are not obvious.

To address these questions, I look to Holmes's pragmatism. Pragmatism is a distinctly American philosophy that was first articulated by men such as Charles Peirce, William James, and – yes – Oliver Wendell Holmes. The key to understanding pragmatism is to recognize that it mandates a different way of thinking about objectivity and subjectivity.

Influenced by British empiricism, we are led to think of these terms in the context of a particular epistemology. Central to this view is the claim that all objective knowledge originates from one of the five senses. For example, if I say that the rose is red, I am reporting the result of an empirical observation. Since this is based on visual input, we treat it as information about an external object and therefore classify it as objective. On the other hand, my judgment about the beauty of the rose is not merely the product of sight. It reports something about me, the speaking subject. It says, in effect: I have an emotional response to the rose that flows from the nature of my subjective self. Therefore, we treat judgments about beauty as subjective. This way of analyzing knowledge leads to a distinction between facts and values. Facts are statements about the world. They are objective because they report information from the five senses. Values, on the other hand, report something about the observing subject and are therefore subjective. And this way of putting it has the additional virtue of explaining why it is that we easily come to an agreement about matters of fact but are not able to do so in assessing value.

The pragmatists turn all of this on its head. For reasons that I explain in Chapter 5, they begin with the idea that something is objectively true if it becomes the object of consensus. Subjective things, on the other hand, are those about which we often disagree. In embracing this idea, the pragmatists do two things. First, they remove the privileged status of sense data as the determinant of objective truth. Second, they confer new importance on things that are subjective. The traditional empiricist might say: In knowing that the rose is red, I know the objective truth, but when I hear you say the Rose is beautiful, all I learn is a relatively transitory fact about you. The pragmatist, on the other hand, believes that the "subjective" realm contains the answer to life's most important questions.

When we put Holmes's views in the context of his pragmatism, the contradiction between the two sets of statements seems less troublesome. The first (law is power; truth is the irresistibility of an idea) statements belong in the objective realm. The truth behind these claims stems from the fact that all matters of personal disagreement have been swept away. As Holmes might say, they have been washed with a cynical acid. The notion of the law as power is true whether or not you are a member of the community whose moral life has defined it. The second set (law is an echo of the infinite; truth is a mystic spiritual tone) records the subjective. For the British empiricist, such thoughts might be hardly worth mentioning. But for Holmes, the second was even more important than the first. It not only defined the substance of his internal life, it also illuminated his connection to the Universe.

Of course, this emphasis on the subjective was not unique to Holmes. It goes back at least as far as the pre-Socratics, and in modern times, it has been the focus of the Romantic poets and their American counterparts – Emerson and the Transcendentalists. Thus, it is not surprising that Emerson plays such an important role in Holmes's intellectual life.

Emerson was also an empiricist, but his view of experience was more complex than that of the British empiricists. On one level, he thought that experience represented a seemingly material world, but on a different level, he believed that it operated metaphorically, offering multiple layers of insight. Experience, he taught, teaches us how best to accomplish our goals. For example, we learn that a stitch in time saves nine – not just when we are mending, but also when we are building bridges and delivering medical care. On an even deeper level, experience becomes a metaphor for life itself as we watch a stream flow or the sun rise. As Emerson put it:

Have mountains, and waves, and skies, no significance but what we consciously give them, when we employ them as emblems of our thoughts? The world is emblematic. Parts of speech are metaphors, because the whole of nature is a metaphor of the human mind. The laws of moral nature answer to those of matter as face to face in a glass. .... The axioms of physics translate the laws of ethics. Thus, "the whole is greater than its part"; "reaction is equal to action"; "the smallest weight may be made to lift the greatest, the difference of weight being compensated by time"; and many the like propositions, which have an ethical as well as physical sense.[5]

Looked at in this way, experience yields both practical knowledge and mystical insight. Thus, the two seemingly disparate parts of Holmes's

[5] Ralph Waldo Emerson, *Nature*, 41 (1836).

character are joined together. On one hand, it makes sense for him to speak of law as a "well known profession":

When we study law we are not studying a mystery but a well-known profession. ... The reason why it is a profession, why people will pay lawyers to argue for them or to advise them, is that [p]eople want to know under what circumstances ... they will run the risk of coming [up] against [public force] and hence it becomes a business to find out when this danger is to be feared.[6]

On the other hand, it is also true that we can look at law as "the witness and deposit of our moral lives," and when we look at law this way, it has a deeper meaning.[7] We gain an understanding of human nature and human aspiration. We learn to admire some things and scorn others. We are able to "connect [our subject] with the universe and catch an echo of the infinite."

We can see, therefore, that Holmes's pragmatism and his admiration for Emerson provide us with clues for understanding how to reconcile the apparent inconsistencies in Holmes's philosophy. But this is not a final answer. We have found one way to interpret Holmes, but is it the right way? Is it possible that Holmes believed in a reductionist theory about law and power, and that he viewed the rest as extraneous – a kind of icing on the cake, a bow to nineteenth-century conventions, or an ex post facto attempt to find meaning in an otherwise reduced world? This is not a question that can be answered by citing additional text.

My answer again involves pragmatism, but this time, it is not Holmes's pragmatism, it is my own. As a pragmatist, when I wish to know the meaning of a concept, I look to its practical effects on action. In this case, I look not just to Holmes's words but also to the way he lived his life, how his beliefs translated into habitual responses to common problems. Looking at these, I find the Emersonian explanation compelling. What convinced me were Holmes's actions. During the Civil War, at a time when he was looking for inspiration and courage, he requested and received an autograph from Emerson. He carried it in his breast pocket throughout combat. Furthermore, when the war was over, he worked day and night to master the law, putting in a kind of effort that could not be justified by practical ambition. In fact, he was struggling to find a meaningful life – one that he felt could only be found in "the roar and bargain of battle." His actions spoke louder than his words, and having spoken, they argued for his sincerity.

---

[6] Holmes, *supra* n. 3 at 457.   [7] *Id.*

In framing the issue this way, I am intentionally blurring the line between conventional biography and intellectual history. We all have a need to understand others, but as philosophers have pointed out for centuries, this goal is problematic. While we may form opinions about what others think and believe, there is no way to check our answers. The result is that understanding others is an inherently speculative process. This being so, it is important to have some principles of interpretation. Philosopher W. V. O. Quine, for example, suggests a principle of charity.[8] This principle states that I should interpret others in a way that maximizes the truth of what they are saying. To this, another philosopher has added a principle of coherence, which requires us to assume a logical consistency on the part of the speaker.[9] The result of adhering to these two principles is inevitably an interpretation that is most favorable to the subject – or at least one that maximizes his or her agreement with the views of the interpreter. While I view this as inevitable, others may think that it is an error to engage in this form of interpretation. For this reason, I offer the following external justification for my interpretation of Holmes.

I believe that my reading of Holmes corresponds with the known facts and with the provocative but incomplete statements that he made about his own beliefs. Even more, my interpretation of Holmes has an explanatory power that many of the other interpretations have lacked. The notion that Holmes was psychologically flawed and deeply ambitious goes only so far in explaining his largely successful life. Indeed, such negative assessments leave it a mystery that he achieved such importance not only to American law but also to America's conception of itself. Neither can they explain why he had such an inspirational impact on so many of the men who knew him. My more positive assessment of him at least has this one significant virtue: it explains Holmes in such a way that we can understand why he continues to engage us in useful and meaningful ways.

---

[8] Quine cites the principle of charity as a maxim of translation. He states it thus: "Assertions startlingly false on the face of them are likely to turn on hidden differences of languages." W. V. Quine, *Word and Object* 59 (1960). It may seem odd to the reader that I need a maxim of translation to interpret the words of a man who spoke the same language as I do. It is important to keep in mind, however, that the notion of "the same language as" is itself problematic. Quine argued that this is the best we can do when we engage in what he calls "radical translation." I leave to another time the question of whether this includes a simple attempt to understand the views of another person.

[9] The principle of coherence assumes the maximum logical consistency in the mind of the speaker. See Donald Davidson, *Three Varieties of Knowledge*, in Donald Davidson, *Subjective, Intersubjective, Objective* 211 (2001).

PART I

THE SOLDIER'S FAITH

PROLOGUE

Memorial Day, 1884

Keene, New Hampshire, is one of those picturesque towns that seems to embody all that is appealing about rural New England. The main street runs into the town square, where a small, park-like area centers around a soldier's statue. Surrounding the square are all the buildings necessary for small town life. And even now, but for the loss of the horse watering trough, the town looks very much as it did in 1884 when Oliver Wendell Holmes arrived to give the Memorial Day address.

Memorial Day that year had perfect weather – it was clear and sunny but not too hot. Most of the businesses were closed, leaving the town's inhabitants with the day off. The local GAR – the Grand Army of the Republic, a veterans' organization dedicated to preserving the memory of America's harshest war – had used the morning hours to place spring flowers on veterans' graves that were too far from the town center to be included in the day's events. After lunch, the members gathered at their headquarters and began the procession to City Hall. They wore uniforms and were accompanied by a military escort. The hall was crowded; nearly all of the local citizens would participate. It had been twenty years since the Civil War, but the town was determined not to forget the men they had lost.

The ceremony opened with a dirge and a prayer. Next, four young women sang an inspirational hymn; and when they had finished, Oliver Wendell Holmes rose to give the address.[1] Holmes had served with the Massachusetts Twentieth and had been in the thick of combat for three

---

[1] Oliver Wendell Holmes Jr., An Address to the Grand Army of the Republic, John Sedgwick Post No. 4, In Our Youth Our Hearts Were Touched with Fire (May 30, 1884).

long years. At the age of forty-four, he had been recently appointed to the Massachusetts Supreme Judicial Court. His father was Oliver Wendell Holmes Sr., a well-known poet and popular speaker. Wendell was a lawyer, but he had his father's gift for elegant phrase-making. His speech that day was barely twenty minutes long, but it was both forceful and profound. Those who listened could not help but be moved. Those who read it in the paper a week later were probably sorry they missed it. And in time, it would become a classic – one of the most quoted Memorial Day speeches ever given.

Holmes's speech was not simply an aimless medley of remembrances; neither was it a collection of platitudes. It was a serious and sincere statement of conviction. In it, he expressed his own understanding about the meaning of life and the place of war in the human experience. Its power lies in the pairing of poignant detail with a spiritual but ecumenical message that seeks to make sense of suffering and sacrifice.

Holmes began with the purpose of Memorial Day:

[I]t celebrates and solemnly reaffirms from year to year a national act of enthusiasm and faith. ... To fight out a war, you must believe something and want something with all your might. So must you do to carry anything else to an end worth reaching. More than that, you must be willing to commit yourself to a course, perhaps a long and hard one, without being able to foresee exactly where you will come out. ... The rest belongs to fate.[2]

In war, then, a soldier must risk everything in the face of unknown odds. He will live or die not through his own efforts, but at the whim of forces beyond his control. Such a wager, if not made recklessly, requires a deep commitment, and, since the odds of success are unknown, the commitment must be to the intrinsic value of heroic action. Such a commitment does not arise on its own; it has to be cultivated:

It is true that I cannot argue a man into a desire. If he says to me, why should I seek to know the secrets of philosophy? Why ... do any great work, either of speculation or of practical affairs? I cannot answer him. ... You must begin by wanting to. But although desire cannot be imparted by argument, it can be by contagion. Feeling begets feeling, and great feeling begets great feeling. We can hardly share the emotions that make this day to us the most sacred day of the year, and embody them in ceremonial pomp, without in some degree imparting them to those who come after us.

[2] *Id.*

Several things are notable about this passage. First, the need for heroism was not limited to military life; it applied equally to civilian life. Indeed, Holmes himself tackled the study of law with much the same attitude that he had brought to battle. Second, we must note the association of heroism with the embrace of "great feeling." Self-discipline alone cannot produce great action. The rigors of high achievement require the motivation that comes with intense desire. Third, Holmes conveys an understanding that "great feelings" are not generated by thought, but by "contagion," and that the ceremonial life of the nation must be crafted in such a way that it cultivates these feelings in each generation.

But, for Holmes, Memorial Day was also a time of remembrance:

As surely as this day comes round we are in the presence of the dead. For one hour, twice a year at least – at the regimental dinner, where the ghosts sit at table more numerous than the living, and on this day when we decorate their graves – the dead come back and live with us. I see them now, more than I can number, as once I saw them on this earth.

And then he proceeded to share the memory of his comrades who had fallen in the war. The first was his cousin Jimmy Lowell:

I see [a] youthful lieutenant as I saw him in the Seven Days, when I looked down the line at Glendale. The officers were at the head of their companies. The advance was beginning. We caught each other's eye and saluted. When next I looked, he was gone.

Another was the company doctor:

I see one – grandson of a hard rider of the Revolution and bearer of his historic name[3] – He fell at Gettysburg ... [and another] ... his brother, a surgeon, who rode, as our surgeons so often did, wherever the troops would go, kneeling in ministration to a wounded man just in rear of our line at Antietam, ... the next moment his ministrations were ended.

Another was his friend Henry Abbott:

There is one who on this day is always present on my mind. He entered the army at nineteen, a second lieutenant. ... His few surviving companions will never forget the awful spectacle of his advance alone with his company in the streets of Fredericksburg. In less than sixty seconds he would become the focus of a hidden and annihilating fire from a semicircle of houses. His first platoon had vanished under it in an instant, ten men falling dead by his side. He had quietly

---

[3] He is speaking of Colonel Paul Revere and surgeon Edward H. R. Revere, grandsons of Paul Revere, the midnight rider who warned of the British attack on Lexington and Concord.

turned back to where the other half of his company was waiting, had given the order, "Second Platoon, forward!" and was again moving on, in obedience to superior command, to certain and useless death, when the order he was obeying was countermanded.[4]

Holmes offers these memories not as individual portraits of particular men, but as illustrations of the type of men lost in the war. He thought that the existence of such men carried a very particular message:

There is upon their faces the shadow of approaching fate, and the glory of generous acceptance of it. ... We who have seen these men ... know that life may still be lifted into poetry and lit with spiritual charm.

Thus, the message of this text is clear. Whether you are a civilian or a soldier, you must approach life with "great enthusiasm and faith." Not knowing in advance what the result of action will be, you should choose the hero's path and push forward with complete devotion in every step. In this spirit, Holmes transformed the suffering and grief of war into the recognition that he and his comrades had received an important gift.

Through our great good fortune, in our youth our hearts were touched with fire. It was given to us to learn at the outset that life is a profound and passionate thing. While we are permitted to scorn nothing but indifference, and do not pretend to undervalue the worldly rewards of ambition, we have seen with our own eyes, beyond and above the gold fields, the snowy heights of honor, and it is for us to bear the report to those who come after us.

This is a beautiful speech and one that reveals much about Holmes's character. Holmes was not a man to rest content with material success. As time went on, he would become both successful and famous, but, as satisfying as this was, he would always feel that there was more to achieve. For Holmes, progress could not be measured by outcomes – by battles won or by appointment to high office. Instead, he viewed the meaning of life as a matter of rising to every challenge with bravery and total commitment. There was, he felt, no reason for anguish when action did not produce the desired result. He would not try to second-guess the hand of fate. Indeed, he believed that the Universe had its own plan – one to which he would willingly defer because he desired a life illuminated with a kind of "spiritual charm."

To modern ears, this is a puzzling attitude. We do not readily understand this idea of heroic action. On one hand, we admire heroes and want them as our soldiers. On the other, we often confuse heroism with reckless

---

[4] Interestingly, Holmes himself could not have observed this as he was confined to the hospital and suffering from dysentery.

courage. In moments of danger, we recognize the need to act with intensity, but at the same time, we seldom admit that the outcome is determined by a power much greater than our own. Instead, we are eager to control what we don't understand, hoping this will secure our safety.

This book contains the story of how Holmes applied his philosophy to his own daily life both in war and in peace. It is my hope that this perspective will bring him into clear focus. But, more than that, important contemporary questions are at stake.

Holmes has an attitude toward life that is very different from our own. As to who is right – Holmes or his modern counterparts – the answer is not clear. Characteristically, Holmes himself recognized that he could be wrong; he therefore offered no abstract justification for his point of view. Thus, the only way to decide the question is to compare lives lived in accordance with these two opposite conceptions. We already know the joys and frustrations of modern life. What we need to understand is how Holmes's vision created a way of life different from our own. Did his approach impart meaning to his efforts? Did it result in a life worthy of praise and emulation?

In addition, serious civic questions are at stake. Holmes was probably the most successful judge in American history. What made him so? How did the commitment to heroism impact his professional life? What made him such an icon of American law? If we begin with the commonsense observation that law cannot be separated from the world that surrounds it, the question remains whether law is simply politics or whether there is some meaning to the command that judges decide the case in accordance with the law. It is worrisome that we have become more and more suspicious about this requirement. For example, it seems wrong that judicial appointments have become hotly contested political issues, and it is unfortunate that we are approaching a time when it will be impossible to fill judicial vacancies. These circumstances suggest that we should reconsider whether the chief qualification for high judicial office should be whether the candidate has the "right" political beliefs.

I can think of no better vehicle for such a reexamination than Holmes's career on the bench. Holmes's chief qualifications for the court were his character and integrity as well as his broad and deep understanding of the law. His career reminds us that a judge can be sensitive to nonlegal realities without becoming a mere politician. Thus, as we begin to understand his life and the jurisprudence it spawned, we begin to see a middle way, and perhaps we will obtain a renewed understanding of the importance of law in deciding human disputes.

I

Our Comfortable Routine

Our comfortable routine is no eternal necessity of things, but merely a little space of calm in the midst of the tempestuous untamed streaming of the world.

Memorial Day Speech, 1884

It was Wendell's father, Dr. Holmes, who coined the term "Boston Brahmins" to describe Boston society in the mid-nineteenth century. The name stuck because it was such an apt caricature of the city's elite. Like their Hindu counterparts, the Boston Brahmins were both materially prosperous and spiritually ambitious. Part of their prosperity came from China trade – a commerce that brought with it ideas and culture as well as wealth. These new ideas permeated the religious atmosphere, and many in Boston sought to blend the whirlwind of Calvinism with the gentler spiritual currents of the East.

The Holmes family occupied a central place among the Brahmins. They were "comfortable" but not extremely wealthy. Their ancestors had come to the city during the Great Migration of the 1630s. Many of them had served in positions of political and religious leadership. Most recently, Abiel Holmes, Dr. Holmes's father and Wendell's grandfather, had been the pastor of the First Congregational Church in Cambridge as well as an American historian of some note. Wendell's mother was Amelia Jackson, the daughter of Justice Charles Jackson of the Massachusetts Supreme Judicial Court. Aside from his medical career, Dr. Holmes was a well-known poet and essayist. As a doctor, he popularized the use of the stethoscope, discovered the cause of puerperal fever, and invented the term "anesthetic." He also was one of the founders of Harvard Medical

School, where he served as the Parkman Professor of Anatomy and Physiology. During a brief tenure as dean of the medical school, he tried – but failed – to admit both the first woman and the first African-American to the school. As a poet, he wrote popular and topical verses. With Longfellow and Emerson, he founded the *Atlantic Monthly* and made regular contributions to its pages. He also wrote several novels. The substance of his work was not profound, but, even if it lacked depth, it was clever and popular. As a result of his literary efforts, he was one of the few Bostonians who was famous on both sides of the Atlantic.

Because young Holmes came from such a distinguished family, it is common for biographers to describe the achievements of his ancestors in considerable detail, lingering nostalgically in nineteenth-century Boston with its famous writers and picturesque scenery. While this creates a pleasing picture, it also presents a vision of Holmes that is more mythical than real. Young Wendell becomes the golden son with the world at his feet, the future icon of the American legal system. Or, alternatively, he becomes the offspring of privilege, squandering his legacy on a self-serving pursuit of fame and glory. In either case, Holmes becomes merely a symbol of his own story, a lifeless icon with big ideas and big accomplishments that lack context and meaning.

Throughout his life, young Wendell – Wendy as his family knew him – had a somewhat uneasy relationship with his father. Part of this was the inevitable difficulties that intelligent and ambitious young men have with successful and famous fathers. The son feared living in his father's shadow – so much so that even at age ninety he would survey his own achievements and exclaim wistfully that he wished his father could have lived to see them.

As he grew older, Wendy was often locked in conversational combat with his father. Meals were boisterous with father and eldest son dominating the conversation. Contemporary observers described them both as people who talked too much, but intellectually, they could not have been more dissimilar. The father's conversation would flit from topic to topic – though, in truth, most of his conversation centered on himself. It was his thoughts, his background, and his experiences that seasoned his volubility. One of his friends remembered him saying: "I am intensely interested in my own personality." When he talked about others, the tone was almost always omniscient and judgmental. He was not, one would suspect, an easy father. Neither was Holmes an easy son. Contemporary observers described him as dreamy and reserved. He spoke little about himself, and more about ideas. While the father raced from subject to subject, the son, scornful of being a dilettante, would stick to one. It is likely that Wendell kept a safe distance from his father – matching him phrase for phrase, but remaining unmoved on the psychic sideline.

Life outside the home was a little less intense. Holmes was an eager student – fond of reading with a quick intelligence. As a child, he loved tales of romantic heroism; Sir Walter Scott was a particular favorite. As he grew older, he explored more serious subjects until, at the age of sixteen, he began a serious study of philosophy and religion.

Wendell grew up well aware of class conflict. His place in Boston's upper crust was secure, but this would do little to earn him respect among the Irish boys who lived in the North End. Boston Common often served as a no-man's-land between the two warring factions, with winter snow-ball fights being a favorite form of combat. As his friend Henry Adams recalled it:

Whenever, on a half-holiday, the weather was soft enough to soften the snow, the Common was apt to be the scene of a fight, which began in daylight with the Latin School in force, rushing their opponents down to Tremont Street, and which generally ended at dark by the Latin School dwindling in numbers and disappearing. ... As long as snowballs were the only weapon, no one was much hurt, but a stone may be put in a snowball, and in the dark a stick or a slingshot in the hands of a boy is as effective as a knife.[1]

There were no known casualties, but the roughness of the "play" suggests that class antipathy was strong.

Holmes's schooling followed a conventional path. At age six, he went to a private primary school run by Thomas Sullivan. At age ten, he moved on to a private preparatory school, with the following note in hand:

O. W. Holmes, Jr ... whom I take delight in calling my young friend has been for four years under my charge as a pupil. He has been uniformly docile, thoughtful, amiable and affectionate. Young as he is, his habits of application are confirmed, while his proficiency in all the English branches, and his love of study are remarkable for his age.[2]

Wendell's new school was "preparatory" in the sense that it centered on subjects that were tested for admission to Harvard College. It was founded and operated by Epes Dixwell, and it is clear that he formed an especially close bond with the young boy. For example, one contemporary remembered that Holmes "often waited for [Dixwell] after school and

---

[1] Henry Adams, *The Education of Henry Adams* 41 (Mass. Hist. Soc'y ed. 1918).
[2] Mark DeWolfe Howe, *Justice Oliver Wendell Holmes Volume I, The Shaping Years, 1841–1870*, at 5 (1957).

walked home across the Common with him, his hand in the older man's." This bond would persist throughout their lives. While at Harvard, Holmes was a frequent visitor to the Dixwells' Cambridge cottage. During the Civil War, he made a special point of visiting Dixwell, and Dixwell, in turn, would note Holmes's visits in his diary, using capital letters followed by a big exclamation point.[3] Eventually, Holmes married Dixwell's daughter Fanny, and this cemented their relationship with the comfortable bonds of familial intimacy.

One suspects that Dixwell posed quite a contrast to Holmes's father. In most ways, the father was conventional. Dixwell, on the other hand, cut a strange figure. His clothing – a dark purple frock coat, a green velvet vest, and a pair of black plaid trousers – was more than notable in conservative Boston. Eccentric but also serious, he was nearly a perfect mentor for a child who loved to read and was interested in cosmic questions. He had trained as a lawyer, but felt that his true vocation was teaching.[4] Indeed, he was a dedicated teacher who was passionate about the classical Greek and Roman texts that were the core of his school's curriculum – a passion that he shared with Wendell, who developed a lifelong interest in reading and rereading the classics.

From an early age, Wendell was preoccupied with difficult questions. Walking through Boston Common one day at the age of seven, he asked his cousin Johnny Morse, age eight, whether it was wrong on every occasion to tell a lie. When Johnny replied that it was, Wendell offered the following hypothetical:

Suppose a man came running along here with terror in his eyes and panting for breath, and hid in this thicket, then the pursuers came along and asked us if we had seen him. Which would be better, to give the man away or to tell a lie?[5]

Johnny of course conceded that the lie would be better and, in this early dialogue, we get a premonition of the kind of lawyer that Wendell would become – he would be attracted to large questions but remain relentlessly skeptical about the equally large answers they seemed to provoke.

---

[3] Epes Dixwell, *Writings*, in *Epes Sargent Dixwell Scrapbooks, Wigglesworth Family Papers* (Mass. Hist. Soc'y 1820–1897).

[4] Thus, when a group from the Boston Latin School approached him about assuming its leadership, he readily agreed. Then, in 1851, he started his own school near Boston Common. Charles P. Bowditch, *Epes Sargent Dixwell*, 35 Proceedings of the American Academy of Arts and Sciences 625, 626 (1900).

[5] Liva Baker, *The Justice from Beacon Hill* 50 (1991).

It seems likely that a young boy who pondered ethical questions would be more than ordinarily interested in religious ones as well. In pursuing these questions, Wendell would have been in tune with his surroundings. New England was awash with religious controversy. Discussion was ubiquitous, taking place at the dining table, in the lecture hall, and even on the streets. Everything was up for debate – even the most fundamental questions. What is real? What is the nature of the human spirit? What is the relationship between science and faith? Religion had always answered these questions, but the Enlightenment had come to Boston and with it the demand that people think for themselves. Educated people were no longer satisfied with the old orthodoxies, and this set loose an enormous rush of intellectual energy.

One immediate effect was that a free-thinking Unitarianism had supplanted Calvinism in the Congregational churches of Boston; indeed, Wendell's own family exemplified this trend. His grandfather Abiel was a Calvinist minister. By 1827, Abiel had spent twenty-five years as the minister of First Church in Cambridge, but had grown radically out of step with his own congregation. As many of them embraced Unitarian principles, he held more firmly to his conservative beliefs. Eventually this difference of opinion escalated to a crisis. The conflict arose over the long-standing practice of area ministers to exchange pulpits on certain Sundays in order to provide variety for their congregations. For a time, Abiel had participated, but, as the new liberal religion spread among the clergy, he grew increasingly troubled by the fact that other ministers were preaching heresies from his very own pulpit. Discontinuance of the practice, however, led to a parish revolt with church members warning that his change in policy would result in disaster. But Abiel could not compromise and, in the end, he was fired.

By the time Wendell was born, Abiel had been dead for nearly a decade, but the Calvinist influence remained present in the figure of Sarah Holmes, Abiel's wife and Wendell's grandmother. Sarah was amiable and cheerful, but nevertheless devoted to her stern religion. No doubt, she would have been pleased if her grandson had come to share her religious beliefs, but this was not to be – even her son, Wendell's father, had long ago abandoned the Calvinist doctrines in favor of a Unitarian faith.

When it came to religion, Dr. Holmes was torn between two great impulses. The first was a love of tradition. He enjoyed going to church and was grateful for the comfort it provided him and many others. He worshipped at Kings Chapel, where the rituals were conventionally Christian and the theology less radical than that preached by Ellery Channing. By temperament, he was a traditionalist – even insisting that the family observe the Sabbath in many of the old-fashioned ways.[6] The second impulse was iconoclastic. He was outspoken in his rejection of the Calvinist doctrine and was particularly critical of the idea that only a few could escape the torments of Hell. Johnny Morse, his nephew and biographer, tells us that he decried a religion that "made a hell of unreasonable spaciousness [yet] made Heaven hardly so big as a modern hotel."[7] He also believed that any religion that passed judgment on others should be prepared to have its own beliefs subjected to rational dissection and, dissecting the Calvinism of his father, he found it wanting.[8] Years earlier, such views would have branded him a heretic, but, fortunately for Dr. Holmes, they had recently become so common that they were considered orthodox.

All of this – his grandfather's faith and his father's skepticism – left Wendell remarkably free to decide for himself what his attitude toward religion should be, and recognizing that his generation was "almost the first of young men who have been brought up in an atmosphere of investigation," he proceeded to actively consider the issue.[9]

It is important to understand that his thinking did not take place in a vacuum. He was surrounded by religious observance. Church attendance – for the most part Unitarian – was mandatory both at home and at college. Nevertheless, he read incessantly, looking for answers to theological questions. One particularly strong influence was Ralph Waldo Emerson, whose work he admired. Emerson was a friend of his father. There has been some suggestion that he was such a close friend that Wendell called him "Uncle Waldo," but this seems unlikely.[10] Nor was it necessary, since Holmes had in his own house exactly the exposure to Emerson that he needed – his father's autographed copy of *Nature*.[11]

---

[6] Dr. Holmes, for example, would not permit himself to read novels on Sunday. *Id.* at 61.

[7] John T. Morse, *Life and Letters of Oliver Wendell Holmes* 269 (2016).

[8] "All persons who proclaim a belief that passes judgment on their neighbors must be ready to have it 'unsettled,' that is questioned at all times by anyone." *Id.* at 272.

[9] Oliver Wendell Holmes Jr., *Books*, 4 *Harvard Magazine* 408, 410 (1858).

[10] In her diary, Ellen Emerson describes running into Holmes on the street. He introduced himself to her father as Dr. Holmes's son – an introduction that would not have been necessary if the families were close enough for Emerson to be an honorary uncle. G. Edward White, *Justice Oliver Wendell Holmes: Law and the Inner Self* 33, 499 (1993).

[11] The book was published in 1849 and, in addition to *Nature*, included "The American Scholar: An Address," "Divinity School Address," "Literary Ethics," "The Method of Nature," "Man the Reformer," "Lecture on the Times," "The Conservative," "The Transcendentalist," and "The Young American." Ralph Waldo Emerson, *Nature; Addresses and Lectures* (James Munroe Co. ed., 1849).

Emerson's impact on Holmes was more than casual, and Holmes himself was not reticent on this point. As a young man, he walked up to Emerson on the street and told him: "If I ever do anything, I shall owe a great deal of it to you."[12] This may have been youthful exuberance, but, nevertheless, Holmes's interest in Emerson cannot be overstated. For example, at seventeen, Holmes requested and received five volumes of Emerson's work,[13] and, as a soldier, he carried Emerson's autograph into battle.[14] Even as an adult, he often said that it was Emerson's influence that had stood the test of time.[15] Emerson's views were complex, and their effect on Holmes was equally complicated. In fact, reading Emerson launched a series of questions and concerns that would animate Holmes's intellectual life for many decades to come.

Emerson's family, like Wendell's, was well situated within the Brahmin community. The father – who had died when his son was only eight – was a Unitarian minister, and it seemed natural that the son would pursue a career in the church. Ultimately, however, even the liberal Unitarian theology would prove too confining for Emerson's expanding vision.

The Unitarians had striven to reconcile religion and rationalism. On one hand, they believed in the Bible as a source of religious revelation and, on the other, they believed its claims were subject to the test of logic and science. As a result, the divinity of Christ became a central issue. Everyone conceded that Jesus was a great and wise prophet – the proof of that was in his teachings. But a rational Christianity required more. It required proof of the idea that Christ was the Son of God incarnate. The Unitarians found this in the miracles that Christ performed. His ability to feed the masses and raise the dead was taken as ample proof of his divine nature. But this resolution of the problem rested entirely on an assumption about the factual accuracy of the Gospels, and this assumption would soon be open to serious dispute.

In Germany, Higher Criticism was in full swing. Not content with studying the Bible in its canonical form, the Higher Critics focused on determining the sources from which it came. Thus, they sought to evaluate the accuracy of the text by comparing it with other historical records from the Middle East. As a result of their efforts, the Bible – and in particular the Gospels – no longer appeared to be

---

[12] John T. Noonan Jr., *Holmes–Sheehan Correspondence: The Letters of Justice Oliver Wendell Holmes and Canon Patrick Augustine Sheehan* 51 (David H. Burton ed., 1976).
[13] Baker, *supra* n. 5 at 85.   [14] *Id.* at 125.   [15] *Id.* at 85, 251.

simple historical records. Instead, educated men began to acknowledge that they had been consciously crafted with political and theological goals in mind. Emerson learned of these developments from his brother William, who was studying in Germany.[16] For some Unitarians, they made little difference, but, for men like Emerson who had rested their faith on the biblical account of miracles, Higher Criticism went right to the core of their Christian faith. He was faced with a choice between an unscientific faith and a rational rejection of Christian doctrine.

Emerson found the choice clear. He came to believe that Jesus was no more divine than an ordinary person. In time, he came to look upon the deification of Christ and the rituals of Christian worship as superstitious practices that stood in the way of true spiritual growth, and this meant that he found himself unable to perform the duties of a Christian minister. Resigning from his pulpit, he retired to his library, where he was determined to examine the full range of philosophical and theological questions. While some of his contemporaries found the loss of their faith dispiriting and demoralizing, the effect on Emerson was just the opposite. Rejecting the divinity of Christ freed him to see the divine nature of every human soul, and this energized him to preach a new set of spiritual doctrines. In this endeavor, he was not alone. There were many individuals whose thinking had followed a similar course. Ultimately, they founded a great spiritual movement that was unique among such movements in lacking both a church and a reigning deity. It was known as American Transcendentalism, and Emerson would function as both its leader and its best-known advocate.

Dr. Holmes was not a Transcendentalist. In fact, he had little interest in theology. He belonged to a church that met his needs and, beyond that, required no coherent statement of belief. Wendell, however, had an abiding interest in religious questions – an interest that was probably intensified by reading a speech that Emerson had delivered to students at Harvard Divinity School. The speech was such an expression of heresy that it marked the end of Emerson's relations with Harvard, but it was just the kind of call to arms that a young man like Holmes would find exciting. In the speech, Emerson challenged his audience to redefine their Christianity and to develop a new sense of spiritual possibility. The problem with traditional Christianity, he argued, was twofold. First, it

[16] Elizabeth Flower and Murray G. Murphey, *A History of Philosophy in America* 404–405 (1977).

assigned divinity to Jesus Christ in a way that blinded ordinary individuals to their own divine nature. Second, its treatment of the Bible as divine revelation suggested that the time for spiritual activity was over. It left modern generations as mere observers of the holy life. By contrast, Emerson's new faith would highlight the sacred in every human experience, and it would call people to participate in the miracles of daily life.

For Wendell, Emerson's speech must have posed a clear alternative to his father's ambivalence. Certainly, the speech's enthusiastic tone and its disdain for the worn-out platitudes of traditional religion would have appealed to a young boy with a romantic temperament, but there would be much more for him to learn before he could share the depth of Emerson's vision.

Wendell's learning would take many forms. First, there was Harvard. In 1857, the intellectual environment at Harvard was far less stimulating than what existed in his own home. By European standards, antebellum Harvard was not a first-class university. Indeed, even its own graduates maintained an attitude of disdain, as the following anecdote reveals:

Charles W. Eliot once disputed with Phillips Brooks the date when Harvard reached its lowest ebb. Eliot said "I think the College struck bottom in 1853." "No," said Brooks, "in 1855." These were the dates when they respectively graduated.[17]

Traditionally, much of the energy of faculty and administration went into keeping order among the students. For example, in 1825, the school's curricular reform amounted to a rearrangement of vacations on the theory that "warm weather produced rioting."[18] Similarly, a Harvard historian boasted that "the close of the commons (1849) and the discontinuance of evening prayers (1855) removed at least half the former occasions for student disorder."[19] In fact, President Walker, who suffered from arthritis, found the duty of quelling the nightly disturbances in the Yard particularly burdensome. Academic performance, on the other hand, was less important than good conduct. The so-called Scale of Merit instituted by President Quincy, awarded points for academic performance,[20] but these could be easily lost for disciplinary infractions.[21] Thus, the primary

---

[17] *See* Samuel Eliot Morison, *Three Centuries of Harvard* 294 (1986). *See also* Adams, *supra* n. 1 at 54–70.

[18] Morison, *supra* n. 17 at 234.   [19] *Id.* at 296.

[20] Note, however, that academic performance was limited to a daily mark (up to eight points) on recitations. *Id.* at 260.

[21] Small deductions were taken for absence from chapel (sixteen) or class (thirty-two) or for missing assignments. Larger ones could be taken for more serious violations. *Id.*

purpose of the grading system was social control and its operation was central to the school – it took a vote of the faculty to determine the penalties, and the president himself calculated the total points.[22]

There was also nothing inspiring about the curriculum of the school. The old guard had successfully defended the ancient system of recitations from reforms that would have allowed students to choose electives and proceed at their own pace. The fixed curriculum was heavily weighted with classics and mathematics, but only lightly seasoned with history, rhetoric, ethics, and the physical sciences. The manner of learning was by rote. For homework, students prepared recitations or wrote highly for-mulaic essays. As one former student complained:

No attempt was made to interest us in our studies. We were expected to wade through Homer as though the Iliad were a bog, and it was our duty to get along at such a rate *per diem*. Nothing was said of the glory and grandeur, the tenderness and charm of this immortal epic. The melody of the hexameters was never suggested to us.[23]

Holmes found a few exceptions to the intellectual dullness that pre-vailed on campus. One was Evangelinus Apostolides Sophocles, a professor of ancient, Byzantine, and modern Greek. Professor Sophocles was raised in a Greek Orthodox monastery on Mount Sinai. As an adult, he immigrated to the United States, and for forty years lived a Spartan existence alone in a single room in Holworthy Hall. He had quite a following among the students, but remained aloof and mysterious – as one writer depicted him, he was "intimate with none and lavish[ed] his affection chiefly on his chickens."[24] Holmes was one of the students who fell under his spell, later describing him as "a beautiful fellow, one of the most learned in the world."[25] Like Epes Dixwell, Professor Sophocles was a founding member of the Oriental Society, and it is likely that it was his influence together with Dixwell's and Emerson's that led Holmes to an early investigation of mystical religion. Later Holmes would recall that "the first adult book" he had read was *Hours with the Mystics* by Robert Vaughn.[26] The book catalogs and describes all the major forms of mysti-cism from Neoplatonism to Islamic Sufism. It is awkwardly written and

---

[22] *Id.*   [23] *Id.* at 260 (quoting James Freeman Clark).
[24] *The National Cyclopedia of American Biography*, v. V at 239 (1894).
[25] Baker, *supra* n. 5 at 78.
[26] Baker, *supra* n. 5 at 89; Robert Vaughan, *Hours with the Mystics: A Contribution to the History of Religious Opinion* (1856).

very dry, and the fact that he read it at all must have reflected a very strong interest in the subject.

Another exception to the general dullness at Harvard was his best friend, Pen. Holmes had come to Harvard with a social life already formed. Most of the young men at Harvard lived on Beacon Hill or attended Dixwell's or were the sons of Holmes's family friends, but Norwood Penrose Hallowell was not a Bostonian. He was from Philadelphia and came from a prominent Quaker family. The Hallowells were well-known abolitionists who had volunteered their home as a stop on the Underground Railroad. This choice subjected them to dangers that were unknown in the comfortable drawing rooms of Beacon Hill. Even the children bore their share of the risk. Consider, for example, the following anecdote that Pen described later in his memoirs:

> Hid away in the barn of our country residence was another fugitive, – a tall, lithe, muscular man, black as anthracite, Daniel Dangerfield by name, now forgotten no doubt, but then enjoying for a brief period a national reputation. The police force of Philadelphia was watching for that man. The detectives looked mysterious as they went about on their false scents and failed to see our Daniel as he passed ... comfortably seated in my mother's carriage, the curtains drawn, my brother Edward on the box quite ready to use his five-shooter, and a younger brother [Pen] in the less heroic part of driver.[27]

To a young man such as Wendell whose ideals had been formed by Sir Walter Scott and Ralph Waldo Emerson, Pen's willingness to defy armed authority for a noble cause must have seemed exotic and heroic. Soon Wendell and Pen were close friends, with Pen exerting considerable influence. It was Pen who was responsible for Holmes's growing commitment to abolitionism; it was Pen's older brother, Edward, who enlisted him in guarding Wendell Phillips from the hostility of a tough Boston crowd; and ultimately it would be Pen who would be his companion during much of the Civil War.

Even with all its shortcomings, a Harvard education had its advantages. Henry Adams, Holmes's friend and classmate, was one of Harvard's severest critics. In writing about his education, he pointed out an advantage that might not have been visible to outsiders:

> [Harvard] was probably less hurtful than any other university then in existence. It taught little, and that little ill, but it left the mind open, free from bias, ignorant of facts, but docile. The graduate had few strong prejudices. He knew little but his mind remained supple, ready to receive knowledge.[28]

---

[27] N. P. Hallowell, *Selected Letters and Papers*, 25 (1896).   [28] Adams, *supra* n. 1 at 55.

For Holmes, this aspect of a Harvard education was of particular benefit since it fitted him for a lifelong journey of self-education. In the meantime, however, he was bored, and, in this respect, he found himself in exactly the position that Henry Adams went on to describe:

[W]ell aware that he could not succeed as a scholar, and finding his social position beyond improvement or need of effort, [he] betook himself to the single ambition which otherwise would scarcely have seemed a true outcome of the college. . . . He took to the pen. He wrote.[29]

Like Adams, Holmes wrote. He found his outlet in *Harvard Magazine*, a semi-independent student publication. By junior year, he was an editor; by graduation, he had published three of his own essays and written a fourth for the *Massachusetts Quarterly*. The first, "Books," extolled the virtues of reading; the second examined Platonic philosophy; the third and fourth shifted to artistic expression – the third, an appreciation of Durer's work and the fourth, a discussion of the Pre-Raphaelites.

These are student essays, and, in the ordinary course of things, hardly worth a read. That being said, they represent our first glimpse of Holmes as an individual distinct from his illustrious family. And indeed, reading the essays, one begins to understand what separated Holmes from his famous father. Each had his own distinctive style of thought and communication. For example, one of the doctor's most popular works was *The Autocrat of the Breakfast-Table*, a series of essays that ran in the *Atlantic Monthly*. His style is peripatetic as the narrator jumps from one subject to another, dropping a clever word here and a metaphor there. For example, one section begins with the observation:

I really believe some people save their brightest thoughts as being too precious for conversation.

Several paragraphs later, he comments on the role of words in shaping our thoughts:

The waves of conversation roll them as the surf rolls the pebbles on the shore.

Stopping briefly to acknowledge the admiration of his listeners, he moves to the theme of higher education, and from there to the state of the clergy, and from there to the difficulties of staying awake during a sermon. Then

[29] *Id.* at 66.

the forward movement jerks to a halt as the narrator notes once again the admiration of those around him.[30]

In contrast, Wendell's essays are finely balanced in their judgments. For example, he offers the following conclusions:

- Books are important opportunities for growth, but one should not become a bookworm.[31]
- Plato lacked an understanding of modern science but he managed to obtain some brilliant insights.[32]
- The sincerity of the Pre-Raphaelites is admirable, but their rejection of refinement limits their aesthetic appeal.[33]

The essays also have a classic form with a beginning, a middle, and an end. The essay on Plato begins with a distinction between the critical method of Socrates and the constructive or synthetic method of Plato. In the middle, Wendell examines Plato's Theory of Ideas as an example of the latter. Finally, he concludes the essay with an emotional paean to the pair:

The spectacle, I say, of these two grand old heathens, the master the inspired fighter, the scholar the inspired thinker, fills my heart with love and reverence at one of the grandest sights the world can boast.

We can see from this comparison why it might have been difficult for father and son to communicate. The father is ever present in his prose. The narrative focuses on *his* observations, *his* feelings, and *his* opinions. In contrast, the son could not be more absent. Everything is presented in such an impersonal way that one is startled at the end of the essay when he tells us that his "heart [is filled] with love and reverence." It is as if an emotional newcomer stumbled into the final paragraph.[34]

---

[30] Oliver Wendell Holmes Sr., *The Autocrat of the Breakfast-Table* 29–33 (1858).

[31] *See* Oliver Wendell Holmes Jr., *Law in Science and Science in Law*, 12 Harvard Law Review 443, 451 (1899).

[32] Oliver Wendell Holmes Jr., *Plato*, 2 *University Quarterly* 205 (1860).

[33] Oliver Wendell Holmes Jr., *Pre-Raphaelitism*, 7 *Harvard Magazine* 345, 346 (1861).

[34] It may seem unfair to make too much of the differences in these essays. They are obviously intended for different occasions and various audiences. However, we know that Dr. Holmes wrote much as he spoke. For example, Charles Eliot described his conversation as being "quick in repartee; he likes to say some witty things in debate – generally comical or pleasant, but sometimes having a sharp point." Wendell too had wit, sharpness, and the ability to turn a phrase, but there is a seriousness and earnestness and sparseness in his essay that must have felt foreign to his father. Furthermore, Wendell himself chose the form of his essay. *Harvard Magazine* published many light and amusing

The essays also tell us something about the way in which young Holmes thought about the world. Holmes grew up in the cusp between two generations. Born a generation earlier, he would have been raised by his parents in a strict Calvinist home, and they would have taught him that the meaning of life is complete conformity to the will of God. Born a generation later, he would have grown up in a more modern world where science had cheapened faith and the desire for material success had undermined religious aspiration. As it was, he was emotionally in the middle. He was entirely committed to science but not to the preoccupation with the material world that it seemed to entail. Commerce never interested him. He loved ideas and their power to shape reality, and it was this love that kept him interested in Emerson.

Emerson too respected science, but for him, the material world represented only a small part of what could be known. Emerson believed that science teaches us about the regularity of nature, but, more importantly, he believed that nature is the foundation for spiritual knowledge. Natural facts, for Emerson, were metaphors that suggest a wide array of nonscientific truths:

Every natural fact is a symbol of some spiritual fact. Every appearance in nature corresponds to some state of the mind, and that state of the mind can only be described by presenting that natural appearance as its picture. An enraged man is a lion, a cunning man is a fox, a firm man is a rock, a learned man is a torch. A lamb is innocence; a snake is subtle spite; flowers express to us the delicate affections. Light and darkness are our familiar expression for knowledge and ignorance; and heat for love. Visible distance behind and before us, is respectively our image of memory and hope.[35]

Thus, the experience of nature is not simply a window on a world of material objects. It is also a lexicon of images that helps us to learn about ourselves and our place in the world. Even more importantly, it teaches us the deepest secrets of the universe. This was the core of Emerson's Transcendentalism. It was based upon a particular kind of experience. This is the example he gives in *Nature*:

Crossing a bare common, in snow puddles, at twilight, under a clouded sky, without having in my thoughts any occurrence of special good fortune, I have enjoyed a perfect exhilaration. I am glad to the brink of fear. . . . Standing on the bare ground, – my head bathed by the blithe air, and uplifted into infinite space, –

pieces and, had he wished, he might have expressed himself in a way that was similar to his father.

[35] Emerson, *supra* n. 11 at 32–33.

all mean egotism vanishes. I become a transparent eye-ball; I am nothing; I see all; the currents of the Universal Being circulate through me; I am part or particle of God.[36]

These were heady thoughts for a young man who aspired to greatness. Like Emerson, Holmes was a romantic idealist. He believed in heroism, and he believed in the value of sacrificing all to a higher calling. His interest in Plato was indicative of this attitude. Modern readers think of Plato as a secular philosopher who urges us to think critically about the world. In the nineteenth century, however, Platonism was a spiritual ideal, representing:

a firm belief in absolute and eternal values as the most real things in the universe – a confidence that these values are knowable by man – a belief that they can nevertheless be known only by whole-hearted consecration of the intellect, will and affections to the great quest – an entirely open mind towards the discoveries of science – a reverent and receptive attitude to the beauty sublimity and wisdom of the creation.[37]

This influence can be clearly seen in Wendell's student writings. Like Plato, Holmes favored the universal over the particular. For example, he praises Plato for his theory of ideas, i.e. for the claim that the idea of a triangle is more real than an actual triangle. Notable in this preference for the general is a distinct system of value. Throughout his life, Holmes would look for truth among the highest and most general aspects of human experience. By contrast, he often disparaged the mundane as gossip, seeing little value in the concrete and particular facts of daily existence. Thus, for example, the two essays on art, "Notes on Albert Durer" and "Pre-Raphaelitism," develop a hierarchy of artistic excellence. Illustration – depictions of a particular scene at a particular time – was at the bottom. At the top, were representations of abstract ideals and idealized human experience such as Durer's depiction of Melancholia – an etching that depicts a person as a general expression of that feeling.[38] Between these two, Holmes saw a middle range that consisted of drawings

---

[36] *Id.* at 12.

[37] William Ralph Inge, *The Platonic Tradition in English Religious Thought* 35 (1926) (quoted by George Santayana, *Platonism and the Spiritual Life* 2 [1927]).

[38] Holmes describes it as a scene where a majestic angel looks overwhelmed by "the many objects of universal study; crowned with the wreath of the elect and beautiful with ideal genius, but grave with thought and marked with the care of the world; winged, yet resting sadly on the earth." Michael H. Hoffheimer, *Justice Holmes and the Natural Law* 103 (1992) ("Notes on Albert Durer").

of real-world figures that could be interpreted as representations of type of human excellence.

Wendell's idealism gave rise to a certain frustration with college life. For example, in one passage, his sense of isolation is clear:

And so we all know well enough the difference, in our various associates between him who lives only in events, and can relish nothing but the College gossip for the day, and him who feels that this is well enough, but that he can find higher food for thought, and who, while still young, passes restless hours longing to find someone who will talk to him of better things.[39]

In another, we can see his internal conflict. Describing one of Plato's most powerful images, he writes:

[The] presentation of the soul ... as a charioteer driving two horses, the one of noble birth and beautiful, the other base and struggling with the reins, and the charioteer, as long as he can command the latter, remaining in the contemplation of the eternal verities and of God; but losing that control being forced to sink to an earthly body.[40]

The self-recognition in this passage is obvious as he concludes: "How sublimely does [this image] set forth the conditions of human life!"[41] But these conditions were about to change.

By the beginning of his senior year, Holmes's literary output was giving way to national events. First, there was the election of Lincoln in the fall of 1860. By the time Lincoln took office in March 1861, seven states had seceded from the Union. Lincoln needed an army and Holmes, with his friend Pen, were among the first to volunteer. In the spring of 1861, they were posted to Fort Independence as a part of the Fourth Massachusetts Battalion of Infantry. This posting entailed missing enough Harvard classes that his graduation was in doubt, being saved only at the last minute by the intervention of his powerful father. But Holmes himself did not care. The war, he knew, would change everything.

[39] Holmes, *supra* n. 9 at 408.   [40] Holmes, *supra* n. 32 at 214.   [41] *Id.*

2

War Is Horrible and Dull

War, when you are at it, is horrible and dull. It is only when time has passed that you see that its message was divine. . . . For high and dangerous action teaches us to believe as right beyond dispute things for which our doubting minds are slow to find words of proof. Out of heroism grows faith in the worth of heroism.

Memorial Day Speech, 1884

Holmes was nineteen when the war began. As soon as the Rebels fired on Fort Sumter, he was ready to enlist. For him, the requirements of duty were clear. He believed in the Union and, increasingly, in abolition. Furthermore, he was committed to a code of chivalry, drawn no doubt from his childhood love of Sir Walter Scott, whose description of the Black Knight summed it up nicely: he would have "no craven fears, no cold-blooded delays, no yielding up a gallant enterprise."[1] Holmes's own strength and courage were as yet untried, but this was the requisite attitude, and the resulting desire to enlist was sure, steady, and accepted no frustration.

Without waiting for graduation, Wendell and Pen joined the Fourth Massachusetts Battalion. They were stationed at Fort Independence on Castle Island, a spare but comfortable camp less than ten miles from Wendell's home in Boston. For two young men bored with college life, their duty could hardly be classified as a hardship. Nevertheless, the assignment presented one serious problem. It became increasingly clear that the Fourth would not see any action – it was destined to stay in

---

[1] Walter Scott, *Ivanhoe* 248 (Oxford University Press ed. 2010).

Massachusetts, performing only ceremonial duties. Since the two young men did not see this as their calling, they soon resigned and began the search for a new unit that had greater prospects of joining the fight.

It was through his father's influence that Holmes obtained a commission in the Massachusetts Twentieth – the unit that would ultimately be called "The Harvard Regiment." The nickname is somewhat deceptive. It was acquired by virtue of the fact that so many of its best-known officers had gone to Harvard. Yet the regiment itself was composed of people from every economic class and from all over the state. This diversity was unusual since recruitment efforts were generally local. Individual towns began the process by forming companies of volunteers and these units would join with others to form countywide regiments. On paper, the governor had the authority to appoint officers, but, in actual practice, he was strongly guided by local appraisals of leadership and by the candidates' contribution to the recruitment efforts. The result was that each unit had a high degree of initial cohesion – soldiers went to war with long-standing friends and acquaintances. This meant that each man was doubly accountable – poor conduct resounded not only in his military unit but also in his civilian life – and a lost friend was doubly mourned – as a comrade and as a companion of youth.

Even though the Twentieth was an exception to this pattern, it had many of the same characteristics. There was, to be sure, no geographic unity. Several of the companies came from Boston; others came from Cape Cod, western Massachusetts, or other areas of the state that were too small or too isolated to field their own regiments. Nevertheless, like other Massachusetts regiments, there was a strong sense of interpersonal connection since most of the soldiers – enlisted men and officers alike – were serving with many people that they had known all their lives.

The real exceptionalism of the Twentieth came from the way its officers were chosen. Governor Andrews was a populist and an abolitionist. Prior to the war, he had not been popular with the wealthy men who lived on Beacon Hill. With war looming, however, he was particularly anxious to ensure their commitment to the cause and could find no better way to accomplish this than to enlist their sons in the struggle. He therefore chose William Lee as the commanding officer. Colonel Lee had all the right connections. As a successful businessman and a Harvard graduate, he was well known, he was widely respected, and he had easy access to Boston's elite.

Once Colonel Lee was chosen, it was a simple matter for Dr. Holmes to petition Lee on behalf of his son. Commissioning the son was not a difficult decision. The father was an influential leader. Wendell himself was smart, capable, and physically strong. In addition, he was an early volunteer who had some training. Thus, in July 1861, Holmes became a first lieutenant and was initially assigned to Company G, under the command of an Irishman named Henry Sweeny. Pen also received a commission. Lacking Beacon Hill connections, he wrote to Governor Andrews directly, and Pen's natural leadership abilities, his training at Fort Independence, and his family's abolitionist credentials were sufficient to convince the governor to appoint him as well.

Once the officers were chosen, it was necessary to recruit enlisted personnel. The regiment set up an office at Camp Massasoit in order to take maximum advantage of walk-ins. But the real work had to be done by the officers. Fortunately, several of the companies were headed by leaders with close ties to the German and Irish communities of Boston. These communities were filled with immigrants who had fled harsh conditions in their own countries, and as a result were extremely patriotic and strongly opposed to slavery. Thus, the German and Irish officers were able to bring hundreds of young men into the regiment. For example, Captain Sweeny, Holmes's superior officer, was able to recruit sixty volunteers from among his community of Irish immigrants.

The Harvard officers, however, were less successful – there was no rush to sign up from Beacon Hill. Nevertheless, a few of them did produce results. Captain Bartlett, for example, who had spent much of his Harvard years in pool halls and bar rooms, was able to capitalize on these connections and recruit twenty-five men. Lieutenant Macy, a Boston business-man and cousin to R. H. Macy the merchandising giant, sailed off to his original home in Nantucket and returned with twenty-four men. Subsequent trips yielded sixty more. Both Wendell and Pen did their share. Pen, with his charm and passionate abolitionism, recruited ten men. Wendell returned to his old summer home in Pittsfield, Massachusetts, and recruited eleven.[2] Finally, on July 18, the regiment was inducted into federal service.[3]

The beginning of its service was not auspicious. Upon inspection, Colonel Lee found "the personal material ... very deficient in stamina and capability."[4] He complained that "the recruiting officers had used such desperately bad judgment" that only one-third of the recruits met the

---

[2] Richard F. Miller, *Harvard's Civil War: A History of the Twentieth Massachusetts Volunteer Infantry* 32–33 (2005).
[3] *Id.*   [4] *Id.* at 35.

expected average. Training soon began in earnest. The soldiers were up at
6:30 AM and in bed by 10:00 PM. In addition to roll calls and the other
routines of camp life, each day included four and one-half hours of drill,
a dress parade, and one hour of regular instruction for both officers and
enlisted men.[5] For the newly minted officers, discipline was not easy.
Initially many of the men were defiant of authority. One man from
Nantucket challenged Holmes: "Why shouldn't a man go where he
pleased when a day's work was done and spend his own money without
asking leave of any God-damned officer?"[6] Answers to such questions had
to be summarily given. For example, a neighborhood saloonkeeper whose
hospitality had caused a fair amount of drunkenness challenged a group of
officers who came to his establishment and poured his whiskey into the
street. In responding, Major Paul Revere – grandson of the famous
Revolutionary rider – did not mince words. He produced his pistol, laid
it on the bar, and said: "This is my authority."[7]

By the end of the summer, all the necessary adjustments had been made
and the Twentieth was ready to report for duty. Despite Colonel Lee's
initial skepticism, it was not a bad fighting force. The soldiers were
physically healthy and adequately trained, though the unit was short-
handed and would remain so throughout the war. The unusual way in
which it had been formed meant that many of its internal relations would
have an aspect of class conflict. A division always existed between the
upper-class Harvard officers and the working-class Irish and German
immigrants. This was apparent even before the regiment had reported
for duty. On the way to Washington, the unit stopped in New York, where
a citizens' group had sponsored a dinner to celebrate their readiness.
Governor Andrews, visiting New York, was the featured speaker.
According to one newspaper account, he gave a speech of "great
power" and put the "house in a complete tempest" when he promised
that even if New York was occupied by Confederate troops,
"Massachusetts would entrench herself behind the hills of Berkshire,
and make the Switzerland of New England the rampart of freedom."[8]
But the Beacon Hill contingent did not hear his speech; they preferred to
arrange their own dinner at an elegant New York restaurant.

---

[5] *Id.* at 38–39.   [6] *Id.* at 36–37.   [7] *Id.* at 38.

[8] Unidentified newspaper clipping in Holmes scrapbook at Harvard Law School in the John
G. Palfrey (1875–1945) collection, 1715–1938. Family and Personal Material, Civil War:
Civil War Scrapbook created by Oliver Wendell Holmes Jr. 1861–1865. http://nrs
.harvard.edu/urn-3:HLS.Libr:1815413?n=18

Sadly, class differences were intensified by a division over the issue of slavery – many of the Beacon Hill officers supported slavery while the German and Irish soldiers were unequivocally opposed. As the regiment moved southward and encountered growing numbers of fugitive slaves, the disagreement became more intense and led to disputes about what to do with them – whether to employ them or return them to their owners.[9] As a result, the administration of the so-called Harvard Regiment became a source of continuing trouble that would run back and forth between the Massachusetts State House and the federal military command.[10]

BALLS BLUFF

On September 7, 1861, the Twentieth arrived in Washington and received their orders. They were to be at Edwards Ferry on the north bank of the Potomac River, just opposite the small city of Leesburg, Virginia. On the other side of the river stood the Confederate Army, and the Union Army was there to hold the enemy in check. For the next two months, both armies stayed in place, maintaining their readiness to fight.

It was not until late October that the Twentieth had their first experience of actual combat, and, as was typical at this stage of the war, their efforts were defeated by confusion and error in the Union leadership. The problems began with an ambiguous order from General McClellan. He had written General Stone that Union forces had occupied Dranesville, a small town on the Virginia side of the Potomac. McClellan's hope was that this move would force the Confederates to abandon Leesburg; he ordered Stone "to keep a good lookout upon Leesburg." He also suggested that Stone might make a "slight demonstration" that would encourage a Confederate withdrawal.[11] Though McClellan later said that this language was not meant to authorize an attack on the enemy, General

---

[9] Given that the North and the South were at war, the notion of Northern soldiers returning slaves to their Southern "owners" seems strange. Nevertheless, that is exactly what Colonel Palfrey (a non-abolitionist Harvard officer) did during the period that Colonel Lee (an abolitionist) was a prisoner of war. This was a difficult time for Pen who, with Holmes recuperating in Boston and the other abolitionist Harvard officers in Southern prisons, remained the only Harvard officer who favored abolition. Never one to sit silently by, Pen challenged Macy:

"By what authority do you make New England soldiers do such work?"

"In pursuance of my orders from Gen. Stone," Macy replied. ...

Hallowell looked at the Nantucketer and said "slowly and sadly" that "I didn't think that any New England Gentleman would do such dirty work." Miller *supra* n. 2 at 97.

[10] *Id.* at 84–104.   [11] *Id.* at 55.

Stone not only ordered his pickets to increase their firing but, in accordance with his more aggressive reading of the order, put together a small force to cross the river at Balls Bluff – an area marked by an incline that rises 100 feet above the river.[12] In the event of trouble, the Twentieth was to serve as reinforcement. They waited on Harrison's Island, a small island that bisected the river and that would serve as a staging area for any attack.

When the exploratory force returned, they reported a small Confederate encampment. This was duly passed on to General Stone, who ordered them to cross the river once again and destroy the enemy camp. Once this was done, they were to return unless they found a tenable position on the Virginia side where they could wait for reinforcements from the Union forces at Dranesville.

This was a dangerous assignment. With the Confederates close by, Colonels Lee and Devens had no way of knowing exactly what the situation would be when their troops returned to the top of the bluff. In addition, the invading force would be particularly vulnerable as they climbed up the steep hill. Once there, retreat would be difficult given the narrowness of the path that descended to the river and the scarcity of boats. There was also the fact – unfortunately unknown to Lee and Devens – that the Union forces had already abandoned Dranesville and that consequently there was no possibility of reinforcement from the Virginia side of the river.

Nevertheless, the Union regiments crossed the river and climbed the bluff without incident. There was no sign of an enemy camp, and this fact was passed on to headquarters. Throughout the day, there were increasing indications of Rebel activity. In the morning, there were small engagements as Union forces encountered enemy pickets. By the afternoon, three Confederate regiments had marched south from Leesburg to confront them. Chaos followed. The Southern forces occupied the higher, sheltered portion of the field and were able to press their advantage. As the Union forces lost ground, they were forced to face the difficulty of their position. To save himself, each man had to scramble down the narrow path and gain a seat in one of the two small boats crossing the river. Since there were not enough boats, some soldiers attempted to swim, but, even for the physically able, the swollen river was extremely treacherous. Many were shot during the escape, and the end result was disaster. From the

---

[12] Baker, *supra* ch. 1, n. 5 at 114.

Twentieth, there were 40 killed, 36 wounded, and more than 100 captured by enemy forces.[13]

Given their inexperience, the Twentieth acquitted themselves with honor. They stayed calm – coolly and efficiently firing their weapons. Pen – now Captain Hallowell – was especially resourceful; he was able to find a flank position where he and his men could fire cleanly into the midst of the enemy force.[14] Holmes himself displayed real courage. With bullets in the air, he stood at the front of his troops and urged them on. Soon, he was hit by a spent bullet that forced him to the ground. He crawled toward the rear, where Colonel Lee suggested that he seek treatment. But Holmes examined his wound, found it was superficial, and decided he could soldier on. By his own account, he rushed forward to the front of his unit and, waving his sword, asked "if none would follow me."[15] Thus Holmes was hit for a second time – this time by a live bullet that pierced his chest and came perilously close to his heart. Amidst considerable doubt as to his survival, he was transported back to Harrison Island and then to the mainland. His consciousness wavered in and out. At one point, he was so certain of his own death that he considered swallowing the lethal dose of laudanum that he carried in his pocket. Sensibly, however, he postponed it, deciding that there was no point so long as there was so little pain.[16] Within a few days, he rebounded. Ten days later, he was well enough to be transported to Philadelphia, where he stayed with Pen's family. In another ten days, he was on his way to Boston.

Wendell's homecoming was worthy of a gallant knight. In Boston, wounded soldiers were still a novelty and, of those who returned, Holmes was by far the most notable. Thus, many people came to pay their respects. In the first three weeks, there were, by his mother's count, 133 visits in all.[17] His callers were not just friends and family, but important men as well. For example, abolitionist Senator Charles Sumner came to see him twice. There was also a visit from English author Anthony Trollop, who happened to be traveling in America.[18] The Harvard contingent was well represented too – both its president, Cornelius Felton, and its best-known professor, Louis Agassiz, made their way to Holmes's door. And, of course, there were the young women who brought gifts of flowers and food.[19]

---

[13] Miller, *supra* n. 2 at 81–82.   [14] *Id.* at 71.   [15] *Id.* at 13.   [16] *Id.* at 13–18.
[17] Baker, *supra* ch. 1, n. 5 at 121.   [18] Howe, *supra* ch. 1, n. 2 at 111.
[19] Baker, *supra* ch. 1, n. 5 at 121.

Holmes no doubt took it all in, enjoying his time in the center of attention. He assumed a sophisticated air, describing army life as an "organized bore."[20] Even so, the experience must have been unsettling. In the course of three weeks, he had gone from a young man who had never experienced serious discomfort to one who had been tested by the reality of war. He had watched friends die and had nearly died himself. Then, in no time, he was back in the safety of Beacon Hill.

We can suppose that a young man's first brush with death is a time for serious reflection. Wendell's response, written somewhat later, sheds light on his innermost thoughts about the nature of life, God, and the Universe. On a page taken from his wartime diary – and one of the few such pages he preserved – he begins with the thought that a "majority vote of the civilized world declared that with my opinions I was en route for Hell." To this, he responds:

Perhaps the first impulse was tremulous ... then I thought I couldn't be guilty of a deathbed recantation. ... Besides, thought I, can I recant if I want to, has the approach of death changed my beliefs much? & to this I answered – No. ... Then came in my Philosophy – I am to take a leap in the dark – but now as ever I believe that whatever shall happen is best – for it is in accordance with a general law.[21]

Thus, Wendell at age twenty is firm in his rejection of Christianity and confident enough to believe in something he calls "my Philosophy." He then goes on to consider the specifics of his fate, wondering:

Would the complex forces which made a still more complex unit in Me resolve themselves back into simpler forms or would my angel be still winging his way onward when eternities had passed?

And this time his answer was almost religious:

I could not tell – But all was doubtless well – and so with a "God forgive me if I'm wrong" I slept."[22]

For all its abstraction, there is something appealing about Holmes's youthful idealism. He was neither dogmatic nor without a sustaining faith. While he believed that the universe ran on mysterious principles, he cheerfully submitted to its plan. And in the end – just in case the world is right and he is wrong – he asked the God he rejected to "forgive me if I'm wrong." All of these thoughts are reproduced without a trace of irony or

---

[20] *Id.*
[21] Louis Menand, *The Metaphysical Club: A Story of Ideas in America* 37 (2002).
[22] *Id.*

anxiety as if to say – I am clueless but confident that all will be well.[23] Thus, in his first moment of real vulnerability, his faith emerges as a simple feeling that the Universe has meaning and that all its energy – all the bustling to and fro – will ultimately result in something beneficial.

While he was at home, he also had time to think about his own conduct. Whatever his doubts may have been about his ability to stand fast in the face of danger, they could now be put aside. While he had begun the battle "all keyed up," his instincts had done him credit – he had not shrunk from his duty.[24] Yet, despite his own sense of success, one disturbing reality must have slowly become apparent. The slaughter at Balls Bluff was meaningless – it had no important objective and it had accomplished nothing. The newspapers were full of it – sketching a narrative where mistake after mistake led young and inexperienced troops to needless slaughter. The public was angry and ultimately forced the government to form a commission to investigate. For one who had been there, this controversy must have struck a discordant note. For him, the battle had been deeply meaningful, but for civilians, he could now see, it was a comedy – or rather a tragedy – of errors. In this new narrative, he was less of a heroic leader and more of a victim; it must have occurred to him that heroic actions lose some of their luster when they prove so entirely pointless.

He had begun his wartime service aspiring to the gallantry of Ivanhoe. But, like many of his comrades, he found this ideal ill suited to the Civil War experience. Ivanhoe fought alone. He chose his battles wisely, always representing good against evil. But Holmes was part of a big war machine – a complex piece of work that, in the beginning at least, malfunctioned more often than it succeeded.

Balls Bluff had been Holmes's first chance to show his gallantry, his first chance to honor his ideal. But his ideal, once fulfilled, could not carry him forward. He needed a more realistic concept of heroism. One element of this was the code of the professional soldier. A few years earlier, Tennyson had written a well-known poem describing an incident in the Crimean War. Like Balls Bluff, the incident was caused by an ambiguous order and subsequent miscommunication, and, again like Balls Bluff, many were

---

[23] It is possible that Holmes's lack of anxiety is at least partly due to the fact that he had no doubt been treated with opiates at the time he had these thoughts. *See* G. Edward White and Oliver Wendell Holmes Jr., Lives and Legacies 25–26 (2006).

[24] Mark De Wolfe Howe, *Touched with Fire: Civil War Letters and Diary of Oliver Wendell Holmes, Jr., 1861–1864*, 75 (2000).

killed and wounded. In the poem, Tennyson described the reaction of the soldiers as they came to realize that they were on a suicide mission.

> Was there a man dismay'd?
> Not tho' the soldier knew
> Someone had blunder'd:
> Theirs not to make reply,
> Theirs not to reason why,
> Theirs but to do and die:
> Into the valley of Death
> Rode the six hundred.[25]

At Balls Bluff, Holmes learned an important lesson – war requires more than swagger. It requires a soldier to obey his orders without question. From this point on, Holmes knew that his fate was not in his own hands, but would ultimately be settled as a small and unintended consequence of a larger plan of battle. Therefore, his will and his judgment had to be suspended in favor of the assigned task – whether that task was foolish or wise.

But if Holmes's actions were to be decreed by others, his determination had to spring from the deepest recesses of his soul. For this, he needed inspiration, and perhaps he found it in Emerson's description of the hero:

Let him hear in season, that he is born into a state of war, and . . . that he should not go dancing in the weeds of peace, but . . . let him take his reputation and life in his hand, and, with perfect urbanity dare the gibbet and the mob by the absolute . . . rectitude of his behavior. . . . To this military attitude of the soul we give the name of Heroism. Its rudest form is contempt for safety and ease.

So far, Emerson might have been quoting Sir Walter Scott, but he adds a very Emersonian element.

There is somewhat not philosophical in heroism; there is somewhat not holy in it; . . . Heroism feels and never reasons, and therefore is always right. . . . [The hero] finds in [himself] a quality that is negligent of expense, of health, of life, of danger, of hatred, of reproach, and knows that his will is higher and more excellent than all actual and all possible antagonists.

What a tall order this must have been for Holmes! In his heart, he was a philosopher with a love of reflection and deeply considered ideals. Circumstances, however, required him to be heedless, to act without thinking, and to disregard the instincts of a careful man. It is no wonder that he sought an outward token to support his inward conviction. Before he left, he wrote to Emerson, asking for an autograph. Emerson complied

---

[25] Alfred Lord Tennyson, *Charge of the Light Brigade* 118 (Norman Page ed. 1995).

and, throughout the rest of the war, Holmes carried the autograph in his breast pocket next to his heart.

THE PENINSULA CAMPAIGN

Holmes returned to the army in March 1862. He found his regiment preparing for the Peninsula Campaign.

Only 100 miles separate Washington, DC, and Richmond, Virginia. In April 1862, McClellan might have simply moved forward toward the Southern capital. At that point, approximately 50,000 Confederate soldiers stood in the way – a not insurmountable force given the superior numbers that McClellan commanded. The somewhat unlikely alternative was to approach the city from the southeast by sailing to Hampton, Virginia, and marching northward up the peninsula formed by the James and York Rivers. While the peninsula route meant encountering fewer enemy troops, it was also longer and logistically challenging. For reasons known only to military historians, McClellan chose the peninsula.

Given the logistics, McClellan's first order of business had to be the fortifications at Yorktown. So long as the Confederates controlled them, necessary supplies and reinforcements could not be transported on the York River. Rather than assault Yorktown, McClellan, ever cautious, opted for a siege. The resulting month's delay gave the Confederates ample time to adjust their forces to the new Union strategy. They drew their troops closer to Richmond and, by the time McClellan was ready for the assault, the Confederate capital was well defended and the Union forces never attacked. They spent one month close to Richmond, and then, after two small and somewhat inconclusive battles, McClellan ordered a retreat.

Inevitably, this pointless trip up and down the peninsula caused much suffering, and the Massachusetts Twentieth was in the thick of it. They spent two months advancing through mud and enemy fire north toward Richmond, a month camped outside of Richmond preparing fortifications, and then five painful days guarding the rear of the Union Army as it retreated down the peninsula. In all this time – much of it in the midst of combat – Wendell was not wounded, but, like many of his comrades, he suffered severe blows to morale and spirit.

For the soldiers, the Peninsula Campaign was a time of extreme privation and danger. The Twentieth began the march toward Yorktown with inadequate shelter – their tents would not arrive for several weeks. This was important because it rained almost continuously. Ultimately, the damp, combined with little food and little rest, made most of the soldiers ill. But ill or not, they had to persevere and this required intense determination – what Holmes called pluck:

It's a campaign now and no mistake – no tents, no trunks – no nothing – it has rained like the devil last night all day and tonight. . . . Marching will have to be slow for the roads have constantly to be made or amended for artillery. . . . The men and officers are wet enough you may believe but there is real pluck shown now as these are real hardships to contend with.[26]

By its very nature, pluck requires an almost delusional optimism. On April 23, Holmes reassured his family that "my cold seems to have finally departed," and "I have been very well." But this was not quite true – "the two rainy days before and while on picket my bowels played the Devil with me owing to cold and wet and want of sleep." The "want of sleep" was particularly miserable:

I forgot to say that as our camp is only about a half a mile from the pickets in the beeline – we are called under arms about every third night by some infernal regiment or other getting excited and banging away for about five minutes – we stand about an hour in the mud and then are dismissed.[27]

That Holmes would describe himself as "very well" in the face of all this bespeaks the level of denial necessary to support the needed "pluck."

The long campaign up the peninsula culminated in the battle of Fair Oaks. For the Twentieth, even getting to the battle proved a struggle. Holmes wrote:

[We] marched for miles I should think – the last part through a stream above our knees and then double-click through mud a foot deep onto the field of battle.[28]

As they neared the fighting, they saw many wounded soldiers, who encouraged them on: "Give it to them, Massachusetts boys, you are just in time." But, as is typical of war, the messages were mixed, as deserters warned them that no one could stand what was in front of them and that they would be "cut to pieces" if they moved forward.[29] Finally at 6:00 PM, they emerged from the woods and joined the battle.[30] Henry Ropes, one of the Harvard officers, described it this way:

The noise was terrific, the balls whistled by us and the Shells exploded over us and by our side, the whole scene [was] dark with smoke and lit by the streams of fire from our battery and from our Infantry in line on each side.

---

[26] Howe, *supra* n. 24 at 38–39 (letter of Apr. 7).   [27] *Id.* at 46 (letter of Apr. 23).
[28] *Id.* at 48 (letter of June 2).   [29] Miller, *supra* n. 2 at 128.   [30] *Id.*

And then there was the human suffering:

Dead covered the field. The sight of the wounded was even more distressing. Some walking, some limping, some carried on stretchers and blankets, many with shattered limbs exposed and dripping with blood.[31]

All in all, it was a horrifying and frightening sight.

As at Balls Bluff, Holmes's courage did not fail. Neither was he willing to tolerate cowardice in his men. Later, he explained the mechanics of courage to his family:

But really as much or rather more is due to the file closers than anything else, I told 'em to shoot any man who ran and they lustily buffeted every hesitating brother. I gave one (who was cowering) a smart rap over the backsides with the edge of my sword – and stood with my revolver and swore I'd shoot the first who ran or fired against orders.[32]

Finally, hours of fighting brought success. Holmes wrote:

Here we blazed away ... till we were ordered to cease firing and remained masters of the field.[33]

There is nothing like victory to test men's souls. First, there was the fleeing enemy. Like the rebel forces at Balls Bluff, the Twentieth now had the opportunity to shoot the enemy in the back as they fled from the battlefield. Pen found this distasteful, believing that men fleeing from the fight should be considered *hors de combat*. He therefore ordered his men to stop firing. This was not a popular order, but it held.

Once the enemy had left, the Twentieth set up camp on the field of battle. The smell was terrible and the sights were worse. Wendell wrote his father:

As you go through the woods you stumble constantly, and after dark ... perhaps tread on the swollen bodies already fly blown and decaying, of men shot in the head back or bowels – Many of the wounds are terrible to look at – especially those fr. fragments of shell.[34]

There was no food to speak of and, distasteful as it was, many of the men were reduced to ransacking the dead bodies for something to eat.

The enemy wounded presented a different kind of problem. Their cries and yells resounded throughout the camp. Remarkably, after a long day of marching and fighting, a number of the soldiers felt compelled to assist.

---

[31] Howe, *supra* n. 24 at 129.   [32] *Id.* at 130.   [33] *Id.* at 131.
[34] *Id.* at 48 (letter of June 2).

They fetched water, gave up their blankets, and spoke with the wounded Rebels, writing down names and addresses so that they could inform Southern families about their sons' final hours. Dr. Revere, brother of Colonel Revere and the company's doctor, even administered scarce opiates to reduce their final suffering. Perhaps, as one writer suggested, the men were just trying to prove a point – they were "determined to show" that they were not just "superior soldiers" but also men of "superior sensibilities."[35] However, long after the point is lost, the compassion remains as one more peculiar aspect of a war among brothers.

After the battle of Fair Oaks, the Union Army began preparing for a siege of Richmond. At one point, the Twentieth was sent three miles back from the front lines so they could get some much-needed rest. Nearly everyone in the unit was sick. Besides the ever-present dysentery, there was an assortment of ailments. On June 13, Holmes wrote that:

Shall I confess a frightful fact? Many of the officers including your beloved son have discovered themselves to have been attacked by body lice.[36]

And on the 19th, he mentioned a different ailment:

The homesickness which I mentioned in my last they say is one of the first symptoms of scurvy.[37]

Ailments or not, the war continued. At the end of June, two events marked the complete reversal of fortune for the Union Army. The first was the wounding of General Joseph Johnston, the Confederate commander, and his replacement by the more aggressive Robert E. Lee. The second was that a skillful use of deception by the Confederates had convinced General McClellan that the Rebel army was three times its actual size. These events, together with two fierce battles fought outside Richmond, were enough to persuade McClellan that the assault on Richmond would be far too risky. As a result, he made the highly controversial decision to retreat.

The Twentieth received the news on the morning of the 28th. Their first order of business was to move a number of railroad cars that had been left at Fair Oaks and were loaded with ammunition. Since no locomotives were available, the orders were to push the heavy cars three miles east to Savage Station so they would not fall into enemy hands. This meant that the Twentieth could not begin their retreat until the next morning, when they were among the last Union soldiers to leave Fair Oaks. As they began

---

[35] Miller, *supra* n. 2 at 132.   [36] Howe, *supra* n. 24 at 53 (letter of June 13).
[37] *Id.* at 55 (letter of June 19).

their march, they could hear the victory shouts of the Rebels entering the Union fortifications.[38] This must have been demoralizing; one can imagine their feelings as they voluntarily – and seemingly without reason – yielded the ground they had so recently fought for and won.

Also demoralizing was the sight of the wounded trying to follow the army. "It was a pitiful sight," one soldier wrote:

to see the wounded men who had been in the field hospital at Savage Station try to follow the army. Some with one leg some with arms gone others with Head tied up trying to escape from being taken prisoner which to many of them meant death.[39]

The Twentieth's placement at the end of the retreating army meant that they were part of the rear guard. Like all retreats, the march was confusing, disorderly, and filled with conflict. At one point, Pen's company was ordered out to harass the advancing enemy. Out in the field, Pen could hear troop movements behind him and gradually realized that the rest of the Union Army was pulling out. He awaited orders but none came. The question then became whether he and his soldiers were expected to follow or whether they were supposed to stay behind and die fighting. Without orders, Pen could only assume the latter. Thus, deep in the forest, fearful and alone with his men, he settled in to do his duty. Much later that night and to his great relief, orders finally came permitting him to abandon his post.

The way back to the main force was not easy. The night was dark and damp; the roads were more than muddy. Paul Revere managed the line and tried to boost the men's spirits by offering encouragement, but not everyone was interested in building morale. Holmes later complained about Tremlett – another Harvard officer – who spread the word that "we must surrender or be cut to pieces within 36 hours."[40]

Finally, at dawn, the men rested for a few hours before continuing their march. Soon they were pinned down by a Confederate artillery attack. They laid down in the mud and waited. They were tired and thirsty from their march, but the only water available came from the muddy pools beside the road. The artillery fire had set the surrounding forest ablaze. Since the trees were damp from the spring rains, there was little danger of the fire leaping to their position near the road, but nevertheless the smoke was terrible and the men were left choking and struggling to breathe. It

---

[38] Miller, *supra* n. 2 at 139.   [39] *Id.* at 145.
[40] Howe, *supra* n. 24 at 60 (letter of July 5).

was several hours before they could resume their march; no sooner had they done this than they received orders to join the battle at Glendale.[41]

Glendale was the last battle on the peninsula and, once again, the Twentieth took many casualties. Holmes lost his cousin Jimmy Lowell – an event he would recall years later in the Memorial Day speech.[42]

After the battle, Holmes and his regiment returned to the safety of Harrison's Landing. As they entered the camp, the unit struck one observer as particularly hard hit; he described them as looking "used up," and, in fact, they were.[43] The Peninsula Campaign had resulted in fourteen killed, seventy-two wounded, and eight missing or captured.[44] Pen and Wendell were both safe, although not without considerable wear and tear. Holmes, in particular, was nearing the end of his endurance. We can hear the fatigue in his July 4 attempt to reassure his mother: "I only want to say I am well after immense anxiety and hard fighting."[45] But it was more than fatigue. The peninsula had taught him that the line between life and death is very thin.

He had also learned a lesson about his own strength. Consider, for example, the extremes of discomfort that he experienced. He had been a healthy boy from a comfortable home. Further, he had been at that age when a young man imagines that he is not only immortal but downright indestructible. Conditions on the peninsula had driven him almost to the breaking point. If he still thought of Emerson and his description of the hero, it must have seemed strangely out of reach. Emerson had written that a hero can maintain his "contempt for safety and ease" because he has a "self-trust which slights the restraints of prudence, in plenitude of [his] energy and power to repair the harms [he] may suffer."[46] But, for Holmes, at this stage in the war, the belief in his own "energy and power" must have been less of a conviction and more of a desperate hope. Furthermore, the reality of human suffering could no longer be ignored. While he told his family that he was increasingly indifferent to the carnage all around him,[47] his indifference did not extend to the cries of the wounded[48] or to

---

[41] Miller, *supra* n. 2 at 147.   [42] Holmes, *supra* prologue, n. 1.

[43] Miller, *supra* n. 2 at 152 (quoting Folsom).   [44] *Id.* at 151.

[45] Howe, *supra* n. 24 at 57.

[46] Ralph Waldo Emerson, *Heroism*, in *Essays, First Series* 270 (McKay ed. 1893).

[47] Howe, *supra* n. 24 at 50–51.

[48] It is interesting that his friend William James uses this phrase to refer to the kind of insistent moral claims that cannot be ignored. William James, *The Moral Philosopher and the Moral Life*, 1 International Journal of Ethics 330, 350 (1891). After the war, Holmes and James spent many hours discussing philosophy, and one wonders whether this shorthand description dates from these discussions.

the loss of people he knew. For example, as the Memorial Day speech makes clear, he was still mindful of the loss of his comrades twenty years after their death.

ANTIETAM

During August 1862, a much-weakened regiment moved from Harrison's Landing to Alexandria, Virginia. It had started the war with 787 men and 39 officers; it was now down to 200 men and 8 officers. This meant there had to be new recruits, and Governor Andrews obliged by sending 344 men.[49] Despite the fact that these recruits were untrained and, in many cases, unarmed, the unit was fighting again by the end of the month – this time as a rearguard action to protect General Pope's army as it retreated from Manassas.

This action was followed by a brief period of inactivity during which Wendell was able to obtain a twelve-hour pass. He spent the time in Washington buying clothing and supplies. Good food and a good night's sleep in a quiet and comfortable bed were restorative. Though he wrote his mother that he was experiencing "spasmodic pain" in the bowels, he nevertheless insisted that he was "pretty well" and then even corrected the phrase with emphasis to "*very* well."[50] Holmes was beginning to heal, but the time of renewal would not last. On September 13, they left for Antietam.

We remember Antietam as the bloodiest day in American history. The battle can be divided into three distinct stages. The first stage took place in the morning, when three successive waves of Union soldiers attacked the Confederate line to the north. At the center of this fight was a cornfield that lay between two patches of woods. The second stage began in the early afternoon, when the Union Army mounted a charge against the Confederate troops at the center of the field. This resulted in a fight over the notorious Sunken Road. Finally, the third stage began in the late afternoon, when General Burnside consolidated his forces and attacked in the southern part of the Confederate line. The center of the third fight was a small bridge that crossed Antietam Creek.

The Twentieth fought as part of the third wave in the morning fight. Henry Ropes recounted the ensuing action in a letter to his father. He began by describing the march across the cornfield:

[49] Miller, *supra* n. 2 at 154.   [50] Howe, *supra* n. 24 at 61–62.

Our division was formed in three lines, the first line Gorman's brigade, the second ours, the third Burns. The principal musketry firing was done of course by the first line. We were under heavy fire, however, and suffered from artillery while advancing. We drove the enemy before us with tremendous loss on both sides. The slaughter was horrible, especially close to the Hagerstown Turnpike where the enemy made a stand by the fences.[51]

Once across the Turnpike, they entered the woods, where there was a momentary halt in artillery fire. As they emerged from the woods, however, they found themselves in an extremely precarious position. Ropes continued:

We finally advanced down the slope, beyond which the enemy held a cornfield and farmhouse with barns and outbuildings, all on an opposite slope. (This was the Poffenberger farm.) The enemy had Cannon planted on the top and constantly swept us down with grape and Shrapnel shell. Our line was advanced close to the first, exposing us to an equal fire, while we could not fire at all because of our first line. The third line was finally advanced close to the second, all this time we stood up and were shot down without being able to reply.[52]

The problem here was that General Summer had ordered the lines formed too close together; as the army fought its way across the cornfield, it had turned leftward. This meant that the left-hand side had become even more tightly packed. Thus, only the soldiers at the extreme left of the formation could fire their weapons. To make things worse, the division was without leadership. Generals Sedgwick and Dana had both been wounded.

In time, their bad position became worse. They found themselves surrounded on three sides. The enemy was in front of them fighting Gorman's brigade, but Rebel soldiers also were attacking both from the side and from the rear.

The enemy in the meantime came round on our left and rear, and poured in a terrible crossfire. Summer came up in time to save the Division and ordered us to march off by the right flank. We did so, but the left regiments gave way in confusion, the enemy poured in upon our rear and now the slaughter was worse than anything I have ever seen before.[53]

Indeed, the situation was dire, but the Twentieth had earned its reputation for grace under fire. Ropes's pride in their conduct is apparent:

---

[51] Henry C. Ropes, *Letter to Father*, in Boston Public Library 265 (1862) (identified as: civilwarlettersoo2rope).

[52] *Id.* A different writer adds color to the scene: "The men leaned quietly on their muskets and the officers chatted and smoked their cigars and pipes." Miller, *supra* n. 2 at 174 (quoting Patten).

[53] Ropes, *supra* n. 51 at 265–266.

Summer walked his horse quietly along waving his hand and keeping all steady near him. Although the regiments in rear of us were rushing by us and through our ranks in the greatest confusion, we kept our company perfectly steady, did not take a single step faster than the regular marching order and brought off every man except those killed and wounded who of course were left.[54]

Pen and Wendell were among the wounded left on the field. Pen was hit in the left arm, and, dressed inconspicuously in a private's shirt, he was able to sneak through enemy lines to a house located in Union territory. Wendell had been shot in the back of the neck and was lying down, drifting in and out of consciousness. He might have been left for dead but for the diligence of a man named William LeDuc, who insisted that he receive attention. They gave him brandy and he revived enough so that he was able to stand; with help, he too made it to safety. As he entered the house, he saw Pen and laid down next to him.

Their relative safety would not last for long. The advancing enemy army had finally overtaken Nicodemus House – the house where Pen and Wendell and countless other wounded had sought shelter. While the Rebels were busy in the yard, one of them performed a quiet act of compassion. As Pen later told it:

The first Confederate to make his appearance put his head through the window and said:
    "Yankees?"
    "Yes."
    "Wounded?"
    "Yes."
    "Would you like some water?" A wounded man always wants some water. He off with his canteen, threw it into the room, and then resumed his place in the skirmish line and his work of shooting retreating Yankees. In about fifteen minutes that good hearted fellow came back to the window all out of breath, saying: "Hurry up there! Hand me my canteen! I am on the double-quick myself now." Someone twirled the canteen to him, and away he went.[55]

After the federal forces reoccupied Nicodemus House, the wounded were evacuated to the temporary hospital in Keedysville. Pen was fortunate to have his arm saved by a surgical procedure called exsection; and, as it turned out, Holmes's wound was not serious.[56] The bullet had gone

---

[54] *Id.* at 266.   [55] Hallowell, *supra* ch. 1, n. 27 at 17.

[56] Miller, *supra* n. 2 at 179. Exsection involves cutting away the damaged bone and placing two healthy cross-sections back together. As a result of the operation, one of Pen's arms became an inch shorter than the other.

straight through his neck without doing lasting injury to his airway or spinal column. Once again, he had been lucky.

Wendell's behavior after his injury suggests that he might have felt relieved to be wounded. The next day, he wrote a short note to his parents, reassuring them:

Usual luck – ball entered at the rear passing straight through the central seam of coat & waistcoat collar coming out toward the front on the left hand side – yet it doesn't seem to have smashed my spine or I suppose I should be dead or paralyzed or something – It's more than 24 hours & I have remained pretty cocky, only of course feverish at times – & some sharp burning pain in the left shoulder.[57]

Apparently, he felt well enough the next day to make his way to Hagerstown, where he could board a train to Philadelphia. Instead, once in Hagerstown, he delayed.

I pulled up in good quarters at Hagerstown ... and not feeling quite inclined to undertake the journey homeward immediately alone – I decided to remain here a few days.

The delay might have been worrisome to his mother but for the fact that it was perfectly clear that he was having a wonderful time. The letter itself had been dictated to a young woman with whom Wendell was clearly enjoying a flirtation. Furthermore, it opened in a joking mood:

Tho unheard from I am not yet dead but on the contrary doing all that an unprincipled son could do to shock the prejudices of parents & of doctors – smoking pipes partaking of the flesh pots of Egypt swelling around as if nothing had happened to me.

Finally, it ended with the promise that "I will be with you shortly for another jollification in Boston."[58]

The lightheartedness of this letter forms a sharp contrast with the rest of Holmes's Civil War correspondence. Because he was wounded, he was exempt from all duties and responsibilities. Since his return in March, there had been considerable suffering; through it all, he had to obey orders, be a good leader, and generally live up to his own code of heroism. Now, wounded, he was free – free to stop in a comfortable home, free to flirt with a pretty girl, and free to hold his parents at arm's length. With respect to the latter, he was explicit: "I neither wish to meet any affectionate parent half way nor any shiny

---

[57] Howe, *supra* n. 24 at 64 (letter of Sept. 18, 1862).   [58] *Id.* at 67–68 (Sept. 22, 1862).

demonstrations when I reach the desired haven."[59] Unfortunately, however, Dr. Holmes could not be so easily deterred. He was already on his way with a pencil in hand. His story, *My Search after the Captain*, became a classic of Civil War literature; Wendell was only saved from embarrassment by the fact that, like so much of what the doctor wrote, the story was chiefly about the doctor himself.

This time, Wendell spent a mere seven weeks at home before he returned for duty. Not surprisingly, he displayed a distinct "nervousness" that was duly noted by his father.[60] Antietam marked a turning point in his attitude toward the war. He had learned an important lesson – one that was difficult for a man of his age and background to internalize. Over the previous nine months, experience had been a strict and ruthless teacher. He now understood that there were limitations on his own strength, power, and spirit. He might aspire to glory in all its forms. With the greatest self-discipline, he might force himself to complete whatever task was at hand. But there was, in the final analysis, a line beyond which he could not go. And what was true for him was also true for the cause he had embraced. He now understood that the Confederate Army was determined to resist occupation; he believed that the Union Army could win a battle but not the war, and, after his seven weeks at home, he was also doubtful that the civilian world of the North was fully committed to victory. These growing realizations must have been hard to swallow, but swallow them he did. From this point forward, his skepticism about the war is apparent in his letters and diary.

His first letter home after his recuperation is a good example of the new attitude. Admitting that he is "blue," he tells his parents that he had had difficulty obtaining directions to his unit and that the army "seems to hold that you are a nuisance for not having stayed at home as indeed but for honor I should suspect I was a fool."[61]

No doubt, his frustration was real, but it represented, for Holmes, an entirely new tone of voice – one increasingly critical of military command.

---

[59] *Id.*

[60] Baker, *supra* ch. 1, n. 5 at 144 (quoting Dr. Holmes, who describing Holmes during subsequent recuperation from his third wound, wrote that he "was not at all nervous as when he was last wounded").

[61] Howe, *supra* n. 24 at 75. See *id.* at 79, where he describes Fredericksburg as an "infamous butchery in a ridiculous attempt."

FREDERICKSBURG I

After the costly stand-off at Antietam, General McClellan was finally relieved of his command. He was replaced by General Burnside, who decided upon a direct route to the Confederate capital. This meant that Fredericksburg, which lay halfway between Washington and Richmond, became the immediate target. Fredericksburg was a small city protected on the north and east by the Rappahannock River. General Burnside planned to cross the river by the use of pontoon bridges sent from Washington. Unfortunately, the bridges were not delivered on time and, by the time they did arrive, the Confederate Army had moved in and fortified the town.

Nevertheless, on December 11, the Union Army attempted to take Fredericksburg. Amidst enemy fire, the engineers began assembling the bridges. As they neared the opposite shore, the firing became so intense they were not able to continue. The Twentieth were assigned to guard them, but were unable to make any progress against the well-hidden snipers. The work soon came to a halt. Burnside faced a dilemma. His army could not cross the river without bridges, and the bridges could not be built so long as no one was fighting the enemy on the other side. To solve this problem, the Michigan Seventh volunteered to cross the river in pontoon boats. General Burnside thought the mission suicidal, but, lacking other alternatives, he permitted it and it succeeded. Next across the river was the Massachusetts Twentieth; to them fell the duty of clearing the main street. This meant running a gauntlet with enemy fire from all sides. Shots came from everywhere – windows, doors, roofs, basements, and alleys. The Union soldiers were an easy target while the Confederates shot from cover. The only way to prevail was for the front to keep moving forward, depending on soldiers from the rear to replace those who were shot. And this is what the Twentieth did. Holmes's friend Abbott became the hero of the day. He stood at the front of his soldiers as they were mowed down by enemy fire. When his first platoon was shot to pieces, he calmly ordered the second one forward and led "them into a storm with the same indifferent air that he has when drilling a Battalion."[62]

For the Twentieth, this was a dreadful day – but it was one that Holmes spent on the sidelines. In a letter to his mother, he recounted his feelings as he watched his regiment go into battle:

---

[62] Miller, *supra* n. 2 at 201.

Yesterday morning the grand advance begins – I see for the first time the Regiment
going to battle while I remain behind – a feeling worse than the anxiety of danger,
I assure you – Weak as I was I couldn't restrain my tears – I went into the
Hospital . . . listless and miserable.[63]

Holmes had a serious case of dysentery. Before the discovery of anti-
biotics, dysentery was a lethal threat. Left untreated, it would cause the
bowels to run with blood, mucus, and half-digested food, leading to
dehydration, starvation, and death. During the Civil War, it killed
60,000 soldiers. Holmes was not only sick, his life probably hung in the
balance. But staying in the hospital was not an easy thing:

We couldn't see the men but we saw the battle – a terrible sight when your
Regiment is in it but you are safe – Oh what self-reproaches have I gone through
for what I could not help and the doctor, no easy hand, declared necessary – And in
it again the Regiment has been – Scarcely anyone now left unhurt . . . – The brigade
went at an earthwork and got it with canister.[64]

When it was all over, he described it as "one of the most anxious and
forlornest weeks of my military career."[65]

Fredericksburg also led Wendell to articulate some of his new attitudes
about the war to his father. He now became openly sarcastic about the
unjustifiable optimism in the Boston papers:

I always read now the D. Advertiser . . . – and I was glad to see that cheerful sheet
didn't regard the late attempt [Fredericksburg] in the light of a reverse – It *was* an
infamous butchery in a ridiculous attempt – in wh. I've no doubt our loss doubled
or tripled that of the Rebs.[66]

Further, while reaffirming his belief in the "rightness of our cause," he
expressed his doubts about ultimate victory:

It is my disbelief in our success by arms in wh. I differ from you . . . – I think in that
matter I have better chances of judging than you – and I believe I represent the
conviction of the army.[67]

He then countered the argument – presumably one made in a letter from his
father – that the Southern devotion to slavery was matched by a Northern
commitment to "civilization and progress," and that the North would
prevail because "progress" is stronger than slavery. Wendell's response
suggests that he is rethinking the role of war in ending slavery.

If civ'n & progress are the better things why they will conquer in the long run, we
may be sure, and will stand a better chance in their proper province – peace – than

---

[63] Howe, *supra* n. 24 at 74.   [64] *Id.* at 76.   [65] *Id.* at 77.   [66] *Id.* at 79.   [67] *Id.*

in war, the brother of slavery – brother – it is slavery's parent, child and sustainer at once.[68]

At this point, Wendell was part of an army that had become thoroughly demoralized. The battle at Fredericksburg and the subsequent retreat brought the Union Army to its lowest point. Desertions were becoming more common and discipline was lax. Abbott may not have been exaggerating when he wrote that:

The state of the army is terrible. Since the intense suffering caused by this advance, things are much worse & almost ready for mutiny.[69]

Morale in the Twentieth was once again threatened by class conflict. One long-standing issue became more intense during the winter of 1862–1863. The Twentieth had lost so many commissioned officers that it was necessary to appoint replacements. Not surprisingly, Governor Andrews preferred to promote from within the ranks, but to the snobbish Harvard officers, this meant sharing their duties with men from immigrant families who had neither breeding nor education. The Harvard officers didn't like it, but they were powerless to stop it.

There was also the question of what to do about a commanding officer. Up until Antietam, Colonel Lee had provided real leadership. In fact, the most fractious time for the unit occurred during his absence after Balls Bluff. Then, it was only his return from the Confederate prison that brought some measure of peace to the warring factions. After Antietam, however, Colonel Lee had had a breakdown. He had disappeared from the battle and been found days later drunk in a stable. Suffering from alcoholism, he was never able to resume command. His formal resignation came soon after the battle at Fredericksburg.[70]

The replacement of Lee was a difficult issue. The Beacon Hill contingent wanted one of their own. Lieutenant Colonel Palfrey was next in line, but he had little support in the unit since he was widely regarded as incompetent. Nor was Governor Andrews inclined in his direction. The next in seniority after Palfrey was Captain Dreher, a German officer, who was also not popular among his fellow officers – partly because he was not from Harvard and partly because his German accent was so thick he had a hard time making himself understood. Third in seniority was Captain Macy, who was the preference of his fellow officers but not the governor's choice. Rumors swirled around the camp. Some thought Dreher would be

---

[68] *Id.* at 79–80 (Dec. 20, 1862).   [69] Miller, *supra* n. 2 at 182.   [70] *Id.* at 218.

named – he was, after all, the governor's favorite. Others thought it might be – God forbid! – an outsider. Such rumors infuriated the Harvard officers and caused them to complain bitterly about civilian interference. Ultimately, however, the governor simply made the appointment in accordance with seniority. First, he appointed Palfrey, but Palfrey was so disabled he resigned. Then he appointed Dreher, who barely lived long enough to receive the appointment. Finally, Macy was appointed acting colonel with every expectation of being appointed to permanent command. Logical as this outcome seemed to the men of the Twentieth, it was not to be. Paul Revere had not yet been officially removed from the rolls of the regiment, and he outranked Macy. He also wished to assume the command, and Governor Andrews, who was still not well disposed toward Macy, was more than willing to have that happen. Technically, since Macy was already occupying the colonel's slot, he had to be mustered out of the unit so that Revere could assume his place. The Harvard officers were so outraged at Revere's interference that they refused to speak to him when he arrived. They were not even assuaged when Revere intervened so that Macy could remain in the unit at the rank of lieutenant colonel. Macy himself behaved with grace, but the rest of the officers nursed their grudge.

Despite the low morale, the officers stood by the unit. Holmes was offered a staff position with General Sedgwick. Traveling with the general would have been somewhat more comfortable than living on the line. Nevertheless, he turned it down, preferring to stay in a unit that, despite its conflicts, commanded both his affection and his respect. Henry Abbott and John Ropes were also offered staff positions. They too turned them down. Pen Hallowell, however, did leave the unit, but he did not transfer to a more comfortable job at headquarters. Instead, he volunteered for one of the most difficult jobs in the army. Together with Colonel Robert Shaw, he would form the command of the Massachusetts Fifty-Fourth – the first black regiment in the Union Army. He asked Wendell to join him, but for reasons nowhere recorded, Holmes declined.[71]

The fiasco at Fredericksburg and the general malaise in the army brought action from Washington. General Burnside was relieved in favor of General Hooker. Hooker sought to improve morale by granting privileges to units that had fought well. Naturally, this benefited the Twentieth. As a reward for their efforts, they were given additional furloughs. They were also moved into comfortable winter quarters in

[71] Baker, *supra* ch. 1, n. 5 at 141.

Falmouth, where Holmes served as provost marshal. As the spring wore on, wholesome food and adequate rest began to have their effect. As their situation improved and the leadership issue stabilized, the officers began to think less of unit politics and more of the coming offensive.

FREDERICKSBURG II

General Hooker had devised a complicated plan for taking Fredericksburg. He divided his army into three sections: the first would cross the Rappahannock well north of the city; the second would cross to the south; and the third smaller unit – which included the Twentieth – would remain near Fredericksburg. The point of the strategy was to leave Lee guessing about where the main attack would come.

On May 2, the pontoon bridges were once again moved into place and the Twentieth crossed into Fredericksburg. This time, they did not attempt passage down the main street, but instead moved to the north and approached the western fortifications from the open plain. This avoided the snipers in town, but exposed them to the Confederate artillery. In a letter to his mother, Holmes gave a vivid description of the scene that followed.

Pleasant to see a d'd gun brought up to an earthwork deliberately brought to bear on you – to notice that your Co. is exactly in range – 1st discharge puff – second puff (as the shell burst) and my knapsack supporter is knocked to pieces … 2nd discharge man in front of me hit – 3d whang the iron enters through garter and shoe into my heel.[72]

And whang! Holmes would be going home once again. He arrived back in Boston in the middle of May. This time, the wound was not life-threatening, but it would take longer to heal and required a course of rehabilitation so that he could walk properly. His father described him as "in excellent spirits [and] not at all nervous, as when he was last wounded."[73] Obviously his life on Beacon Hill was more comfortable than life in the Army. On the other hand, the revolving contrast between home and battle must have been somewhat disorienting. The war looked one way viewed from the comfort of Beacon Hill, and looked quite different from the battlefield. As the war went on, these two perspectives must have seemed more and more at odds. For example, there were all those mutilated corpses. Remember his letter from Balls Bluff, reporting

---

[72] Howe, *supra* n. 24 at 92.   [73] Baker, *supra* ch. 1, n. 5 at 144.

that corpses were everywhere – "you stumble constantly, . . . perhaps tread on the swollen bodies already fly blown and decaying."[74] Compare this with the tenderness and delicacy of the letter John Ropes sent to Wendell asking him to be a pallbearer at his brother Henry's funeral:

The body arrived this morning. It is, I am afraid to say, not in a state to be seen. It would not do to open the coffin. All that can be seen through the glass-plate is the breast, which is bare, and in which there is a fearful wound in the region of the heart, which must have caused instant death. I think I can discern a fragment of shell embedded in the breast. It is a sad and shocking sight – nothing of the face can be seen but the chin, round which is a handkerchief.[75]

Home and war are two different worlds, and it is painful to hold both in one's heart. Back at war, Holmes himself described the problem:

The duties & thoughts of the field are of such a nature that one cannot at the same time keep home, parents and such thoughts as they suggest in his mind at the same time as a reality – Can hardly indeed remember their existence.[76]

LEAVING THE WAR

Holmes returned to the war at the end of January 1864. Then, after six more months of active service, he was on his way home for good. He made the decision in May 1964, sometime between the Wilderness and the battle at Spotsylvania Courthouse.

One way to understand Holmes's decision is in terms of his evolving view of his duties as a soldier. We have seen that Holmes began the war with an image of himself as a gallant knight who fought for virtue and honor. We have also seen that this image did not survive the battle at Balls Bluff. He then developed a new narrative that tied him to the war – one that drew on the duties of a professional soldier, loyalty to one's unit, and the Emersonian ideal of heroism. Slowly over the ensuing years, all three of these motivations became less forceful.

The first to go was the code of the professional soldier. The army had become impersonal and ruthless in its warlike mission. Grant was now in charge of the Union forces, and with him came a new strategy for ending

---

[74] Howe, *supra* n. 24 at 36 (June 2).

[75] Letter from John Ropes, at Harvard Law School, the John G. Palfrey Collection (1875–1945) *in* Oliver Wendell Holmes Jr. *Papers, 1715–1938, Family and Personal Material, Civil War: Civil War Scrapbook Created by Oliver Wendell Holmes, 1861–1865.* http://nrs.harvard.edu/urn-3:HLS.Libr:1815413?n=18

[76] Howe, *supra* n. 24 at 123.

the war. Union plans were no longer centered on occupying Richmond. Instead, Grant recognized that the destruction of Lee's army would mean an end to the Confederacy. And so he began a long war of attrition. It began on May 5 at the battle of the Wilderness. For two days, there was intense fighting in difficult terrain. Toward the end of the second day, the Confederate Army outflanked the Union Army on the right side, inflicting much damage. That night, Grant disengaged his forces from the fighting and resumed his march southward toward Spotsylvania Courthouse. This began the series of flanking maneuvers in which battle followed battle with little time in between.

At this point, it must have been obvious to Holmes that the days of infantry charges were over. It was not heroism that would win the day, but a daily grind of mechanized killing. As Nathan Hayward, Holmes's "mentor," had put it in a letter home:

A general order from General Grant, to Meade, to Hancock, to Gibbon, to the brigade commanders, to regimental commanders – nothing to arouse enthusiasm – not the presence of generals to encourage and inspire their men with the example of their own determination – but as I say this cold-blooded official order.[77]

Furthermore, Holmes was seeing a new kind of fighting. Battles dragged on for days. Troops were digging in – building barricades and trenches. It was also true that Holmes was learning, for the first time, the terrible extent of the fighting. As he rode around attending to his duties, he was seeing more of the destruction. He wrote in his diary:

In the corner of woods ... the dead of both sides lay piled in the trenches 5 or 6 deep – wounded often writhing under superincumbent dead. ... The losses of our Corps in these nine days are ten thousand five hundred & forty seven![78]

All of this clearly took its toll. Cold-blooded orders and impersonal, ruthless combat could not inspire a worn-out soldier to reenlist.

But there was also the question of loyalty to his regiment. After Fredericksburg, however, the sad and simple truth was that he had no place there. The Civil War had its share of red tape. Colonel Revere had been killed at Gettysburg, and Lieutenant Colonel Macy had been wounded. Holmes was next in line for the position of lieutenant colonel. He suggested that he waive it in favor of his friend Abbott, who was at that point commanding the unit. Abbott, however, gracefully declined and Holmes accepted the promotion. This created an anomaly in the chain

---

[77] Miller, *supra* n. 2 at 399.　[78] *Id.* at 117.

of command. Abbot was a major, but, if Holmes returned as a lieutenant colonel, he would have to serve under Abbott – essentially taking orders from one of lower rank. The obvious solution – that Holmes accept a temporary demotion – was not available since the Twentieth already had its full allotment of captains.[79] There was no solution except for Holmes to leave the unit and accept a staff position at Sixth Corps Headquarters.[80]

The final blow to Holmes's regimental loyalty came during the battle of the Wilderness when Abbott, his last remaining tie to the unit, was killed. In some ways, the two men were an odd pairing. Abbott was a copperhead and one of the more snobbish men in the unit. He would complain, for example, about officers who were not also "gentlemen."[81] Wendell, on the other hand, usually joined his friend Pen in bridging the divide between the anti-abolition "gentlemen officers" and the pro-abolition "non-gentlemen officers." Nevertheless, despite their differences, it is clear that Holmes loved Abbott:

I observed him in every kind of duty, and never ... did I see him fail to choose that alternative of conduct which was most disagreeable to himself. He was indeed a Puritan in all his virtues, without the Puritan austerity; for, when duty was at an end, he who had been the master and leader became the chosen companion in every pleasure that a man might honestly enjoy.[82]

---

[79] Baker, *supra* ch. 1, n. 5 at 145.

[80] Holmes may have contemplated that his absence from the unit would be temporary. As late as mid-April 1864, he wrote Charles Eliot Norton of his plan to return to the Twentieth as a lieutenant colonel under a recovered Colonel Macy: "In all probability from what I hear of the filling up of the Regt. I shall soon be mustered in for a new term of service as Lt. Col. Of the 20th" (Howe, *supra* n. 24 at 122, n. 1 [Autograph letter, Houghton Library, Harvard University]). Note that the "new term of service" was contingent on the circumstance that the regiment was "filling up." This refers to the fact that the regiment would go out of existence on its three-year anniversary unless two things happened – it had to persuade half of its remaining volunteers to reenlist for a new term, and it had to recruit enough men to bring the unit up to fighting strength (844 men) (Miller, *supra* n. 2 at 315). Given that the Twentieth had been decimated by its years of service, these were two difficult requirements, but remarkably the regiment passed both these tests. The result, however, was a unit that barely resembled the one Holmes had left. After the slaughter at Gettysburg, all that remained of Holmes's friends in the officer corps were Macy and Abbott. Furthermore, thanks in part to the growing practice of foreign recruiting, German was replacing English as the most spoken language in the regiment. *Id.* at 320–321.

[81] Generally, the term "copperhead" was applied to those who were so opposed to the war that they encouraged various forms of resistance. Obviously, the soldiers in the Twentieth who were called "copperheads" were not so extreme in their views.

[82] Holmes, *supra* prologue, n. 1.

Since Abbott was the last of Holmes's close friends to serve in the regiment, his death terminated what was left of Holmes's attachment to the unit.

The final barrier to Holmes's reenlistment was his own physical condition. Essential to the Emersonian ideal was a steadfast confidence in one's own ability to withstand discomfort and injury, but Holmes's confidence had slowly eroded during three long years of war. Holmes had not held anything back – he required himself to push to the limits of his endurance. Years of this had taken their toll. While his wounds may have recovered, the wear and tear from the day-in-and-day-out punishment of his body had not.[83] Only a few men had suffered what he had suffered and were still able to perform their duties.

On May 16, Holmes finally found a quiet time to write to his parents. It is no surprise that he was not "in the mood for writing details." Instead he summed up the situation:

Enough that these nearly two weeks have contained all of fatigue and horror that war can furnish – The advantage has been on our side but nothing decisive has occurred & the enemy is in front of us strongly entrenched ... nearly every Regimental off – I knew or cared for is dead or wounded.

And then he told them he had had enough:

I have made up my mind to stay on the staff if possible till the end of the campaign and then if I am alive, I shall resign.[84]

Apparently, Holmes's father, growing more and more ardent in his support of the war, wrote to express his disapproval. Holmes replied:

I can do a disagreeable thing or face a great danger coolly enough when I *know* it is a duty – but a doubt demoralizes me as it does any nervous man – and now I believe the duty of fighting has ceased for me – ceased because I have laboriously and with much suffering of mind and body *earned* the right ... to decide for myself how I can best do my duty to myself to the country and, if you choose, to God –[85]

This response, however, hides more than it discloses. Holmes emphasizes his right to decide for himself the extent of his duty, but does not recite the reasons why he believes his duty has ceased. Unfortunately, his

---

[83] About this, Holmes sought advice. The medical director of his unit was skeptical about his ability to continue. He felt that Holmes was "not keeping up by the strength of [his] constitution but by the stimulus of this constant pressure to which [the unit] had been subjected." *Id.*

[84] *Id.* at 112.   [85] Howe, *supra* n. 24 at 143.

silence on this question has led some commentators to suggest that he had given up on his ideals. This is, however, not the only possible explanation.

In retrospect, we know that the war was over soon after Holmes left the army. At the time, however, it did not feel like the war was winding down. Instead, it must have seemed that the fighting had shifted into high gear. Holmes would have been justified in feeling that another enlistment would have meant the end of his life. The odds in favor of being killed must have seemed extremely high. And, if he was not killed, he was certainly mindful of the risk of receiving a crippling wound or worse. As he wrote to his parents, "Many a man has gone crazy since the campaign begun from the terrible pressure on body and mind."[86]

But these considerations simply spoke to the sacrifice involved in reenlisting, and sacrifice was what duty was all about. Holmes had to think hard about the nature of his duty and what it required from him. Did the same duty that required him to enlist also require him to reenlist? The answer lies in his changing attitude toward the war.

Holmes certainly did not become a pacifist. In fact, throughout his life, he praised the military spirit that brings men to war. On the other hand, we have seen that he had arrived at an important insight – that war is "the brother of slavery." More than that he wrote: "[War] is slavery's parent, child and sustainer at once."[87] In short, he had come to believe that slavery arose from a state of war and was sustained by violence. Thus, he doubted that more war and more violence could eradicate it. Some will argue that Holmes was simply mistaken in this judgment. Within a year, the war would be over and there would be no slavery in the South. But it was equally true that justice would not prevail in the South. Plantation slavery would be replaced by systems of peonage, sharecropping, segregation, and lynching trees.[88] The war may have abolished slavery but it had not eliminated the cruel oppression of those who were formerly enslaved. Indeed, the face of white supremacy may have changed, but it had not been eliminated. This would be exactly as Holmes might have expected. If he had learned one thing from the war, it was the determination of his Southern opponents to maintain their previous ways of life.

---

[86] *Id.* at 150.   [87] Howe, *supra* n. 24 at 79–80 (Dec. 20, 1862).

[88] Douglas Blackmon, *Slavery by Another Name: The Re-Enslavement of Black Americans from the Civil War to World War II* (2008).

3

The Great Chorus of Life and Joy Begins Again

As I listen, the great chorus of life and joy begins again, and amid the awful
orchestra of seen and unseen powers and destinies of good and evil our
trumpets sound once more a note of daring, hope, and will.
Memorial Day Speech, 1884

Wendell returned to Boston in the summer of 1864. He found his family
little changed. Happily, his sister, Amelia, and his younger brother, Ned –
now a student at Harvard – were both living at home. His father was still
pursuing two successful careers at once; his mother, who had spent the
war years organizing volunteer workers, had returned to her chosen role
as wife and mother.

But, indisputably, Wendell himself had changed. Those closest to him
saw it as positive. Fanny Dixwell, his future wife, declared that without
the war, Wendell would have been a coxcomb – a pretentious young man
full of his own good luck and fine pedigree.[1] It is easy to understand her
concern. Wendell, the son and namesake of a famous father, was surely in
some danger of becoming one more expendable member of Boston
society. But two things militated against this. As Fanny said, one was the
hardening effect of his Civil War service. The second, present long before
the war, was the intensity of his ambition.

There can be no doubt that the war shaped Holmes's character. The
burning question over several decades of scholarship has been the exact
nature of the influence. Was it positive as Fanny suggested? Or was it
negative and, if negative, exactly how negative?

---

[1] Baker, *supra* ch. 1, n. 5 at 105.

To understand the importance of this debate, it is necessary to fast-forward to a time when lawyers began to reexamine Holmes's legacy. Holmes was a nineteenth-century man who lived well into the twentieth century. His legal sense was shaped in a time when conflicts between the state and federal governments were a source of instability and rebellion. Today, we are more likely to see the combined strength of the state and federal governments as a potential problem. From this perspective, Holmes sometimes seems out of step with conventional wisdom; indeed, in a few cases, his opinions seem inconsistent with a fundamental regard for human rights. But some modern writers were not content to simply criticize his views. Holmes had become such a treasured icon of our jurisprudence that reasoned examination – no matter how salient – was insufficient to break the spell of his influence over American law. Lessening the Holmesian influence meant dismantling the myth of Holmes the war hero, scholar, and judge. Thus, as scholars began to reassess his reputation as a jurist, they also began reinterpreting his wartime experience and the effect it had on his subsequent life. Holmes may have been a Civil War hero, but today's critics have portrayed him as its victim. They see him as a wounded spirit who emerged from the war with numerous character defects; he was, they argue, self-centered, excessively ambitious, and even at times misanthropic.

The debate began with the publication of Holmes's war letters in 1946. Mark Howe, Holmes's biographer and former law clerk, started the discussion with a relatively positive assessment; he viewed the war as the source of Holmes's intellectual humility:

[Holmes] had seen a number of his own convictions crumble when they felt the impact of reality. He had seen opposing convictions withstand the strain of war. It would always be hard for one who had been sensitive to this experience to consider that his own principles of morality were sanctioned by a cosmic or universal authority.[2]

On the other hand, some began to question both Holmes's heroism and his conduct in civilian life. The general charge was that his wartime experience diminished his idealism and made him skeptical about the requirements of morality. For example, in *Patriotic Gore*, Edmund Wilson suggested that the war had fostered a number of unappealing characteristics – detachment, cynicism, and single-minded ambition.[3]

---

[2] Howe, *supra* ch. 2, n. 24 at 285.
[3] Edmund Wilson, *Patriotic Gore: Studies in the Literature of the American Civil War* (1962) is an iconic study of the effect of war on famous men.

Another scholar echoed this judgment, arguing that Holmes suffered psychological injuries that caused:

the deadening of sympathetic feelings, the Olympian aloofness, the spectator view, [the need for] books to calm the nerves, the sentiment of honor, the belief in heroic action, the disbelief in causes – all these, by which he can somehow gain distance from the world, can be seen in him by the end of the war.[4]

Soon, each of his biographers attempted armchair psychology, and as time went on, the resulting commentary seemed more and more implausible. For example, in 1993, G. Edward White published a biography of Holmes in which he portrayed Holmes as a soldier obsessed with his own survival. Thus, Holmes's statement that continued service on the line of battle "was a greater strain" than he was "called to endure," became, in White's interpretation, proof that:

Holmes ... had evolved to the point where he saw war principally as a threat to one's being. In the end the central duty of wartime [became] the duty to do one's best to ensure the survival of self.[5]

White also drew a marked contrast between the self-interested Holmes and his heroic friend Henry Abbott:

The one, Abbott, the very personification of soldierly duty and honor. The other, Holmes, a soldier who after being shot in the heel had hoped his foot might be amputated so that he could avoid returning to war, who had chosen to leave service before Union victory was certain, who had admitted to his parents that he could no longer endure the blows and hardships of being a line officer, [and] who had reproached himself for missing the battle that produced Abbott's legendary bravery.[6]

Thus, what earlier writers had seen as "survivor's guilt" became, for White, real guilt caused by real failures of spirit.[7] Holmes had not just lost his idealism, White suggested; he had become an amoral egoist, who thought only of himself.[8]

While it is true that Abbott became a kind of heroic figure to Holmes, White's contrast between Abbott and Holmes surely misses the mark. Holmes too had been wounded – not once but three times. He too had rushed fearlessly into the thick of battle. He was on the sidelines at Fredericksburg not because he was malingering, but because he had

---

[4] Saul Touster, *In Search of Holmes from Within*, 18 Vand. L. Rev. 437, 470 (1965).
[5] White, *supra* ch. 1, n. 10 at 70. [6] *Id.* at 79. [7] Touster, *supra* n. 4 at 472.
[8] White, *supra* ch. 1, n. 10 at 70 ("His concept of duty had thus progressed from the idea of fidelity to a cause to that of loyalty to a regiment and finally to that of loyalty to oneself").

a case of dysentery that disabled him for months and might have proved fatal. Furthermore, the reason why Abbott became such a symbol to Holmes was not his intense courage – which Holmes certainly admired – but the impetus that brought him to war. Abbott was a copperhead – he did not believe in abolition; neither was he committed to saving the Union. He fought solely to fulfill his duty to his country. It was this aspect of Abbott's bravery that fascinated Holmes. Holmes had enlisted because he believed in the cause, but, as his commitment waned, he searched for things to sustain his courage. Abbott, fighting solely to vindicate his sense of honor, became a powerful example that stiffened Holmes's resolve.

Also negative is Albert Alschuler's treatment of Holmes's wartime experience. Noting that negative interpretations "now seem conventional,"[9] he restated many of them without analysis or criticism. For example, he portrayed Holmes as a man obsessed with "war, power, and struggle."[10] He also suggested that Holmes had an "attraction to morbidity."[11] But, for Alschuler, Holmes was not just a coward; he was almost a psychopath. "Imagine," he writes,

that your Uncle Bob is a postal clerk whose career has never been interrupted by military service, and imagine that Bob begins one day to voice the thoughts once voiced by Oliver Wendell Holmes. For example, at the dinner table one evening, Bob announces, "[W]hen men differ in taste as to the kind of world they want the only thing to do is to go to work killing." The next day, Bob praises suicide as a more "uneconomic" form of expression than charity to the poor. You and other family members are likely to consider whether Bob needs help.[12]

This comparison seems far-fetched. Holmes is not sitting at the dinner table philosophizing about mass murder and suicide. He made these statements in a context in which his hearers understood that he was

---

[9] Albert Alschuler, *Law Without Values: The Life, Work, and Legacy of Justice Holmes* 45 (2002). The conventional view to which he refers is not White's harsh judgment but the milder one by Robert Gordon:

The war experience may have laid the foundations of Holmes's aloof detachment, his disengagement from causes and distrust of enthusiasms, and the bleakly skeptical foundations of his general outlook, according to which law and rights were only the systems imposed by force by whatever social groups emerged as dominant in the struggle for existence. (Robert W. Gordon, Introduction: Holmes's Shadow, in *The Legacy of Oliver Wendell Holmes, Jr.* 1 [Robert W. Gordon ed. 1992])

[10] Alschuler, *supra* n. 9 at 50.   [11] *Id.*

[12] *Id.* at 50. The quotes from Holmes are obviously taken out of context. Neither statement was casually made at a dinner table. The first, for example, comes from a letter in which he was explaining why he found Jane Austen dull. *See* Wilson, *supra* n. 3 at 761.

making a larger point, one driven home by a provocative exaggeration. Even more notable is the fact that Alschuler chooses to compare Holmes to "Uncle Bob," who has spent his days delivering mail rather than fighting a war. Fighting a war is a significant experience – one that normally colors our estimation of those who do it. Note, for example, Touster's treatment of this issue:

Holmes was . . . a profoundly injured spirit, and his greatness as a human being can be justly viewed only in the light of this fact. . . . He had been there and come back! We are all in awe of such spirits.[13]

One way to understand the difference between Touster and Alschuler is in terms of the intervening Vietnam War. That war filled our streets and shelters with men who had been devastated by combat and forced us to see that the psychological wounds of battle are often worse than the physical ones. Thus, Alschuler, writing before the most recent Gulf War increased our esteem for returning veterans, accorded such wounds a kind of condescending sympathy.[14] As a result, he wondered "how and why a man brutalized by war became the great oracle of American law."[15] In asking this question, Alschuler was not wondering how Holmes rose to the challenge. Rather he was inquiring how someone who was not suitable for high office could receive so much public esteem.[16]

With Alschuler we have come full circle. In 1934, Holmes had been lionized as a symbol of American greatness. People were not just appreciative of his many achievements; they were also captivated by his persona – they saw him as a war hero, a great wit, and a man of grace and wisdom. Sixty years later, the image had become severely tarnished. His detractors argued that public admiration of Holmes was misplaced because, in reality, he was a coward, a crackpot, or worse. The centerpiece

---

[13] Touster, *supra* n. 4 at 471.

[14] In fact, Alschuler's sympathy seems a little ambivalent: "If Bob were a war hero, however, your response might be somewhat different. The crusty talk of soldiers is part of their charm. This talk may be a way of reminding an audience of an old soldier's history without quite boasting." Alschuler, *supra* n. 9 at 50.

[15] *Id.* at 181.

[16] That this is the nature of his question is evident in the answers he gives. According to Alschuler, Holmes has an undeservedly good reputation because of: (1) "his height (six foot three), his eyes, his bearing, and his mustache"; (2) "the lack of plausible liberal heroes on the bench of the U.S. Supreme Court"; (3) "the public relations efforts on Holmes's behalf . . . by Felix Frankfurter and other young admirers of Holmes." *Id.* at 181–182.

of this latter account was the war and the way in which his wartime experience left him selfish and unfeeling.

It seems to me that both views of Holmes are equally unrealistic. Holmes was never quite as grand as his original biographers declared, neither was he as psychologically damaged as his modern critics suggest. Holmes's experience in the war *was* devastating. After the war, he *was* skeptical about conventional morality. He was also distrustful of simple idealism, and he was certainly ambitious. But none of these characteristics is pathological, neither do they require a patronizing explanation. Many of Holmes's Boston contemporaries shared these qualities. Many of these qualities were part of Holmes's character well before his Civil War experience. Furthermore, the idea that Holmes was emotionally disabled by three years of combat is simply inconsistent with the facts of his subsequent life.

It is a painful truth that the hardships of war do not run off a young man's back like so many drops of rain, but what is striking about Holmes is that – as horrific as his experiences had been – he was not severely damaged. Within a year of his return, he had enrolled in Harvard Law School and begun work on his career. After law school, he visited Europe. In London, he led an active social life – his wit and striking personality making him a popular guest at fashionable dinners and weekends.[17] In Paris, there were no social engagements, but he actively explored the city, studying its art and history. In Switzerland, he did some serious climbing in the Alps.[18]

Neither did he seem troubled when he came home. A depressed man might have lapsed into a desultory practice of law, but he did not. He remained energetic and engaged. While legal practice did not excite him, he spent his free time studying legal history and building relationships with others who were committed to intellectual pursuits. He spent long evenings with William James discussing philosophy.[19] He went to New Hampshire with Henry James and, while there, befriended a young child who went hiking with them every day.[20] He edited a law review and discussed legal theory with his friends. He reached out to George

---

[17] Baker, *supra* ch. 1, n. 5 at 179.

[18] He went climbing with Leslie Stephen and the climbs were difficult enough to earn him membership in the London Alpine Club. *Id.* at 185–186.

[19] *Id.* at 193. *See also* Ralph Barton Perry, *The Thought and Character of William James* 113 (1935).

[20] Baker, *supra* ch. 1, n. 5 at 199. *See also* Sheldon M. Novick, Henry James, *The Young Master* 75 (1999) for a fuller account of this relationship.

Shattuck as a mentor and friend.[21] Furthermore, as time went on he patiently worked his way through mountains of case law, and provided the annotations for a new edition of Kent's *Commentaries*.[22] He also read most of the existing literature on legal theory. He married Fanny Dixwell, a woman with whom he had much in common, and they formed a lifelong bond of engagement and comfort.[23] He wrote articles for the *American Law Review*,[24] and, by the time he was forty, he had completed *The Common Law*.[25] At this point, he stood poised for appointment to the Harvard Law faculty, and soon thereafter, to the Supreme Judicial Court of Massachusetts.[26] Twenty years later, he was appointed to the Supreme Court. Indeed, this is a remarkable record of achievement for one who had endured some of the most difficult experiences that a war can provide.

Perhaps Holmes was lucky. Perhaps he was one of those men who are able to forget the horrors of war. But the truth is he did not forget. He remained mindful of the war throughout his life. He mentioned it to friends, observed its anniversaries, and often thought in terms of military metaphors. The war stayed very much with him, but it did not prevent him from moving forward. Holmes had returned from the war with his energy and enthusiasm intact. Understanding Holmes requires that we acknowledge this fact because if we treat him – as others have treated him – as a wounded warrior, we will miss the vitality and fortitude of his character.

---

[21] In a memorial to Shattuck, Holmes wrote: "Young men in college or at the beginning of their professional life are very apt to encounter some able man a few years older than themselves who is so near to their questions and difficulties and yet so much in advance that he counts for a good deal in the shaping of their views or even of their lives. Mr. Shattuck played that part for me." Oliver Wendell Holmes Jr., *Memoir of George Otis Shattuck 10* (1900). He also said: "From the time when I was a student in his office until he died, he was my dear and intimate friend." *Id.* at 22.

[22] James B. Kent, Commentaries on American Law (Oliver Wendell Holmes Jr. ed., 12th edn. 1873).

[23] For a description of the relationship between Oliver Wendell Holmes Jr. and Fanny Dixwell, *see* Baker, *supra* ch. 1, n. 5 at 218–230.

[24] His major writings during this period include: *Codes and the Arrangement of the Law* 5 Am. L. Rev. 1 (1870); *The Arrangement of the Law – Privity* 7 Am. L. Rev. 46 (1872–1873); *Misunderstandings of the Civil Law*, 6 Am. L. Rev. 37 (1871); *Theory of Torts*, 7 Am. L. Rev. 652 (1872–1873); *Gas Stokers Strike* 7 Am. L. Rev. 582 (1872–1873); *Primitive Notions in Modern Law I*, 10 Am. L. Rev. 422 (1875); *Primitive Notions in Modern Law II*, 11 Am. L. Rev. 641 (1877); *Possession*, 12 Am. L. Rev. 688 (1877); *Common Carrier and the Common Law*, 13 Am. L. Rev. 609 (1879); and *Trespass and Negligence*, 14 Am. L. Rev. 1 (1880).

[25] Oliver Wendell Holmes Jr., *The Common Law* (1881).

[26] He was appointed to the Harvard Law faculty in January 1882, and to the Massachusetts Supreme Judicial Court in December 1882.

We can begin separating fact from fiction by discarding the biographical debris generated by the construction of myth and countermyth. Leaving this behind, we must focus our attention on what we know about the young man who returned from war in 1864, and we must be careful not to confuse him with the much older man who resides in our collective memory. If Holmes in his nineties seemed somewhat reserved and reclusive, we should attribute it to his age rather than his personality. Thus, we turn to Wendell's friends in the postwar period to assemble a more accurate picture.

The evidence from this period suggests that he was generally outgoing and charming. He was well liked by his contemporaries and made friends easily. Even as late as 1903, when he moved to Washington, he was considered a congenial and gregarious figure. In fact, President Theodore Roosevelt – a "strenuous" man with high standards of friendship and fun – frequently invited him to the White House simply for the pleasure of his company.

Part of what fueled his popularity was a certain lightheartedness. For example, he was delighted by Fanny's propensity to play practical jokes. And it is clear that his relations with friends also had a playful element. We can see this in a letter from William James to Holmes and John Gray after they had removed some of the wrong outerwear from the James foyer:

Gents! – entry-thieves – ... – beware! The hand of the law is already on your throats and waits but a wink to be tightened. ... My father and self have pledged our lives, our fortunes and our sacred honor to see the thing through. ... Gurney and Perry have been heard to go about openly declaring that "if they had known the party was going to be that kind of an affair, d—d if they would have started off earlier themselves with some of those aristocratic James overcoats, hats, gloves and canes!

Young Holmes was also capable of great exuberance. It is hard to imagine the isolated, cynical, workaholic described by Wilson, Alschuler, and White writing a letter to William James that began with this celebration of spring:

Now are the waters beneath my window of a deeper and more significant blue. ... Now do the fields burn with green fire – the evanescent hint of I know not what hidden longing of the earth. Now all the bushes burgeon with wooly buds and the elm trees have put on bridal veils of hazy brown. Now the chorus of the frogs answers the chorus of the birds in antiphony of morning and evening. ... Spring is here, Bill, and I turn to thee, – not with more affection than during the long grind of the winter, but desiring if it may be to say a word to thee once more.[27]

Holmes, however, was a man of contradictions – a trait Bill James noted in a letter to his brother Harry:

I think [Wendell is] composed of at least 2 ½ distinct human beings and how they inhabit his own narrow skin without quarreling and trying to shove each other out of doors [is] a [mystery] to me.

Of the "2 ½ distinct human beings," one was gregarious while another was an introvert. Like many young men, Holmes had both a public and a private self. He acknowledged this in an early letter to William James: "In spite of my many friends, I am almost alone in my inner thoughts and feelings."[28] Thus, to get beyond his public affability, we have to delve more deeply into his character, his ambition, and even into the spiritual beliefs that fueled his achievements.

Unfortunately, it is not easy to understand this aspect of Holmes's personality. Holmes was not a man who felt comfortable discussing himself. This may have been New England reserve or it may have been a reaction to his father who erred so much in the other direction. His Civil War letters – at least those that were not burned – were affectionate to his family but terse when it came to his inner struggles, and, while there are volumes of letters to professional associates, little remains of his correspondence with his wife and family.

Whatever the reason, Holmes's reticence poses a difficult problem for someone seeking to understand the depth of his character. We know a great deal about his ideas, but very little about his personal concerns. We can see that he pursued his goals with fierce discipline and real passion, but the nature of these goals and the substance of his motivation remain obscure. Even to those who were close to him, Holmes remained somewhat of an enigma.

Nothing illustrates this more clearly than Holmes's friendship with William James. Wendell met James soon after the Civil War and they became close friends. They would often meet on Saturday night, smoke cigars, drink brandy, and discuss philosophy into the early morning hours. As is so often true with men of a certain age, philosophical questions could be substitutes for more personal ones. Later, for example, when James went through an intense struggle with depression, he saw it in

---

[27] Perry, *supra* n. 19 at 92.   [28] *Id.* at 90.

terms of free will. If men had free will, James thought, life was worth living. If they did not, then suicide would be the better alternative.

Despite the fact that Wendell and Bill were close friends, Wendell found it hard to express himself fully. This was a matter of some sorrow for Bill, who had been brought up in a family where inexhaustible self-expression was the currency of the realm. This is evident in their correspondence. In 1866, Bill had gone to Germany to look after his health. He did not hear from Holmes for many months. Finally, Bill wrote to Wendell when he found a note from him tucked into a letter from Minnie Temple.

I received a letter from home, containing amongst other valuable matter, a precious specimen of manuscript signed O.W.H. Jr, covering just 1 page of small note paper. ... Now I myself am not proud ... but by Jove, Sir! – there is a point ... to which it seems to me hardly worthwhile to condescend – better to give up altogether [than] to write to a friend after six months, in another person's letter, hail him as "one of the pillars on which life rests" and after 12 lines stop short.[29]

Bill's response was partly playful. Its tone was reminiscent of the letter sent to Holmes and Gray about the mix-up in the coat closet. However, there was also a note of wounded feelings. Bill wanted more than an affectionate note from Wendell; he wanted fellowship and self-disclosure. Bill himself was a model of this kind of communication. His letter was extremely long, recounting the details of his trip, the difficulties posed by his illness, and his most recent thoughts on philosophy. He concluded the letter hopefully with a p.s. – "Why can't you write me the result of your study of the *vis viva* question? I have not thought of it since I left. I wish very much you would, if the trouble be not too great."[30]

It was two and a half months before Wendell responded. Part of the problem was that he was faithfully trying to honor Bill's request that he write about the *vis viva* question. He noted that he had started three long

---

[29] Letter from William James to Oliver Wendell Holmes Jr. (Sept. 17, 1867). The lightness of tone is even more apparent in the next sentence: "[This may seem to you] an action replete with beauty and credit. To me it is otherwise. And if perchance, O Wendy boy, there lurked in any cranny of thy breast a spark of consciousness, a germ of sham, at the paltriness of thy procedure ... I would fain fan it, nourish it till thy whole being should become one incarnate blush, one crater of humiliation."

[30] *Id.* The *vis viva* question involved a formula proposed by Leibnitz to describe the conservation of energy. It differed from a similar formula proposed by Isaac Newton. Generally, Newton's formula is accepted today, but Leibnitz's is correct for a certain class of cases. It is hard to know why James and Holmes were interested in this question. Did Holmes have an opinion about which of the formulas was correct or were the young men simply interested in the concept of a living force?

letters but was "compelled to destroy" them because the reasoning in them "on reflection, appeared ... unsound."[31] Ultimately, it was Fanny who suggested that Bill would be pleased to hear from him even without a solution to the *vis viva* problem.

As Wendell continued with the letter, it is clear that he is unsure how to please his friend. After noting Fanny's comment, he writes, "So here goes," and then admits his difficulty with self-disclosure – "writing is so unnatural to me that I have never before dared to try it to you unless in connection with a subject,"[32] and follows it up with:

Ah dear Bill – do me justice – my expressions of esteem are not hollow nor hyperbolical – not put in to cover neglect. ... whether I ever see you much or not, I think I can never fail to derive a secret comfort and companionship from the thought of you – I believe I shall always love and respect you whether we see much or little of each other.[33]

Having said this much, Holmes hastily searches for a subject. He begins with Fanny, who has postponed art school because of trouble with her eyes. From there he goes to his recent read of *The Critique of Pure Reason* and what he sees as the problems with Kant's theory. Only toward the end does he return to personal matters. After one more burst of affection:

Oh Bill my beloved how have I yearned after thee all this long time – How have I admired those brave generous and magnanimous traits of which I will not shame thee by speaking – I am the better that I have seen thee and known thee.

He adds, "Let that suffice," and concludes the letter by transmitting his sister's affection for Bill and reporting on a trip to see Bill's father.

What is striking about this letter is that despite its length – about four large printed pages – and despite the fact that it was written to his best friend, there is no real self-disclosure. The discussion of Kant is interesting and sheds considerable light on Holmes's interpretation of Kant, but we don't know why he has read it or what he finds useful in it. Furthermore, even though he has no trouble expressing his love for Bill, Bill seems to have no place in his life. Note, for example, that Holmes claims to be comforted by Bill's existence whether he ever sees him or not.

A similar pattern emerges in his later correspondence with professional colleagues. In these letters, Holmes resolved the problem of self-expression by always having a subject at hand. Indeed, the collected volumes of his correspondence perfectly illustrate this strategy. Unlike

[31] Letter from Oliver Wendell Holmes Jr. to William James (Dec. 15, 1867).   [32] *Id.*
[33] *Id.*

his letters to Bill, there are few effusive expressions of affection, but each letter is an economical pairing of conventional pleasantries with substantive discussion. Even when he speaks of his own feelings, his expressions are limited to a few well-worn phrases borrowed from his own public speeches. Thus, what was private for Holmes has remained private.

To understand Holmes, we must recognize that he was, first and foremost, an intellectual. From an early age, he read voraciously. Indeed, by the end of his life, he had read all the books that mattered – many of them several times. Ideas moved him, but, unlike many intellectuals, he was not moved by one great idea. Holmes was a pluralist – a man who enjoyed looking at life through many lenses. In fact, Holmes was an intellectual of a particular stripe. To put it in his father's terms, he was a "third story man."

"There are," Dr. Holmes wrote, "one-story intellects, two-story intellects, [and] three-story intellects with skylights."

All fact-collectors ... are one-story men. Two-story men compare, reason, generalize, using the labors of fact-collectors as well as their own. Three-story men idealize, imagine, predict; their best illuminations come from above, through the skylight. There are minds with large ground floors that can store an infinite amount of knowledge ... Your great working lawyer has two spacious stories, his mind is clear, because his mental floors are large, and he has room to arrange his thoughts so that he can get at them, – facts below, principles above, and all in ordered series.[34]

When he came to the three-story men, Dr. Holmes described them as "often narrow below, incapable of clear statement, and with small power of consecutive reasoning, but full of light."[35] A third-story man, he thought, delighted in the power of metaphysical insight. Emerson, perhaps, might have been a good example.

When we think about Holmes in this way, we can see that he was competent on all three levels. On the first floor, he seemed to collect and store a prodigious number of facts; on the second, he was more than capable of rational and orderly thought. But it was on the third level that his spirit found its true home. For Wendell, the most important question would always be – what are the most general ideas that give order and form to the universe? When it came to law, this meant that he would not be content with mastering the details; he would push forward

---

[34] Oliver Wendell Holmes Jr., *Poet at the Breakfast Table* 44 (Houghton Mifflin & Co. and J. M. Dent & Company ed. 1902).

[35] *Id.* at 492.

to discover the deeply buried truths of jurisprudence. He would become not just a lawyer but also a scholar and a scientist of the law.

Holmes was not just casually interested in these questions. In fact, he was driven; he would sacrifice all his comfort and ease to satisfy this need for achievement. This has given rise to the notion that he was self-seeking and cynical. For proof, we have Bill's statement to his brother Henry that Holmes was "a powerful battery, formed like a planning machine to gouge a deep self-beneficial groove through life."[36] But, of course, this assessment leaves open an important question: what was the "deep self-beneficial groove" that Holmes was trying to cut? How did Holmes understand his own well-being? After the war, what aspirations had he formed? What did he think of as a meaningful life?

We can begin to understand Wendell's ambition by comparing him to his cousin Johnny Morse. Together, Wendell and Johnny attended Dixwell's. Together, they went to Harvard. But, when the war came, they parted company. Johnny was too busy to enlist – he had fallen in love. He met his future wife during his senior year while ice skating with friends. Immediately he was committed. As he later explained: "After that I had but one purpose in life . . . to have a profession . . . so that I could have the right to propose to marry." And so he pursued legal training.

Note the contrast. Morse was impulsive – he met a woman and immediately dedicated his entire life to making her his wife. By comparison, Holmes could not have been more deliberate. First, he did his duty to his country. Then, he decided his vocation. Then, he did all that was necessary to prepare himself for success. Only after he had done all this did he propose marriage to Fanny Dixwell, who had been a close friend since childhood.

Furthermore, the cousins were different in their attitude toward their chosen profession. Neither one of them loved the practice of law. Morse, in fact, was quite emphatic: "I hated the law with all my wicked little heart," he said and soon he turned his attention to history.[37] He edited a series of biographies called *The American Statesmen* and wrote a number of the volumes, but his work was mediocre at best.[38] Holmes,

---

[36] Baker, *supra* ch. 1, n. 5 at 232.

[37] John T. Morse, *Incidents Connected with the American Statesman Series*, 64 PROC. OF THE MASS. HIST. SOC'Y 371 (1931).

[38] One historian summed it up this way: "He was, as you know, the editor of the American Statesmen Series and the author of several of its volumes. But the Series is not much read today, even if we may agree that it served its purpose well in its time. Oscar Handlin in his *Dictionary of American Biography* article on Morse is fairly severe on him as an

on the other hand, continued practicing law while he spent his free time trying to understand its history and foundations. He slowly built a reputation as a distinguished scholar and it was this reputation that led to his success.

It is also apparent that the two cousins had very different conceptions of what life is about. Johnny thought of it as a pleasant affair that occasionally required the performance of specific obligations. For him, duty was a gentle taskmaster. For example, he faithfully attended his wife, who had fallen physically and mentally ill – reading to her and taking her for drives. But his understanding of marital obligation was limited to these small acts of kindness; it did not prevent him from "keeping company" with a much younger woman.[39] For Wendell, on the other hand, duty was everything. It infused every aspect of his life with the claims of obligation. But there was nothing grim about his attitude. His conscience rarely led to foul-tasting medicine. Instead it voiced a call to arms, urging him to higher and higher ground until, at last, he could enjoy the view.

In later years, Morse regretted that he had not made more of himself. At ninety, he wrote to his cousin:

As I review my life it seems to me little better than a desert – horses, boats, dinner parties – what has been the use of them all? They don't even give me any real memories! How profoundly wise you have been. A life of labor, of profound interests, of distinction. Well, so it has come about and we are winding up as we began, side by side – you one of the distinguished men of the world; I, nobody in particular. I find it difficult and painful to appreciate quite what a damned ass I have been.

When Morse wondered why their lives had been so different, the answer seemed obvious to him: "you [Wendell] had more brains than I did; but I had enough ... if I had only had the good sense to make the effort."[40]

Morse's explanation does not seem adequate, especially in view of the fact that Wendell had made far more of an effort than simple "good sense" would have required. He was not merely dedicated to his studies. At times,

---

historian, and so are others whom I have consulted. Let us at least grant him his excellent *Life and Letters of Oliver Wendell Holmes* and his *Memoir of Colonel Henry Lee* and there as an historian leave him for this afternoon." Alexander Williams, *The Letters and Friends of John T. Morse, Jr.*, 79 PROC. OF THE MASS. HIST. SOC'Y 97 (1967).

[39] Her name was Charlotte Silber, and he built a house for her on his farm outside of Boston. When his wife died, he did not marry Charlotte but instead adopted her as his child, and lived with her in a big house outside of Boston. *Id.* at 99–100.

[40] Williams, *supra* n. 38 at 101.

his devotion seemed almost obsessive, as is clear in a description Alice James wrote to her son Henry:

Wendell Holmes dined with us a few days ago. His whole life, soul and body, is utterly absorbed in his *last* work upon his Kent. [Holmes was editing Kent's *Commentaries* at the time.] He carries about his manuscript in his green bag and never loses sight of it for a moment. He started to go to Will's room to wash his hands, but came back for his bag, and when we went to dinner, Will said, "Don't you want to take your bag with you?" He said, "Yes, I always do so at home." His pallid face, and this fearful grip upon his work, makes him a melancholy sight.[41]

We get a similar picture of young Holmes from his father. Dr. Holmes wrote essays that had many fictional characters, and some of them were based on people he knew. In fact, one of them – the Young Astronomer – was remarkably like his eldest son. Thus, in the following story, we get a glimpse of Wendell as a young man. The story begins when a flirtatious woman visits the Astronomer in his observatory and asks to see a "double star." When he shows it to her, she exclaims:

How charming! It must be so much pleasanter than to be alone in such a great empty space! . . . Does not a single star seem very lonely to you?

To which the Astronomer replies – "Not more lonely than I am myself." And this led the narrator (Holmes's father) to comment:

To see a pale student burning away, like his own midnight lamp, with only dead men's hands to hold, . . . when all this time there are soft, warm, living hands that would ask nothing better than to bring the blood back into those cold thin fingers . . . is pitiable enough. . . . But our young man seems farther away from life than any student whose head is bent downwards over his books. His eyes are turned away from all human things. How cold the moonlight is that falls upon his forehead!

Wendell too was wrapped up in his studies and made little time for romantic involvements. But it was more than just a question of conscientious study. Dr. Holmes continued:

I cannot say that the Young Astronomer seemed particularly impressed with a sense of his miserable condition. He said he was lonely, it is true, but he said it in a manly tone, and not as if he were repining.[42]

Like the Astronomer, Wendell had made his lonely studies a solemn duty. Indeed, his commitment to legal work was every bit as robust as his commitment to the army. If he was going to be a lawyer, he was going to

[41] Perry *supra* n. 19 at 98.   [42] Holmes, *supra* n. 34 at 145.

be the best lawyer, and, for him, this was not simply a matter of professional excellence. He would not rest content with practical questions.
Instead, he wished to climb the peak of intellectual insight. In this respect,
Dr. Holmes's portrayal of him as an astronomer is especially apt; after all,
what could be "higher" than the things that are examined through the lens
of a telescope?

If Wendell had been born in an earlier age, he might have dedicated his
life to searching for the truth. But, given the time and place, he knew from
the beginning that such a quest was impossible. He had been born into the
ruins of a zealous religious movement. At college, he had studied Plato and
Kant – two men who had warned against confusing appearance and
reality. He had fought in a war where both sides had equally strong but
opposite convictions. All of this tended toward the realization that it
would not be within his power to know the truth.

Also pointing in this direction was Wendell's study of history. Like his
childhood friend Henry Adams and his cousin Johnny Morse, he was an
historian of some depth. His motivation, however, was quite different
from theirs. They each had a very personal stake in the history they
studied. For example, Morse wrote to vindicate his pride in Boston and
his admiration for the ancestors who had built the city. Adams, on the
other hand, was more ambivalent about his heritage. His grandfather,
John Quincy Adams, had married a Southerner who was charming,
creative, and affectionate. As a result, Henry came to regard the Boston
family as a continual source of repression and the Southern family as
a representative of all that was wholesome and good. As one writer
described it: "his [Adams's] emotional and ideological compass bore due
south."[43] Adams wrote about Southern men – Washington, Jefferson,
Monroe, and Madison – men who had been his family's opponents, but
whom he nevertheless admired. It was the Southerners, he thought, who
were responsible for the success of the American enterprise. When he was
older, he returned his attention to Boston. It was then that he wrote his
most famous work, *The Education of Henry Adams* – a memoir of his
early life that presented a largely negative portrait of the community in
which he was raised.

Both Morse and Adams studied history to prove a point. Morse used
it as an excuse to retire to his clubs and languish in the notion that
Boston's finest times were behind it. Adams used it to convey

---

[43] Garry Wills, *Henry Adams and the Making of America* 11 (2005).

a particular message – the superiority of Southern culture and the falsity of Boston's inflated self-conception.

Holmes too was interested in history, but he had no axe to grind. He did not study history in order to find meaning in his own life or to impose judgment on the past. In studying legal history, he investigated Roman and medieval practices rather than modern times. As John Morse would explain during the First World War: "I think he [Holmes] has heard of the war, but so has he heard of the invasion of Greece by Xerxes; and I doubt whether he cares for one more than for the other." Furthermore, he had little interest in facts. Morse continued: "He and I certainly make odd kindred. He cares no more for concrete facts than for the moon; whereas I fear that I care for little else."

For Holmes, facts were little more than historical gossip. He was interested in ideas and the ways in which they influence events. He studied the past with the expectation that it would be useful in understanding the present and the future. History would become an important tool for studying the law. It would sharpen his sense of possibility and help him to identify worn-out contrivances. As he would later write:

[C]ontinuity with the past is only a necessity and not a duty. . . . Continuity simply limits the possibilities of our imagination, and settles the terms in which we shall be compelled to think.[44]

The word "simply" in this comment is deceptive. It suggests that Holmes is merely making the obvious claim that historical developments color one's sense of the present. But, overlooking the word "simply," the full force of his statement becomes apparent. Anything that "limits the imagination" and "settles the terms in which we shall be compelled to think" is a very powerful force indeed. It does not merely *color* the present; it essentially *creates* the present from the past. Like the war, history taught Wendell an important lesson. In college, he had begun by embracing Plato's theory of ideas, believing that abstraction might lead him to the highest truths. History, however, reinforced his growing sense that the ultimate truth was beyond his grasp. He would study history and use it to explain contemporary life, but he would never forget that his own ideas were destined to become antiquities. Thus, Holmes inhabited a paradox. Because he was a third-story man, he would not be content

---

[44] Oliver Wendell Holmes Jr., An Address Delivered before the New York State Bar Association, Law in Science and Science in Law (Jan. 17, 1899), in *Collected Legal Papers* 211 (1920).

with simple facts or rational dissection. He yearned to discover universal truths, but, at the same time, he knew that such truths were unobtainable. Even knowing this, he labored intensely at obtaining a certain kind of transitory wisdom. He would always be most comfortable on the third floor of human thought and he toiled there day after day, in the hope that it would bring him the satisfaction he sought. This conundrum makes Holmes's postwar years all the more poignant. He was a pilgrim with no destination, and lacking this, what drove him forward?

This is not an easy question. Holmes was not driven by material success. With his career and his family resources, he did not fear poverty. Further, coming from his background the idea of amassing a fortune or commanding an industrial empire would seem almost vulgar. Nor was it success in conventional terms. True, he hoped to follow his grandfather Jackson's path to the highest court in Massachusetts, and perhaps even to surpass him by obtaining a seat on the Supreme Court, but, given his family connections, war record, and natural abilities, he could have achieved conventional success without spending every spare moment in the Social Law Library. Indeed, if a judgeship measured the extent of his ambition, then his evenings would have been better spent on the social circuit, cultivating the kind of political contacts that would ensure an appointment.

On the other hand, he longed for a different kind of success. In his letters, he sometimes complained that the world had not given him the recognition he deserved. He bemoaned the fact that his labors were so invisible. We have all known people like this – people who confuse the legitimate claims of ambition with the greedy demands of the ego – and a piece of Wendell's personality was prone to this human frailty. But, for him, this was a sideshow – he did not spend all those hours studying law simply to earn the admiration of others. The goal was more internal. There was something he needed to discover – an investigation that he had to pursue. This was the secret of his ambition – he could not rest until he had satisfied his destiny.

At times, Holmes needed help understanding his destiny, and this was why Emerson was so important to him. Emerson would guide him into the innermost regions of the spirit. Thus, in deciding on his future life, Holmes paid a visit to the great man. A recent Holmes biographer reports it as follows:

The young man seemed to be testing his new resolve: Would the philosopher's glowing talk seduce him once again? Or could he maintain the momentum?

Emerson's discourse was, as always, captivating, but Wendell did not succumb. When he left Concord that night, he gave the door to a contemplative career a final slam.[45]

Perhaps it happened this way, but I doubt it. When Holmes visited Emerson, they certainly discussed his intellectual ambitions. What seems unlikely, however, is that Emerson – or indeed Holmes himself – would have seen it as a simple choice between law and philosophy. They would not have seen these as separate choices. Emerson was a philosopher but he was also a farmer, a public lecturer, and a volunteer fireman. Indeed, he had written an essay that urged men like Holmes to integrate their academic pursuits with their practical lives.[46] In it, he had argued for a new conception of scholarship – one that took the entire natural world as its text. Thus, at a time when European philosophers were focused on analyzing the scientific method, Emerson was seeking to articulate a different kind of relationship between the scholar and the universe he studies. His fundamental insight was that nature and spirit were two sides of the same coin and that knowledge of the two was inextricably connected.[47] He believed that a sympathetic understanding of the natural world was the first step toward knowledge of the spirit world. From this starting point, a person might apprehend the resonance between nature and spirit. This resonance, he wrote, is "the key which unlock[s] my thoughts and make[s] me acquainted with myself."[48] Thus, as the scientist must go to the laboratory, the philosopher had to engage ordinary life. Emerson described it this way:

I run eagerly into this resounding tumult. I grasp the hands of those next to me, and take my place in the ring to suffer and to work, taught by an instinct, that so shall the dumb abyss be vocal with speech. I pierce its order; I dissipate its fear; I dispose of it within the circuit of my expanding life.[49]

This passage shows Emerson as the ultimate third-story man – "incapable of clear statement" but "filled with light." An ordinary person might wonder what it means to be "taught by an instinct," or

---

[45] Baker, *supra* ch. 1, n. 5 at 163.

[46] Ralph Waldo Emerson, *Oration to Harvard Phi Beta Kappa Society: The American Scholar* (Aug. 31, 1837).

[47] Modern readers generally think of the natural world as babbling brooks, grazing sheep, and other bucolic sights, but Emerson's conception was not limited in this way. He used the term in a wider sense to include everything in the universe that was material rather than spiritual. It included man-made items like belching factories and stinking dumps. Emerson, *supra* intro., n. 5 at 15–17 (1836).

[48] Ralph Waldo Emerson, *On the American Scholar* 13 (1837).   [49] *Id.*

to "pierce [the] order" of the "dumb abyss." But Wendell understood perfectly. He, like Emerson, heard the echo of a spiritual world calling forth from the bustle of daily life.

For many, the spiritual world is a matter of faith that needs no form of rational justification. This, however, was not the Puritan way. Both Emerson and Holmes were descended from men who did not rest their beliefs on simple faith. Faith had to be redeemed by personal experience, and one could not get this experience without rigorous work. If it were simply a matter of finding a beautiful place and absorbing the natural rhythm, then it would be right to imagine that Holmes faced a clear choice between law and philosophy. But Holmes learned from Emerson that an indifference to the material world would only serve to alienate him from the spiritual. Thus, by practicing law, Holmes would be facilitating rather than hindering his philosophical quest.

Keeping this in mind, it seems unlikely that Emerson advised Holmes that he must make a choice between law and philosophy. Instead, it seems more likely that Emerson advised him to practice law, but to always maintain a receptivity to the infinite. Thus, Holmes probably left Emerson's house not so much with a determination to choose law over philosophy, but rather with the understanding that the path of the law would also be his route to philosophical and spiritual truth.[50] What was the nature of this path and what was the truth at which it aimed? There was no clear vision, but Emerson and Holmes seemed to share a sensibility that illuminated the journey to come.

[50] This interpretation of the visit with Emerson seems confirmed by a letter Holmes wrote to Emerson enclosing a copy of his article "Primitive Notions in Modern Law." He wrote: "It seems to me that I have learned, after a laborious and somewhat painful period of probation[,] that the law opens a way to philosophy as well as anything else, if pursued far enough, and I hope to prove it before I die. Accept this little piece as written in that faith, and as a slight mark of gratitude and respect I feel for you who more than anyone else first started the philosophical ferment in my mind." Letter from Oliver Wendell Holmes Jr. to Ralph Waldo Emerson (Apr. 16, 1876).

4

For the Puritan Still Lives in New England, Thank God!

For the Puritan still lives in New England, thank God! ... New England is not dead yet. She still is mother of a race of conquerors – stern men, little given to the expression of their feelings, sometimes careless of their graces, but fertile, tenacious, and knowing only duty.

Memorial Day Speech, 1884

Like most elite Bostonians, Holmes belonged to the Unitarian Church. As his wife, Fanny, explained, "In Boston one has to be something and Unitarian is the least you can be."[1] It is not hard to understand what she meant. The Unitarians were liberal in their attitudes and did not require conformity of religious belief. For Holmes, this was fortunate because he was deeply agnostic and could not have made a sincere confession of Christian faith. He did, however, have a "theology" of his own. We see it, for example, in declarations like the following:

I often say over to myself ... "O God be merciful to me a fool," the fallacy of which ... is in the "me," that it looks on man as a little God over against the universe, instead of as a cosmic ganglion, a momentary intersection of ... streams of energy such as gives white light at one point and the power of making syllogisms at another, but always an inseverable part of the unimaginable, in which we live and move and have our being, no more needing its mercy than my little toe needs mine.[2]

---

[1] John S. Monagan, *The Grand Panjandrum* (1990) at 58.
[2] Mark DeWolfe Howe (ed.), *Holmes Pollock Letters*, v. 1, 172 (1961). I have chosen this passage as representative of many such comments. Several iterations of this statement can be found in Holmes's correspondence. None of them adds any clarity to the sentiment expressed.

What could he mean by such a statement? Why, for example, does Holmes suggest saying "Oh God, be merciful to me a fool" sets him up as a "little god over against the universe"? And what exactly does he mean by calling himself a "cosmic ganglion"? Notwithstanding the obscurity of this statement, some of his critics have regarded it as emblematic of Holmes's failings. It is demeaning, they say, to describe members of the human race as "ganglia"; it shows, they argue, that he had little feeling or compassion for his fellow man.[3] Furthermore, it is tempting to dismiss such statements as sophomoric – a childish attempt at provocation rather than a mature statement of belief. It is hard to assess the merit of these criticisms without a better grasp of what Holmes is trying to express.

Taking his words at face value, several things are apparent. First, it is obvious that Holmes was not an atheist; he believed in the "unimaginable" as something transcendent and meaningful. Second, there is a definite statement about the nature of the relationship between God and man. Many religions portray this relationship as one of lord to servant or father to son. Holmes, however, views it as part to whole – seeing himself as an "inseverable part of the unimaginable." Third, and most significant, the term "unimaginable" suggests that he was an agnostic.

The depth of Holmes's agnosticism cannot be overstated, but even extreme agnosticism does not equate to atheism. Atheists believe that nothing exists except the physical universe. They therefore view religion as a cultural expression based on a reassuring fiction. An agnostic, on the other hand, believes that there is something beyond the material world – something that remains unknown and undefined. For some, this means that they view theology as little more than idle speculation. For others, theology is more metaphorical – giving expression to feelings that they could not otherwise articulate. Holmes was in the second camp; he maintained a lifelong interest in religious questions. Indeed, the subject fascinated him, although his enthusiasm would quickly wane in the presence of rigid doctrine. Like many skeptics, he was an almost religious man – a man of faith whose deep spiritual impulses resisted articulation and particularity. Thus, the essence of his agnosticism was belief in a creative spirit whose presence he felt but whose character remained beyond his comprehension. Consider, for example, this statement about the value of studying law:

---

[3] White, *supra* ch. 1, n. 10 at 355.

[T]hrough [it] you not only become a great master in your calling, but connect your[self] with the universe and catch an echo of the infinite, a glimpse of its unfathomable process, a hint of the universal law.[4]

Such "hints," "glimpses," and "echoes" were highly personal. Holmes felt they were sufficient to justify an indefinable faith for him, but it was not a faith that he would urge on others. As usual, he expressed it with a military metaphor:

I think one should accept one's ultimates (i.e. one's firm beliefs) as governing one's life but not require assurance that they govern the universe. It is enough that one embodies one's little fraction of cosmic destiny – and I think one is wise to keep the humility of a soldier in the ranks and not ask to be told the final secrets of the strategy.[5]

Note that even this degree of skepticism did not silence all questions. The soldier on the line must ponder his duty whether or not he is privy to the full plan of battle, and Holmes, as a young man, had already begun a lifelong search for the meaning of his life and its relationship to the wider universe.

This aspect of Holmes's life has been largely overlooked by his biographers. Given his reticence about personal matters, it is easy to focus on his skeptical – sometimes cynical – statements and conclude that Holmes had no deep beliefs. This, however, is a mistake. The truth is that a thoroughgoing skepticism can only go so far. Whatever our doubts, we must act, and actions require belief – not just about individual facts (Is it raining; should I take an umbrella?) but also about the big questions of life (What is real; what matters?). If a person is religious, his faith can provide the answers. If he is unreflective, he may rely on the surrounding culture. But for a man like Holmes – skeptical, intentional, and full of energy – it was necessary to seek out the answers for himself.

In keeping with his agnosticism, the answers Holmes found are somewhat general. Nevertheless, we can see the basic outline. First, he believed in a transcendent spirit that he sometimes called "god." Second, this spirit was not a personal god. It did not speak to him; it did not require his prayers. Nevertheless, he clearly understood that *its* business was *his* business, and thus he recognized an obligation to act as a useful part of the whole. In this respect, the ganglion analogy is especially apt. Ganglia

[4] Holmes, *supra* intro., n. 3 at 478.
[5] Baker, *supra* ch. 1, n. 5 at 76 (Letter from Oliver Wendell Holmes Jr. to Albert J. Beveridge, July 8, 1916).

are bits of nervous tissue that exist outside of the central nervous system. While their communicative function is necessary to sustain bodily function, they play no role in command and control. Thus, by describing himself as a ganglion, Holmes is acknowledging the essential but limited nature of his role. He is part of the process whereby the Universe pursues its own inscrutable purposes, but he is not part of its guiding sensibility.

For all of its arcane expression, there is nothing extraordinary about Holmes's philosophy. Many in postwar Boston shared his faith. In fact, it was the result of two very pronounced local influences. The first was the Calvinist religion that had brought his ancestors to the shores of North America; the second was the Buddhist and Hindu texts that had arrived in Boston on the ships of the China trade. Emerson and Thoreau were the most famous exponents of this philosophy, but many among Boston's educated class – including Epes Dixwell, Holmes mentor, father-in-law, and friend – embraced it. To understand what they believed, we need to examine its various parts.

THE EASTERN INFLUENCE

In terms of theology, the Buddhist philosophy provided a model. Buddha taught that the material world – *samsara* – is an illusion and that all human suffering comes from the false belief that *samsara* is real. This being the case, Buddha argued, we should not look to the material world for meaning and satisfaction. Instead, we should fix our gaze on the world beyond. In this latter world we come to understand that all sentient beings are interconnected and that we will suffer whenever we bring harm to others. This is karma – the general law of the universe that ensures a state of justice and ultimate peace. As Holmes describes his religious sense, we can see the parallels to Eastern thought. For example, the part–whole relationship is common to both. And we might also remember the words he used at Balls Bluff when he thought he was dying – "I believe that whatever shall happen is best for it is in accordance with a general law." His calm acceptance of his fate suggests an optimism based on something like the karmic principle.

The Eastern influence in the spiritual life of Boston makes it crucial that we recognize a distinction between consciously chosen religious belief and those habits of piety, gratitude, and adherence to duty that are part and parcel of religious life. The first are matters of religious doctrine; the second are part of religious culture. Both are important components of a person's spiritual identity. Keeping this in mind, we must not overstate the influence of the Eastern texts. Clearly, Holmes was not a Buddhist in any real sense. He did none of the things that committed Buddhists do. He did not spend his time chanting or meditating. Neither did he live in a monastery or beg on the streets. In fact, he led an active American life that would have certainly seemed foreign to Eastern members of a Buddhist sect. The substance of his beliefs may have been vaguely Eastern, but he himself was deeply embedded in a Puritan culture.

THE PURITAN HERITAGE

Holmes was descended from Puritans and lived in a city shaped by their influence. It is no wonder that his portrait of the Puritans – "stern men, little given to the expression of their feelings ... but fertile, tenacious, and knowing only duty" – seems equally to describe himself. He had grown up surrounded by religious observance. Church attendance – for the most part Unitarian – was mandatory both at home and at college. Boston – or at least the elite of Boston – formed a tightly knit community whose bonds were strengthened by shared values, shared culture, and a shared religious tradition. He may not have believed in the old religion, but it had nevertheless created the habits of thought and feeling that defined his character. Obviously, there is nothing unusual about this kind of religious influence. We understand, for example, that a lapsed Catholic is different from someone who did not grow up in a Catholic home, and that a nonobservant Jew remains Jewish. And it is not surprising that Holmes, coming as he did from a long line of Puritans, would always be influenced by an inner Puritan voice that would enable him to inscribe, along with his contemporaries, a new chapter of what it meant to be Puritan in America.

In seeking to understand this voice, we must be careful not to oversimplify the Puritan tradition. Puritan belief is frequently summarized in terms of three main characteristics. First is the concept of original sin; or, as it was famously explained in a children's primer: "In Adam's fall, we sinned all."[6] Second is the belief in predestination – the idea that God chooses a few individuals to save from the consequences of original sin. Third is the insistence on hard work and repression of bodily pleasure. While the early Puritans embraced each of these beliefs, this oversimplified view is misleading – it creates an almost cartoonish version of what is, in fact, a complex spiritual tradition. Religion in New England was not

---

[6] *The New England Primer* (ed. 1784).

a static set of beliefs. As it guided the original Pilgrims through the hardships and rewards of the New World, it would morph and adapt to the
new conditions. We must see the complexity of this process before we can
understand its effect on Holmes.

The original Puritans based their faith on the teachings of John Calvin,
a sixteenth-century French theologian and a major figure in the Protestant
Reformation. The basis of his theology was a belief in the absolute
authority of the Bible as the source of all knowledge about God.
Without the Bible, Calvin thought, we would live with only the vaguest
sense that there is a God who created us and we would know nothing
about him or our obligations to him.

Scripture, gathering together the impressions of Deity, which, till then, lay
confused in our minds, dissipates the darkness, and shows us the true God
clearly. God therefore bestows a gift of singular value ... when he not only
proclaims that some God must be worshipped, but at the same time declares
that He is the God to whom worship is due.[7]

The idea of worship was foundational. It established the basic requirement that man must obey God in all things.[8] This was the explanation for
original sin. Adam had disobeyed the word of God and therefore deserved
a punishment that was swift and severe. Not only was he exiled from the
Garden of Eden but he was also transformed from an innocent creature
into a sinful beast – a change that would affect not only him but all of his
descendants. Thus, God punished Adam by corrupting his soul and making both him and his descendants "obnoxious to the wrath of God."[9]

With respect to this corruption, Calvin emphasized two points. The
first is that we ourselves are not punished for Adam's sin. We are instead
punished for our own sinful natures.

This is not liability for another's fault. ... [It] is not, that we, who are in ourselves
innocent and blameless, are bearing his guilt, but that ... [t]hrough him, not only
has punishment been derived, but pollution instilled, for which punishment is
justly due.[10]

---

[7] John Calvin, *Institutes of Religion*, 64 (Catholic Church Ethereal Library ed. 1995). www
.ccel.org/ccel/calvin/institutes.iii.ix.html

[8] *Id.* at 212–213. ("The prohibition to touch the tree of the knowledge of good and evil was
a trial of obedience, that Adam, by observing it, might prove his willing submission to the
command of God. For the very term shows the end of the precept to have been to keep him
contented with his lot, and not allow him arrogantly to aspire beyond it.")

[9] *Id.* at 217.   [10] *Id.*

For this reason, even a newborn babe could justly be sent to Hell – the sin was in *being* corrupt, not in *doing* corrupt things.

The second point is that original sin is not an abstract condition. It is a powerful force in human motivation:

[T]his perversity in us never ceases, but constantly produces new fruits ... just as a lighted furnace sends forth sparks and flames, or a fountain without ceasing pours out water. Hence, those who have defined original sin as the want of the original righteousness ... do not significantly enough express its power and energy.[11]

There was therefore no moderation in our sinful tendencies. Calvin taught that, without God's intervention, the evil in our souls would drive us to unspeakable acts of wickedness.

Despite this, Calvin's religion was not without hope. The Bible provided two sources of human betterment. The first came from the Old Testament. After Adam's expulsion, God chose the people of Israel to be his people and gave them his law to govern their lives. He sent them into the wilderness to purify their souls, and then led them to the Promised Land. To be sure, this purification did not restore their original state of innocence; neither was their arrival in the Promised Land a return to the Garden of Eden. But the law was central – so long as they obeyed, they could live in harmony with God and avoid the evil that would otherwise be generated by their own corruption.

The New Testament reaffirmed God's law but added mercy and grace. The death and resurrection of Christ brought with it the possibility of true redemption, but God, Calvin believed, had chosen only some for salvation. Those selected received the Holy Spirit in their hearts; because of this, they could rise above their sinful state and find their place in Heaven. As Calvin explained it, "The covenant of life is not preached equally to all."[12] The proof of this, Calvin thought, was in the Bible,[13] but the reason for it could not be known: "It displays the unsearchable depth of the divine judgment."[14] Why are some people chosen while others are not? To even ask the question was to repeat Adam's sin by seeking knowledge that could only be held by God.

---

[11] *Id.* at 218.   [12] *Id.* at 2208.

[13] For example, he cites Paul's teaching on the subject of divine grace: "But if it is by grace, it is no more of works: otherwise grace is no more grace. What then? that which Israel seeketh for, that he obtained not; but the election obtained it, and the rest were hardened: according as it is written, God gave them a spirit of stupor, eyes that they should not see, and ears that they should not hear, unto this very day" (Romans 11:7).

[14] Calvin, *supra* n. 7 at 2202.

There was, however, one important effect of God's selectivity. By leaving some souls unredeemed, God made clear that salvation was a matter of his grace rather than human effort. A person who believed otherwise was guilty of false pride. A true saint – those who were among the elect were frequently referred to as "saints" – had to maintain a proper attitude. There could be no complaining, no vain pleasure in salvation, and, most importantly, they had to love God and the divine justice that condemned other souls – perhaps even the souls of their own infant children – to eternal torment. Thus, the life of a saint entailed perpetual effort. Even those who are saved, Calvin taught, "are still beset by many vices and much weakness."

Given this reality, many have been troubled by a seeming inconsistency in the Puritan faith. On one hand, Puritans believed in working hard and fulfilling their duties. On the other, they believed that hard work availed them nothing – because of predestination, their fate was sealed no matter what they did. Together, these concepts seemed to create a paradox. One had to struggle to live a good life, but a good life was without reward. Why struggle? If you are destined for eternal damnation, why not make the best of the few earthly years that separate you from your fate? And if you are predetermined for salvation, why not enjoy yourself while you wait? Given this reality, what motivated Puritans to maintain the strict discipline their religion demanded? If they lived a life of liberty and license, wouldn't they still be saved in the end?

To understand the resolution of this dilemma, it is necessary to place one's self in the shoes of the original Puritans. Given the hardship of their chosen course, it was inevitable that doubts would surface. Puritans regularly confronted a central fear – were they in fact among the saved? They had to admit that there were occasional mistakes. Sometimes even the elders had been fooled. For reassurance, those with doubts could only look to their own behavior. Consider, for example, the metaphor that Augustine used for contrasting the nature of a godly life with one driven by a devilish spirit. Imagine a horse awaiting his rider:

If God mounts, he, like a temperate and skillful rider, guides it calmly, urges it when too slow, reins it in when too fast, curbs its forwardness and over-action, checks its bad temper, and keeps it on the proper course; but if the devil has seized the saddle, like an ignorant and rash rider, he hurries it over broken ground, drives it into ditches, dashes it over precipices, spurs it into obstinacy or fury.[15]

---

[15] *Id.* at 266.

Thus, in order to reassure himself of salvation, a Puritan had to consider whether he experienced life as well ordered and satisfying or as disordered and frustrating. The former suggested salvation while the latter might mean an eternity of suffering.

The fact that doubts could only be resolved in this fashion provided a powerful catalyst for good behavior. Those who were saved had the Holy Spirit in their hearts, making them aware of their sinful nature and generating a willingness to change. Thus, a desire to do good actions would bring with it reassurance of salvation, while an interest in sin would produce fears of damnation. It was this cycle of fear and reassurance that furnished the motivation for practicing virtue. Puritans met their obligations not as a stepping stone to Heaven but as a way of experiencing their hopes for salvation.

This view of duty survived well into the late nineteenth century despite the decline of the theology that had fostered it. For example, one nineteenth-century writer made a distinction between "superstitious" and "true" religion. A religious duty is superstitiously undertaken, he wrote, if a person conforms in order to avoid sanction in an afterlife, but "if immediate happiness in doing his duty, or misery in not doing it, is the ultimate sanction, then his religion is real, or a part of his character."[16] Thus, duty was not a means to an end or a matter of simple obligation. It was instead a matter of internalizing an obligation to the point where fulfilling it became the source of deepest joy and the cornerstone of a good life.

THE ANTINOMIAN HERESY

It is often assumed that the Puritans were entirely homogenous in matters of belief, but there was a dispute among them that went to the very heart of their religion. At issue was the question of proper conduct for those who were saved. On one hand, there were those who believed in a doctrine of works. They thought that saints were required to follow biblical law, because this was the only way to honor the God who had saved them. A second group favored a doctrine of faith. They believed that those who were saved had received the Holy Spirit in their hearts and, as true saints, they should look to this inner voice to illuminate the path of righteousness.

---

[16] Joseph L. Blau, *Chauncey Wright: Radical Imperialist*, 19 New England Quarterly 495, 498 (1946) (quoting from Letters of Chauncey Wright to Charles Eliot Norton, Aug. 18, 1867).

In England, there had been advocates for both views and little conflict between them. This is probably because the English Calvinists felt besieged on all sides and the differences between the two camps would have seemed minor compared to their conflict with the English Church. Besides, there were no great differences in outward behavior. The Antinomians, despite their name, were not rowdy and lawless. Indeed, they often felt bound to a higher standard of obligation. The conflict was really one of emphasis. Both sides believed in salvation by God's grace and the need for good behavior. The Nomians wanted to stress that obedience to God was the fundamental virtue. The Antinomians sought to remind everyone that salvation was a matter of God's grace and to encourage humility and gratitude among those who had received it.

In America, however, there were several reasons why the antinomian issue became a matter of intense controversy. First, in America, the Nomian faction had a clear majority. This was partly because the Antinomians in England were more deeply embedded in the English Church and therefore less likely to emigrate. Second, there was the problem of maintaining law and order. In England, the king had soldiers to keep the peace. In America, settlers had to rely on religious orthodoxy for social control. This meant that the Antinomians posed a real threat to the established order. Finally, and most importantly, the American Antinomians had a passionate and charismatic leader – a woman named Anne Hutchinson.[17]

Anne had come to Boston with her husband, eleven children, and a substantial household of servants. She and her husband immediately joined the Boston congregation. By local standards, they were wealthy. Arriving at a time when most settlers were living in small thatched-roof huts, the Hutchinsons had brought the materials necessary to build a comfortable home. She was a woman of remarkable energy. Despite her large household, she found time to help her neighbors in various ways. She nursed them through illnesses; she was midwife to their births; and she was ever present with advice and reassurance. Soon, she was holding weekly Bible meetings in her home where she expounded freely on her religious views. Anne's views on religion were decidedly fixed. Her father was Francis Marbury, an English minister who publicly denounced fellow members of the clergy. Unfortunately, his aggressive criticism offended the bishop of London so much that he sentenced Francis to a two-year

---

[17] According to the website Famouskin.com, Holmes is the great (x7) grandson of Anne Hutchison. The line extends back through Holmes's maternal grandfather, Charles Jackson. Of course, at this remove, her descendants would number in the thousands.

prison term. It was only after his release that Francis settled down and raised a family. His experiences, however, were not lost on his daughter Anne. Her father had taught her to read and write, and, since most of the texts were biblical, she absorbed much of his religious thinking. In addition, Anne herself believed in a particularly charged form of antinomianism. Her conversion experience had been so vivid that it convinced her that she had a direct line to God and to the Holy Spirit. Because of this, she viewed herself as a prophet and claimed to see events before they happened.

The intensity of Anne's advocacy transformed the controversy over antinomianism. What had always been an abstract argument about the relative importance of good works and God's grace became in her hands a question about the nature of God and his relationship to saved souls. To Anne, God was not a master or a father. She did not think of redemption simply as a form of divine leniency. Rather she believed that God was capable of absorbing those he had saved. Thus, when the Holy Spirit entered her heart, she was transformed from the proverbial sinful beast, separate from God, to a spiritual being who was already a temporal manifestation of God's divine grace. She was obedient, to be sure, but she was obedient to the will of God as expressed directly to her through the Holy Spirit. It was this "part-to-whole" relationship that gave her the right – and the confidence – to follow her heart.

The strength of her faith made her unwilling to compromise and ultimately caused her expulsion from the Massachusetts colony. It is hard to say what her offense was.[18] Anne herself was very pious. She observed all the requirements of church membership. Indeed, she was exemplary in her concern for others. The problem, however, was in her attitude. Her "sins," as alleged by the church authorities, were contained in her thoughts and expressed in terms of her contempt for certain ministers. Her disdain for them was based on their seeming embrace of a doctrine of works. About this, Anne could not be silent. She could not respect their authority because she felt that her highest duty was to obey the inner voice – the voice that came directly from God. In the end, even though Anne and her followers had done little to disrupt community life, the elders saw them as a threat and expelled them.[19]

---

[18] Despite the fact that there is considerable documentation of her "trial," there are significant variations in the accounts of Anne's conduct and expulsion.

[19] In recent years, Hutchinson's reputation has improved. Eighteenth- and nineteenth-century writers saw her as a symbol of the dangers of religious enthusiasm. By the late twentieth century, she was more often portrayed as a feminist icon.

It is important to see the connections between Hutchinson's heresy and American Transcendentalism.[20] Both are antinomian in sense that they reject the idea that salvation requires obedience to an external law. In Hutchinson's case, this was because the Holy Spirit spoke to her directly. In Emerson's case, it was because the Divine Spirit illuminated the world and made him receptive to the message. Thus, the difference between them came down to two things: the question of divine selection and the nature of salvation. Where Hutchison believed that God selected individuals who would be saved from the tortures of Hell, Emerson believed that freedom from spiritual alienation was open to all. All they had to do was listen to the voice within. This is the message of *Self Reliance* – the highest goal should be to discover and follow your individual path.[21]

Perhaps the most important connection between the early Antinomians and the later Transcendentalist was the enthusiasm and commitment they had for the spiritual life. The antinomian strain in Calvinist thought reminds us that the Calvinists were often ecstatic in their love of God. To be saved was not just an assurance of heaven; it was also an experience of life on earth as something enchanted. Calvinists did not love God in order to save their souls. Neither was their love entirely one of gratitude. Rather, it was driven by God's majesty and goodness as they were revealed in his creation. This had been the feeling that propelled Anne Hutchison. Emerson had found this feeling by observing nature. Holmes too had embraced this feeling and found in it a meaning for his life.

Holmes's expressions of this may seem cold-blooded and impersonal. For example, his description of himself as a "momentary intersection of … streams of energy such as gives white light at one point and the power of making syllogisms at another" is so abstract that it is almost unintelligible. But, for Holmes, such conceptions were not merely

[20] For a discussion of the relationship between Transcendentalism and the early Antinomians, *see*, e.g., Amy Schrager Lang, *Prophetic Woman: Anne Hutchinson and the Problem of Dissent in the Literature of New England* 119 (1987). Eve LaPlante, *American Jezebel: The Uncommon Life of Anne Hutchinson, the Woman Who Defied the Puritans* 196–197 (2004). For a source that connects the development of Transcendentalism with the history of controversy in the Puritan Church, see Phyllis Cole, *Mary Moody Emerson and the Origins of Transcendentalism: A Family History* (1998).

[21] In *Self Reliance*, Emerson is careful to contrast the concept of self-reliance to "mere" antinomianism. His argument is based on the idea that the standards imposed by self-reliance are often higher than those imposed by external authorities. This does not, however, distinguish it from the antinomianism of Hutchinson, which too was based on the high demands of the redeemed soul.

intellectual statements. His religious heritage had infused them with a mystical glow that assured him of his place in the universe and inspired him to follow the long and difficult path toward his destiny.

UNITARIANISM

In one sense, Unitarianism was a rejection of Calvinism. Indeed, they are at the opposite poles of Protestant belief. Calvinists believed that religion was a matter of faith, while Unitarians thought it must be rational. Calvinists believed that only the elect could be saved, while Unitarians thought that the opportunity was open to all. And finally, Calvinists believed in the Holy Trinity, while Unitarians (as their name suggested) did not. Nevertheless, it is important to recognize the close ties between them. It took only one generation for the Calvinist churches in Boston to become Unitarian. This may seem astonishing, but if we ask how it happened, it is not hard to find the answers.

The change had its roots in the seventeenth century. It began with church doctrine. The Calvinists believed that saved souls could recognize other saved souls, and they restricted membership in the church to those who had been saved. This created some ambiguity about children.[22] On one hand, children were part of the parish and could be baptized. On the other hand, one could not make a judgment about their salvation until they had their own conversion experience. As generations began to multiply, the grandchildren and great-grandchildren of church members had an uncertain status. To deal with this, a group of churches adopted the Halfway Covenant in 1662. This provision allowed children of saved members to be baptized in the church and to become limited members who could not vote or receive communion until they had demonstrated their own sainthood.[23] As limited members, their children too could attend church services and become limited members. This meant that all descendants of saved souls were included in the church, but that the church had two types of members – those who were known to be saved and those who were not.

Not everyone, however, accepted the Halfway Covenant. Most notably a group of churches in the Connecticut River Valley adopted a different

---

[22] In general, they based their judgments upon the applicant's testimony about their personal conversion experience.

[23] Technically, the Halfway Covenant applied only to grandchildren of full church members since children had been routinely admitted to membership in the church.

approach. Under the leadership of Solomon Stoddard, they opened the church doors.[24] Being saved was no longer a requirement for church membership. Any person with a sound reputation was welcome to join. Stoddard was well regarded in the religious community, and it was his prestige that guaranteed that his policies would be cheerfully tolerated by the congregations to the east. Thus, the situation stood until the Great Awakening. In New England, the Awakening was fueled by the charismatic preaching of Jonathon Edwards, who was the son-in-law of Solomon Stoddard. Under his leadership, two things happened – either one of them might have strengthened the church, but together, they produced a serious crisis. The first thing was his vivid style of preaching. His sermons were carefully crafted to produce maximum fear in his listeners. For example, he would describe the dangers of bad conduct:

> They [the wicked] are now the objects of that very *same* anger and wrath of God that is expressed in the torments of hell. .... Yea, God is a great deal more angry with many that are now in this congregation. .... The devils watch them; they are ever by them, at their right hand; they stand waiting for them, like greedy hungry lions that see their prey, and expect to have it.[25]

The second was that he reversed his father-in-law's practice and barred church membership to anyone who could not show that they had been divinely selected for salvation. As a result, many whose ears were ringing with the terrors of damnation were deprived of any hope of salvation. This caused anger as well as a number of suicides, and created a scandal in which Edwards was ultimately fired. For many Calvinists, this experience taught an important lesson. The idea that church membership and eventual salvation was limited to a few of the elect became, for them, increasingly untenable. As Wendell's father would write nearly a century later:

> Anything that is brutal, cruel, heathenish, or makes life hopeless for the most of mankind and perhaps for entire races, anything that assumes the necessity of the extermination of instincts which were given to be regulated ... ought to produce insanity in a well-regulated mind.[26]

Many agreed, and this change ultimately culminated in the Unitarian movement.

Unitarianism arose from the practice of some churches in opening their membership to all – saved and sinner alike. This small change in

---

[24] Flower and Murphey, *supra* ch. 1, n. 16.
[25] Jonathan Edwards and Mark Trigsted, *Sinners in the Hands of an Angry God* 40 (2003).
[26] Oliver Wendell Holmes Sr., *Religion and Insanity*, 1 *The Atlantic* 175–184 (1857).

church practice ultimately destabilized church doctrine as one Calvinist domino fell after another. It was, for example, only a small step from opening the church door to embracing the idea that salvation is open to all, that it can be earned by pure thoughts and good deeds. With this simple change, there was no longer any reason to believe in the doctrine of original sin because there was no further need to explain the punishment of newborn babes. Neither was there any need to believe in a Holy Spirit. If the human soul is not depraved, then, as God's creation, it is inherently capable of good action. This means that sin is a voluntary choice that earns a sinner a just punishment. Conversely, virtue is possible and, if practiced, will be rewarded with the joys of heaven. Furthermore, as some congregations ceased believing in the Holy Spirit, it was no longer accurate to call them Trinitarians; they had become de facto Unitarians, whether or not they spoke of themselves as such.

Prior to 1800, the only Unitarian church in Boston was King's Chapel, an Anglican church that had modified its liturgy to comport with Unitarian principles.[27] By 1825, however, all but one of the Congregational churches in Boston identified as Unitarian. The actual schism took place between 1815 and 1825. It began with the publication of a pamphlet titled *A Brief History of the Progress and Present State of the Unitarian Churches in America*.[28] This pamphlet was unremarkable in many ways, consisting mainly of excerpts from letters written by American ministers to their colleagues in England. Nevertheless, the pamphlet caused quite a stir. The reason for this is described in one contemporary account as follows:

That such a pamphlet should produce such an effect, proves two things beyond contradiction; first that the evangelical party [the conservative Calvinists] up to that time, did not know the depth to which Unitarianism had struck its roots in this soil; and secondly, that the liberal party [the Unitarians] were not yet intending to let them know it.[29]

---

[27] King's Chapel, as the name suggests, was originally affiliated with the Church of England. During the Revolutionary War, it had been occupied by the congregation from the Old South Meeting House, which had been displaced by the war. In 1783, the church was returned to its original parishioners who were now formally separated from the Church of England. They hired George Freeman as a minister and he modified the Anglican Book of Common Prayer to conform to Unitarian principles – a change the congregation formally adopted in 1785.

[28] Thomas Belsham, *American Unitarianism, or, a Brief History of the Progress and Present State of the Unitarian Churches in America* (1815).

[29] Joseph S. Clark, *Historical Sketch of the Congregational Churches in Massachusetts: From 1620 to 1858*, at 248 (1858).

In short, to the surprise of all, the disagreements that had been bubbling under the surface had become public and undeniable.

Rapid change followed. In 1819, William Ellery Channing, the brilliant pastor of the Arlington Street Church, delivered a sermon titled *Unitarian Christianity* that set out the principles of liberal Congregational thought.[30] A few short years later, the liberal congregations founded the American Unitarian Association and the schism was complete.[31]

It seems extraordinary that such a dramatic change in the religious life of Boston had been accomplished with so little controversy. The explanation for this is complex. First was the decentralized character of church governance. Boston's churches were congregational in the sense that each congregation was self-governing. Since there was no higher authority to insist on doctrinal conformity, the religion was whatever the local parishioners said it was. Second were the changes brought by the Revolutionary War. When the British were still in Boston, they appropriated churches as armories and sometimes disassembled them for firewood. In addition, the war dislocated both families and parishes, and the end of the war brought rapid changes to Boston life. Calvin's theology, which had been well suited to the pioneer life of early New England, was no longer suited to the new realities of Boston. The changing times had put considerable pressure on the old Calvinist ways, and one by one, the congregations responded to these changes with doctrinal adjustments.

The rise of Unitarianism meant that believers had become more hopeful. Their lives were no longer dominated by a cycle of fear and reassurance. Gone was the strict code of behavior based on biblical law. As a result, religious duty became a kind of conventional morality. So long as one did not ruffle any feathers, strict adherence to God's law was no longer required. Remember, for example, Johnny Morse, who cheerfully fulfilled what he took to be his spousal duties while simultaneously living openly with his mistress. Despite this laxity, there were those – men such as Holmes – who felt themselves governed by a more demanding sense of duty. The question is obvious: what separated them from their contemporaries? For Holmes, it was certainly not a mere "vestigial

---

[30] William Channing, Remarks Delivered at the Ordination of Rev. Jared Sparks in the First Independent Church of Baltimore (May 5, 1819), in The Complete Works of William Ellery Channing 278 (1884).
[31] George Willis Cooke, *Unitarianism in America: A History of Its Origin and Development* 117 (1902).

Calvinism," as one writer has suggested.[32] He was not someone who simply fell into established patterns. Instead, it came from what he called his "philosophy" – that melded blend of Unitarianism, Buddhism, and Transcendentalism that he had found in Emerson.

It was this set of beliefs that committed him to extremes of courage and effort. Like the soldier he had been, he stood ready to fight even though he did not know the objectives of the battle. What he did know, however, was that discharging his obligations with honor and enthusiasm was the very meaning of life. He would work hard at learning law because that was his function; he would spend every evening in the Social Law Library because that was how he connected to the wider universe; and he would labor over the annotations in Kent because that was the only way that he could feel the joy of playing a small part in the universal pageant. Thus, he wrote:

The rule of joy and the law of duty seem to me all one. I confess that altruistic and cynically selfish talk seem to me about equally unreal. With all humility, I think "Whatsoever thy hand findeth to do, do it with thy might"[33] infinitely more important than the vain attempt to love one's neighbor as one's self.[34]

Note that like his Puritan ancestors, he equates the "rule of joy" and the "law of duty." Note also the reference to Ecclesiastes 9:10. The verse is part of a narrative in which the author reports upon his efforts to find wisdom, justice, and meaning. After a long search, he concludes that there is no justice in the distribution of earthly rewards and that human achievements ultimately dissolve in the grave. As a result, he decides that all earthly ambition is vanity. From this follows the guidance given in 9:10:

Whatsoever thy hand findeth to do, do it with thy might; for there is no work, nor device, nor knowledge, nor wisdom, in the grave, whither thou goest.[35]

Holmes, who had an ardent spirit and energy to spare, must have welcomed this advice. But it was not simply a matter of temperament; it was also a matter of conviction. Regarding earthly achievement as unreal, he believed that there was an encompassing reality beyond the physical where heroic action met a proper response. This would become the touchstone of his life – the image he remembered in times of struggle and doubt.

---

[32] White *supra* ch. 1, n. 10 at 23.　　[33] Ecclesiastes 9:10.　　[34] *Id.*　　[35] *Id.*

FIGURE 1 In February 1884, Wendell Holmes posed for a photograph by Clover Adams. Holmes was a personal friend of Clover and her husband, historian Henry Adams. The result of this session was two photographs that she placed in a photographic scrapbook. They are currently in the files of the Massachusetts Historical Society. This photograph is labeled Oliver Wendell Holmes Jr., seated, facing right.

FIGURE 2 Oliver Wendell Holmes Jr., seated, facing left.

PART II

THE JOURNEY TO THE POLE

Brown University Commencement, 1897

During the winter of 1897, Holmes read a book that impressed him very much. That book, *Farthest North*, was written by Fridtjof Nansen and it was an account of his attempt, beginning in June 1893, to reach the North Pole.

Nansen had left Norway with twelve men and a ship that had been specially designed to withstand the pressures of being frozen into Arctic waters. His plan was to sail north until the boat became stuck in the ice and then to rely on the polar current to move it due west over the pole. This, he knew, would be a slow process, and he had provisioned the ship with food and fuel sufficient for a twelve-man crew and a five-year trip.

During the summer, all went as planned. On September 21, they finally lifted the rudder and surrendered to the surrounding ice. But the progress toward the pole was slower than Nansen had thought. Even five years would not be sufficient. After six months of slow progress, Nansen hatched a second plan. He would build dog sleds and kayaks, and make his way to the pole on cross-country skis. After six more months of preparation, he and another Norwegian, Fredrik Johansen, left the boat. At first, they made good progress. But, as ice conditions deteriorated, their speed slowed and the pole faded from reach. They reached latitude 86°13.6' north – three degrees further north than any previous expedition – before they abandoned the attempt.

They skied southward toward Franz Joseph Land, a series of islands in the Arctic Circle. In July, they sighted land and, lashing two kayaks together, left the ice and sailed southward. They arrived safely in a remote and unsettled area. By September, however, winter had set in, and they were forced to establish a winter camp.

Not until the following May did they resume their journey. By a series of fortuitous events, they were rescued when Nansen encountered British explorer Frederick Jackson. On August 13, 1896, they arrived back in Norway, receiving a triumphant welcome.

In the spring of 1897, Holmes gave the commencement address at Brown University. In it, he compared Nansen's journey with his own exploration of the law. Wedded together in this account are two of Holmes's most prominent characteristics – first, his love of adventure and conflict, and, second, his commitment to a life of the mind.

My way has been by the ocean of the law. On that I have learned a part of the great lesson, the lesson not of law but of life. There were few of the charts and lights for which one longed when I began. One found oneself plunged in a thick fog of details – in a black and frozen night, in which there were no flowers, no spring, no easy joys. Voices of authority warned that in the crush of that ice any craft might sink. One heard Burke saying that law sharpens the mind by narrowing it. ... One doubted oneself how it could be worthy of the interest of an intelligent mind. And yet one said to oneself law is human – it is part of man, and of one world with all the rest. There must be a drift, if one will go prepared and have patience, which will bring one out to daylight and a worthy end. Most men in some form or other have to go through that experience of sailing for the ice and letting themselves be frozen in. In the first stage one has companions, cold and black though it be, and if he sticks to it, he finds at last that there is a drift as was foretold. When he has found that, he has learned the first part of his lesson, that one is safe in trusting to courage and to time.

But he has not yet learned all. So far his trials have been those of his companions. But if he is a man of high ambitions he must leave even his fellow adventurers and go forth into a deeper solitude and greater trials. He must start for the pole. In plain words he must face the loneliness of original work. No one can cut out new paths in company. He does that alone.

When ... he has turned misgiving into success, he is master of himself and knows the secret of achievement. He has learned the second part of his lesson and is ready for the consummation of the whole. For he has gained another knowledge more fruitful than success. He knows now what he had divined at the outset, that one part of the universe yields the same teaching as any other if only it is mastered. That the difference between the great way of taking things and the small – between philosophy and gossip – is only the difference between realizing the part as a part of a whole and looking at it in its isolation as if it really stood apart. The consummation to which I referred comes when he applies this knowledge to himself. He may put it in the theological form of justification by faith or in the philosophical one of the continuity of the universe. I care not very much for the form if in some way he has learned that he cannot set himself over against the universe as a rival god, to criticize it, or to shake his fist at the skies, but that his meaning is its meaning, his only worth is as a part of it, as a humble instrument of the universal power. It seems to me that this is the key to intellectual salvation, as the key to happiness is to accept a like faith in one's heart, and to be not merely a necessary but a willing instrument in working out the inscrutable end.

5

A Black and Frozen Night

My way has been by the ocean of the law. . . . There were few of the charts and lights for which one longed when I began. One found oneself plunged in a thick fog of details – in a black and frozen night, in which there were no flowers, no spring, no easy joys. . . . [At least] one had companions, cold and black though it be.

Commencement Speech, Brown University

One day in the fall of 1864, Wendell left his family's home on Charles Street and went to the omnibus stop at the foot of Beacon Hill. There he boarded the streetcar for Harvard Square. Emerging at the square, he walked past his grandparents' house and made his way to the law school. Once there, he paid his fee and signed the official register. That would be all that was required for admission. To become a lawyer, he would ultimately have to pass an oral examination administered by a justice of the Supreme Judicial Court. But the school itself had no requirements. Like a modern-day bar review course, it did not compel attendance and gave no exams. The students attended whatever lectures they wished and participated in a series of moot court exercises if they found them helpful.

As a law student, Holmes would have learned the traditional subjects.[1] In the mid-nineteenth century, these included agency, pleading, equity, contracts, evidence, real property, wills, criminal law, and constitutional law.[2] Each subject had a corresponding treatise and the professors

---

[1] Since no records are available and since no courses were required, it is impossible to know what lectures Holmes actually attended. *See* Howe, *supra* ch. 1, n. 2 at 188–189. By this time, however, he had become a conscientious student and it is therefore likely that he attended most of what was offered.

[2] Daniel R. Coquillette and Bruce A. Kimball, *On the Battlefield of Merit: Harvard Law School, The First Century* 436–462 (2015).

lectured by explaining and commenting on the assigned text. The treatises were dull and dry, but Holmes applied himself to mastering the material. As a result, he learned what he later called a "ragbag of rules." What he did not learn was how to think about law as a whole or its place in society. This left him disappointed. He had not made his decision to study law with half a heart. He had firmly and fully committed himself to something beyond professional training. He would not just be a lawyer. He wanted to be a legal scholar, and this meant grasping not only *the law* but the theory behind it. He wanted to know: What made the law? Where did its authority come from?

At Harvard, the answers to these questions could only come from Blackstone, whose *Commentaries* claimed to present a science of law. For Blackstone, however, the word "science" had a particular meaning. Today, it conjures up a secular world of lab coats, experiments, and sophisticated equipment, but Blackstone's conception was neither secular nor experimental. In this respect, it complied with the theological expectations of the university. Louis Agassiz, the Swiss naturalist, was a good example of the Harvard scientist. He scoured the earth for all kinds of biological phenomena. He went to the Amazon to collect specimens, keeping meticulous records and drawings. People from all over the country would send him plants and fossils. But his particular genius was organization. Every sample had to be identified. Every living thing had its place on a giant chart of species and subspecies; to know the chart, Agassiz felt, was to know the mind of God and to understand his creation.

Blackstone had a similar feeling about law. He began by tracking down every common law decision and every legal custom. Then he bisected it all. Thus, the *Commentaries* was structured on a pattern of logical dualities. For example, when one section dealt with "rights," a second would discuss "wrongs." Each of these two parts was further subdivided – the first part into the rights of persons and the rights of property; the second part into private wrongs and public wrongs. Within each of these subdivisions, further distinctions were made. For example, the rights of persons were divided into individual rights and the rights of bodies politic; individual rights were divided into "absolute" and "relative"; relative rights were divided into those of magistrates and ordinary persons; and even magistrates were divided into superior and subordinate. This organization served a practical purpose. Blackstone was not only a teaching text; it was also a research tool. Mastering its structure became the key to finding relevant legal authority. First a lawyer would locate the problem in Blackstone's conceptual scheme. Then he could find the section of the treatise that discussed the subject and provided citations. Beyond the practicalities, however, there was a loftier purpose. Like Agassiz, Blackstone felt he had found the natural order of law – the one that revealed God's plan for ruling human society.

Blackstone's theory was too deeply embedded with theories of natural law and intelligent design to satisfy Wendell's intellectual demands. Like most knowledgeable men of his generation, he wanted to find an explanation that went beyond: "And God made it so." His idea of science was more modern and empirical – he wanted facts, explanations, and theories that could be tested by experience. In short, he wanted the kind of theory that was revolutionizing the physical sciences. "What about law," he would wonder, "could it be studied in this way?" It seemed that no one at Harvard could answer such a question.

Without answers, Wendell continued to work diligently on the law school curriculum. He read the treatises, attended class, and was enough involved that he could not help discussing legal questions with everyone he met. Summing it up, he wrote to poet H. H. Brownell, "I think my first year at law satisfies me. Certainly, it far exceeds my expectations both as gymnastics and for its intrinsic interest."[3] Nevertheless, he remained ambivalent about surrendering his interest in philosophy, and sometimes his patience wore thin. Thus, he confessed in the same letter that he sometimes yielded to the temptation to "turn over a few stones in some new mind or read some new poem or (worse) write one." Finally, he ended the letter on an ambivalent note. On one hand, he claimed to know "the danger [of distraction] well and tried to avoid it." On the other, he seemed to suggest that the fault did not lie with him but with the law. "Truth sifts so slowly from the dust of the law," he wrote, using an image that fairly reeked of frustration and impatience.

In writing about philosophy as a temptation, Holmes was oversimplifying his dilemma. To some extent, he would always view law as a duty and philosophy as a diversion, but there was more to it than that. If law was to provide him with a window on the world, he would need more than detail. In truth, he would need a theory of the law – one that connected it to human experience. Not finding one at Harvard, he would have to invent his own. He began to read more widely. One book in particular made an impression. It was Henry Maine's *Ancient Law*. Maine had stated that his purpose in writing the book was "to indicate some of the earliest ideas of mankind, as they are reflected in Ancient Law, and to point out the relation of those

[3] Howe, *supra* ch. 1, n. 2 at 196 (letter of May 1865).

ideas to modern thought."[4] Thus, it was responsive to some of Holmes's questions. And, as Holmes's later work would show, there was also a methodological affinity between the two men. Consider, for example, Frederick Pollock's description of Maine's book:

Maine's work is not architectural but organic. His ideas are not presented in the form of finished propositions that can be maintained and controverted in the manner of a thesis. Rather they appear to grow before our eyes, and they have never done growing. The roots are the same, the flowers and fruit are various. We are constantly brought home again after digressions and excursions, often in quite unexpected ways.[5]

This would be an equally apt description of Holmes's *Common Law*. Both men saw law not as a logical system but as a living part of the universe. Both were seeking to understand its growth rather than its internal logic, and both generated theories of law that had more in common with Darwin's theory of evolution than with Agassiz's analysis of God's creation.

As appealing as this method was, it did not yield answers to all of Wendell's questions. Whether he recognized it or not, philosophy was not simply a diversion. To understand law not just on its own terms but in terms of its relation to the rest of the world, he would need a broader understanding of human knowledge and human obligation. At the same time, he meant to ground himself in a scientific view of the world. This was a complicated task. A broader understanding of human life had to be paired with an understanding of the methods of science. Thus, with a growing sense of need meeting inclination, he would find it necessary to study philosophy.[6] Luckily for Wendell, this was the time in his life when he would have many companions who were as eager as he was to understand the world in terms of modern science and philosophy.

BILL JAMES

Wendell met Bill James soon after his return from the war in 1864.[7] It is not clear when or how they met, but it is not surprising that they did.

---

[4] Sir Henry Sumner Maine, Ancient Law, xv (J. M. Dent & Sons LTD ed. 1917).

[5] Frederick Pollock, *Sir Henry Maine as a Jurist*, 178 Edinburgh Rev. 100, 102 (1893).

[6] Philosophers of the time were concerned not only about epistemology but also about questions of scientific methodology. Furthermore, scientific discoveries were creating increased urgency about ontological topics.

[7] Even this date is subject to dispute. Menand, *supra* ch. 2, n. 21 at 204 suggests that they were friends by 1862, when Wendell mentioned in a letter to his father that he had written "James." On the other hand, Mark DeWolfe Howe, the editor of Holmes's Civil War correspondence, notes that "it is unlikely that it [the letter] refers either to William or

Henry James Sr. was a friend of Wendell's father. Bill was studying medicine and was one of Dr. Holmes's students. Both Wendell and Bill had a burning interest in philosophy and both were exceptionally well read. Though they shared intellectual interests, they were temperamentally opposite. Wendell was often ebullient while Bill tended toward depression. Wendell had committed himself to a profession, but Bill could never make up his mind. In fact, he was professionally adrift – never sure where he wished to go. Nevertheless, they became best friends.

The centrality of these discussions and their personal importance to James are evident in a letter he wrote to Wendell from Berlin in January 1868.

My dear Wendle
  I don't know why it is that I am so sad,[8] – tonight. The ghosts of the past all start from their unquiet graves and keep dancing a senseless whirligig around me. ... Good golly! How I wd. prefer to have about 24 hours talk with you up in that whitely lit room ... I should like to have you opposite me ... so that the oyster shells which enclose my being might slowly turn open on their rigid hinges under the radiation, and the critter within loll out his dried up gills into the circumfused ichor of life until they grow so fat as not to know themselves again.

These early discussions were formative for both men. No longer schoolboys, they were embarking on a life of intellectual discovery, and their discussions were serious and earnest. Although there are no records – no "Proceedings of the Wendle and Bill Club" – we know quite a bit about these discussions from their correspondence and from other contemporaneous records.

One thing we know is that both men admired Emerson. Like Wendell, Bill had a personal connection. His father, Henry Sr., was a friend of Emerson's; some have claimed that Emerson was Bill's godfather.[9]

Henry James, for there is no evidence of Holmes's friendship with either of them before 1864." Howe, *supra* ch. 2 n. 24 at 75. This argument is weakened by the fact that the postulated third James remains unidentified. In any case, by March 1866, Wendell is writing to a friend, "The only fellow here I care anything about is Holmes, who is on the whole a first rate article and one that improves by wear." Baker, *supra* ch. 1, n. 5 at 174.

[8] James wrote it in the German: Ich weiss nicht was soll es bedeuten, dass ich so traurig bin. Heinrich Heine, Lorelei (1822). The song recounts a beautiful night enhanced by "the air is cool under nightfall. The calm Rhine courses its way. The peak of the mountain is sparkling. With evening's final ray."

[9] Like the story that Wendell called Emerson "Uncle Waldo," the idea of Emerson being Bill's godfather is most likely untrue. It probably stems from a time in New York City when Bill was an infant. His father took him to one of Emerson's lectures. At the end of the program, his father went to greet his friend and took the child with him. At the podium, Emerson gave the child a blessing. White, *supra* ch. 1, n. 10 at 35.

Wendell and Bill had both read Emerson and been inspired by his vision of life as a spiritual quest. However, in keeping with their temperamental differences, Wendell's enthusiasm was matched by Bill's doubts. These doubts centered on two philosophical questions. The first question was metaphysical; the second involved the nature of the human spirit.[10]

The first question was really a series of questions: What is the nature of reality? Is it composed of physical objects in a world bounded by space and time? Or is it ideational? Do our mental pictures have physical counterparts in an external world or are they merely a series of representations in consciousness? These are ancient metaphysical questions that date back to the pre-Socratics, but, more recently, the British empiricists had resurrected them in the context of a focus on perception. As they conceived it, the dispute was between materialism on one hand and idealism on the other.

Materialism reflects the common understanding that there is a physical world that exists separate and apart from our perception of it. It holds that our knowledge of the external world is based on experience and, in particular, on the evidence of the five senses. According to materialism, knowledge is possible because of interactions between our physical selves and the physical world. For example, we can see physical objects because they reflect light to the eye and this light causes chemical changes on the retina and ultimately in the brain. Thus, they believed that the five senses were generally trustworthy – that what they saw, heard, touched, smelled, or tasted provided reliable testimony about an outside world.

Idealists, on the other hand, reject the idea of a material world. Experience, they argue, consists of ideas, and there is simply no reason to suppose that these ideas are copies of something else. From their perspective, the material world exists solely as a hypothesis, as a convenient way to order perception. In Holmes's

[10] A third issue interested Holmes with James acting as the willing listener. This was the *vis viva* question – a dispute that had broken out a century before between the Newtonians and the Leibnitzians. It concerned the exact formula to be used in expressing the conservation of energy or, as they called it, *vis viva* (living force). It is unclear what aspect of this controversy interested Holmes. At the time, many scientists had concluded that it was simply a semantic dispute, i.e. a disagreement over the definition of energy. A more modern appraisal, however, suggests that it was more substantive; that it was what Kuhn might consider a paradigm conflict. David Papineau, *The "Vis Viva" Controversy: Do Meanings Matter?* 8 Stud. in the Hist. and Phil. of Sci. 111–142 (1977). My own guess is that what intrigued Holmes was the combination of an interest in the nature of the "living force" and the fact that the question seemed inaccessibly technical.

time, English philosopher Bishop George Berkeley was one of the chief proponents of this point of view.[11]

The problem with idealism is that it seems counterintuitive and difficult to accept. Note, for example, Boswell's famous account of how Samuel Johnson expressed his disagreement:

> After we came out of the church, we stood talking for some time together of Bishop Berkeley's ingenious sophistry to prove the nonexistence of matter, and that everything in the universe is merely ideal. I observed, that though we are satisfied his doctrine is not true, it is impossible to refute it. I never shall forget the alacrity with which Johnson answered, striking his foot with mighty force against a large stone, till he rebounded from it – "I refute it *thus.*"[12]

While Johnson's "refutation" has seemed persuasive to some, it is not a very good argument. From an idealist standpoint, all it shows is that there is a conjunction between visual and tactile sensations. It certainly does not prove that there is anything outside the stream of consciousness. Someone might, if he likes, suppose that there is a real physical stone that causes both sensations. He might even suppose that the supposition of a stone represents a convenient first step in ordering his experience. But, from a metaphysical standpoint, what has he accomplished? His explanation (a physical world outside of experience) is surely more baffling that what he seeks to explain (things that are part of our sensual experience).[13]

The issue of idealism and materialism may seem like a semantic quibble, but to those who are philosophically minded, they represent serious questions about the meaning of life. In a material world, nothing exists but physical objects and forces. There is no God, and no such thing as the

---

[11] Berkeley argues for idealism as follows:

> It is indeed an opinion strangely prevailing amongst men, that houses, mountains, rivers, and in a word all sensible objects have an existence natural or real, distinct from their being perceived by the understanding. But with how great an assurance and acquiescence soever this principle may be entertained in the world; yet whoever shall find in his heart to call it in question, may, if I mistake not, perceive it to involve a manifest contradiction. For what are the forementioned objects but the things we perceive by sense, and what do we perceive besides our own ideas or sensations; and is it not plainly repugnant that any one of these or any combination of them should exist unperceived?

> George Berkeley, *Treatise Concerning the Principles of Human Knowledge* 31 (Dover, 2003).

[12] James Boswell, *Life of Johnson* 333 (Oxford University Press 1970).

[13] This is the argument that Charles Peirce made in *Questions Concerning Certain Faculties Claimed for Man.* Charles S. Peirce, *Six Questions Concerning Certain Faculties Claimed for Man*, 2 J. of Speculative Phil. 103 (1868).

human spirit. Even the existence of consciousness and reason are problematic. Idealism, on the other hand, seems to suggest that we are alone in the universe. For instance, a person might think that they have friends, but all they really have are ideas of friends. Berkeley had resisted this conclusion by appealing to faith. He argued that our mental lives do not take place in isolation. Human ideas, he thought, are copies of God's ideas, and the ultimate reality is the divine mind and all it contains.

Emerson had a different approach. In an essay called *Nature*, he had set out the foundations of his Transcendentalism, and there we find his concession to idealism:

A noble doubt perpetually suggests itself, ... whether nature outwardly exists. It is a sufficient account of that Appearance we call the World, that God will teach a human mind, and so makes it the receiver of a certain number of congruent sensations, which we call sun and moon, man and woman, house and trade. In my utter impotence to test the authenticity of the report of my senses, to know whether the impressions they make on me correspond with outlying objects, what difference does it make, whether Orion is up there in heaven, or some god paints the image in the firmament of the soul? ... [W]hat is the difference, ... [w]hether nature enjoy a substantial existence without, or is only in the apocalypse of the mind, it is alike useful and alike venerable to me.[14]

Emerson did not agree with Berkeley that human ideas are simply copies of divine ideas. Rather, he relied upon a metaphor: God is the teacher and humans are his students. For Emerson, it is this relationship between humans and God that must be taken as the ultimate reality. Thus, he cautions:

Idealism saith: matter is a phenomenon, not a substance. ... Idealism is a hypothesis to account for nature by other principles than those of carpentry and chemistry. Yet, if it only deny the existence of matter, it does not satisfy the demands of the spirit. It leaves God out of me. It leaves me in the splendid labyrinth of my perceptions, to wander without end.

And then he urges that we understand experience this way:

that behind nature, throughout nature, spirit is present; one and not compound, it does not act upon us from without, that is, in space and time, but spiritually, or through ourselves: therefore, that spirit, that is, the Supreme Being, does not build up nature around us, but puts it forth through us, as the life of the tree puts forth new branches and leaves through the pores of the old.

---

[14] Emerson, *supra* intro., n. 5 at 59.

From this perspective, finding truth is not a simple question of copying reality. Instead, it is a matter of participation, of transcending the phenomenal world to see oneself as a part of the divine.

In addition to idealism, Bill and Wendell were particularly interested in a second philosophical issue. This was the problem of free will. And this issue too had major implications for their own lives. Bill, in particular, was troubled because of his studies in psychology and anatomy. To him, these posed a fundamental challenge. If there was a science of human behavior, how could man be free? And, more personally, what could be the meaning of his life if an impersonal fate had dictated not only his problems, but the exact nature of their resolution?

Indeed, by 1870, James had become despondent with the possibility that he stood as nothing before the great forces of nature. We get a glimpse of his fears in the story he tells of "the French man" in *The Varieties of Religious Experience*. James's son, Harry, reported that his father had confided to him that this story was in fact a description of his father's own experience during this period.[15] The account begins:

While in this state of philosophic pessimism and general depression of spirits about my prospects, I went one evening into a dressing room in the twilight to procure some article that was there; when suddenly there fell upon me without warning, just as if it came out of the darkness, a horrible fear of my own existence. Simultaneously there arose in my mind the image of an epileptic patient whom I had seen in the asylum, a black-haired youth with greenish skin, entirely idiotic, who used to sit all day on one of the benches, ... with his knees drawn up against his chin and the course gray undershirt which was his only garment, drawn over them inclosing his entire figure.[16]

James felt terrified because, in that moment, he understood how thin was the line between his own prosperous life and the pitiful man he had seen earlier in the day:

That shape am I, I felt potentially. Nothing that I possess can defend me against that fate, if the hour for it should strike for me as it struck for him. There was such a horror of him, and such a perception of my own merely momentary discrepancy from him, that it was as if something hitherto solid within my breast gave way entirely, and I became a mass of quivering fear. After this the universe was changed for me altogether.[17]

---

[15] Gay Wilson Allen, William James: A Biography 166 (1967).
[16] William James, Lectures VI and VII: *The Sick Soul*, compiled in *Varieties of Religious Experience* (1902) (quoted in Allen, *supra* n. 15 at 166).
[17] *Id.*

Thus, James felt the philosophical problem of free will as a deep spiritual abyss. He was powerless against the forces of nature that could at any moment line up against him. He understood that it might only take a small chemical change in his brain for him to become similarly debased. His study of psychology and religion were both stimulated by this reality. He hoped to understand why some men were visited with this kind of disaster while others lived normal lives. But it would be a philosopher who would ultimately set his mind at rest. The philosopher was Charles Renouvier.

In his diary, James credited Renouvier with inspiring a new faith in freedom of the will. On April 30, 1870, he wrote:

I finished the first part of Renouvier's 2nd Essays and see no reason why his definition of free will – the sustaining of a thought because I chose to when I might have other thoughts – need be the definition of an illusion. At any rate, I will assume for the present – until next year – that it is no illusion. My first act of free will shall be to believe in free will.[18]

This response to a problem that had been deeply troubling him for some time may seem flip and superficial, but, underneath the surface, Renouvier was helping James to form a new philosophical stance that recognized, on one hand, the legitimacy of scientific prediction and, on the other, the open and chosen aspect of human action.

As Bill worked on these issues, Holmes stood steadfast in his beliefs. Since he had first read Emerson at age sixteen, he had been an idealist. In addition, he had firmly believed that risk and ambition freely chosen were the path to a meaningful life. As he debated these points with his confused and uncertain friend, he must have felt relieved that he had been given the joy of a trusting and certain faith. This faith, however, did not leave him satisfied. Unlike his Puritan ancestors, he did not feel that his journey could end with certainty. He was a curious student. His goal was to understand as much as he could about the world. Thus, his faith became the stepping stone on which his journey began. Therefore, Wendell and Bill continued their discussions and eventually widened them to a group of like-minded friends. In these discussions, Renouvier's strategy would form the basis of their own.

---

[18] Diary of William James (Apr. 30, 1870); Menand, *supra* ch. 2, n. 21 at 219 and many other places.

THE METAPHYSICAL CLUB

The first hint that something was up came in a letter from Bill to Wendell. Writing from Europe in 1868, Bill suggested:

> When I get home let's establish a philosophical society to have regular meetings and discuss none but the very tallest and broadest questions – to be composed of none but the very topmost cream of Boston manhood. ... [I]t will give each one a chance to air his own opinions in a grammatical form, and to sneer and chuckle when he goes home at what damned fools all the other members are, and may grow into something very important after a sufficient number of years.[19]

Eventually, it happened pretty much as he had said.[20] In 1871, Bill James and Charley Peirce formed such a club. During 1871–1872, the group met twice a month in James or Peirce's study. The members called themselves "The Metaphysical Club," even though the one thing they agreed upon was that traditional metaphysics was not possible.

Charley Peirce, the cofounder of the club, was a remarkably gifted logician and chemist. He was the son of Benjamin Peirce, a Harvard mathematician with an international reputation, who raised his son to believe in his own genius. Unfortunately, as this belief took hold, it produced a predictable result – Charles's brilliance was hampered by the fact that he was annoying. Many years later, when Charles Hartshorne, the editor of Peirce's papers, asked Holmes for his recollection of Peirce, Holmes replied as follows:

> I think I remember his father saying to me, "Charles is a genius," and I remember the august tone in which ... Charles prefaced his opinion with "Other philosophers have thought."[21]

William James was more charitable. He offered his brother Henry advice for dealing with Peirce:

> Grasp firmly, contradict, push hard, make fun of him, and he is as pleasant as anyone, but be overawed by his sententious manner ... and you will never get a feeling of ease with him.[22]

---

[19] William James, *The Correspondence of William James*, v. IV at 245 (Letter to Oliver Wendell Holmes Jr., Jan. 1868).

[20] Max Fisch, *Was There a Metaphysical Club in Cambridge?* in *Studies in the Philosophy of Charles Sanders Peirce*, Second Series 3–33 (Edward C. Moore and Richard S. Robin eds. 1964) (a review of the evidence supporting the existence of The Metaphysical Club); *see* Menand, *supra* ch. 2, n. 21 at 201–232 (extended discussion of its members and their individual views).

[21] Fisch, *supra* n. 20 at 10–11.   [22] Menand, *supra* ch. 2, n. 21 at 204.

He then concluded by saying: "I confess I like him very much in spite of his peculiarities, for he is a man of genius and there's always something in that to compel one's sympathies."[23]

In addition to Peirce, James, and Holmes, there were two other members of the group. Nicholas St. John Green and Chauncey Wright had been childhood friends. They were a decade older than the other three. Green was a Boston lawyer who had a strong interest in philosophy. Wright was a well-known Cambridge intellectual, but he was a classic underachiever. He was brilliant and relentless in pursuing whatever attracted his interest, but also indolent and indifferent when it came to everything else. He was a man of contradiction. He had many friends but was deeply lonely and prone to long – but not very frequent – bouts of alcoholic intoxication.[24] When sober, however, he had an extremely fast and agile mind. He supported himself as a "calculator," making long and complicated calculations for the *American Ephemeris and Nautical*, a Cambridge-based organization that provided information for seagoing navigators. He was, in fact, so adroit at this that he was able to do a year's work in six months. This left him plenty of time to hang out at Harvard College and chat with whomever would listen. He occasionally wrote papers for local publications. He even sent one – a work on the evolution of consciousness – to Charles Darwin, who pronounced it brilliant and urged him to expand it into a book.

In 1875, Wright suffered a stroke, and then a second stroke. Henry James Sr. reported to William that "he [Wright] had been drinking moderately for a few days but not harmfully."[25] Nicholas Green and Henry James Jr. rushed to his bedside, but he did not regain consciousness. One year later, Green also died, having taken a fatal dose of laudanum. Louis Menand, the renown American cultural historian, speculates that Green, like Wright, had been an alcoholic. Sadly, these two men never achieved lasting fame, but there can be no doubt that they were a strong and vital influence on the younger men.

The starting point for the Club's discussions was the philosophy of Immanuel Kant. Writing a century earlier, Kant had produced an analysis of knowledge that was meant to provide a firm foundation for science and, at the same time, to retain a place for human freedom and morality. The

---

[23] *Id.*

[24] Menand, *supra* ch. 2, n. 21 at 231 also speculates that Green too was an alcoholic.

[25] James, *supra* n. 19 at 519 (Henry James Sr. to William James, Sept. 12, 1875) (cited in Menand, *supra* ch. 2, n. 21 at 231, n. 6).

key to his position was a division between the phenomenal world – the world of things as they appear to us – and the noumenal world – things as they are in themselves. The phenomenal world reveals itself through sensation and reason; we can therefore study it scientifically. But the noumenal world, by its very definition, cannot be known in this way. Kant believed that it was only accessible through the use of pure reason. Pure reason, he argued, demonstrated that the noumenal person was autonomous and free, responding only to the dictates of reason and never to human desire. Thus, Kant thought that the basis of all morality was an aspiration to behave as the noumenal person. He argued, for example, that we should "act only according to that maxim whereby you can at the same time will that it should become a universal law."[26] And, since noumenal persons were always more real than anything else, he required that one should: "act in such a way that you treat humanity, whether in your own person or in the person of any other, never merely as a means to an end, but always at the same time as an end."[27]

Kant's philosophy was so successful that a century later, philosophers – even those who disagreed with him – were still working within a Kantian framework. In France, for example, Auguste Comte used the distinction between phenomena and noumena to draw a boundary around possible knowledge. He argued for what he called positivism, declaring that we could know nothing about a noumenal world and that therefore we must content ourselves with a world of observable physical objects. On the other hand, philosophers in Germany did believe in a knowable noumenal world, but they could not agree on its nature. Schopenhauer, for one, thought that Kant's account of the noumenal person was unrealistic. Instead, he believed that base desire was at the heart of human motivation and that nothing but disciplined abstinence could free the human soul from its bondage to the willful self. On the other hand, Hegel chose a third alternative. He rejected the idea that the human will was either autonomous or enslaved; that it was either rational or appetitive. Instead, he argued that there was an all-encompassing spirit – the Absolute – that could bridge the dualities of human nature. These various responses made the problem with Kant's view apparent. By consulting pure reason, different philosophers had come to different conclusions. This meant that

---

[26] This is the first formulation of the maxim. From this, Kant derived several others. Immanuel Kant, *Grounding for the Metaphysics of Morals* 4:421 (James W. Ellington ed. 1993).

[27] *Id.* at 4:429.

Kant's distinction between the noumenal and the phenomenal relegated important areas of human concern – namely, morality, law, and the nature of personhood – to an a priori method that was proving undependable. Thus, what Kant had touted as a path to certitude had become instead an opportunity for speculation in the face of ignorance.

This result was unacceptable to the small band of philosophers meeting in Cambridge, and they soon found their own way of addressing it. Peirce was the first to describe this alternative vision.

CHARLEY PEIRCE AND THE ORIGINS OF PRAGMATISM

In 1867, Peirce published a series of papers in which he rejected the conception of a noumenal world.[28] His argument for this was simple. Like Emerson, he began with the concept of experience as a series of ideas. Then he asked an important question: what is the point of supposing that these ideas correspond to something that exists outside of experience? If we think that it explains these ideas, it is a peculiar form of explanation. In fact, we would be explaining something familiar to us – our own ideas – in terms of something we understand not at all – a thing in itself that can never enter human consciousness. Such an "explanation" does not generate any insight. Therefore, Peirce concludes, the supposition of a noumenal world is pointless and we must be satisfied with the original set of mental ideas. He thought that we should give up worrying whether our ideas related to anything but each other and instead concentrate on how these ideas could lead to something we call knowledge.

In this respect, Peirce's argument is similar to the one advanced by Renouvier, the philosopher who freed Bill James from his fears of determinism. In fact, Renouvier believed in free will precisely because he thought that knowledge was possible only if a human being was free to choose between competing beliefs; it was this assertion that lay at the heart of his philosophy. As Renouvier expressed it: "I place myself at the point of view of knowledge, not at the one of being without knowledge."[29] Since Renouvier trusted personal experience and the beliefs it generated, he saw no need to provide a Kantian foundation for human knowledge. Instead he took knowledge as a given and rejected all

---

[28] Peirce, *supra* n. 13 at 103–114, and Charles S. Peirce, *The Fixation of Belief*, 12 Popular Sci. Monthly 1 (1877).

[29] Jeremy Dunham, *Idealism, Pragmatism and the Will to Believe: Charles Renouvier and William James*, 23 Brit. J. for the Hist. of Phil. 756, 759 (2015).

views that seemed to render it unattainable.[30] Like Renouvier, Peirce began with the cognitive value of our experience, and understood his project in terms of describing the relationship between scientific truth and the experience that generates it. It is no wonder, then, that the two men reached a similar result. They both found that they could explain knowledge only by rejecting materialism.[31]

Peirce's rejection of materialism had the benefit of abolishing the need to explain how phenomenal experience could lead to truth about an external world. But, at the same time, the move came at a cost – ideas in the mind could only represent other ideas in the mind, leaving human beings alone in a world of disembodied images. The problem is not hard to see. The common-sense realist thinks of truth in terms of accuracy, believing that an idea is true if it accurately portrays some real state of affairs. Thus, a belief that there is a large stone in front of the church is true if in fact there really is such a stone. But Peirce could not speak so casually of "facts," "truth," and "reality." He had to explain the use of these terms without appealing to a noumenal world that was beyond human experience.

To address this, Peirce formulated a non-noumenal conception of truth. He began by noting the way in which we distinguish reality from fiction in ordinary life. What do I think if I see a pink giraffe in the corner of my study? If no one else sees it, I might be convinced that it is a hallucination. Even if everyone sees it, I may still hesitate to call it real as it might be a group hallucination or perhaps a prank. We believe that something is real only when we can fit it into our preexisting understanding of the world. Thus, I find it hard to believe in the reality of the giraffe without the testimony of others and a suitable explanation of its appearance in my study. In short, I need a coherent picture, and I will not toss aside my preexisting worldview for the sake of this one visual image.

Thinking of reality in this way, Peirce formed a distinctive notion of truth. He did this by assuming that the goal of investigation is the production of stable belief. He then argued that in view of man's social nature, no belief can be stable unless it has the power to persuade others. If each person arbitrarily selects his own opinions, he reasoned, the result will be

---

[30] *Id.*

[31] See, for example, Dunham, who portray Renouvier's position in this light: "The point of view of 'being without knowledge' is the position of substance realism. This position, [Renouvier] maintains, regards our phenomena as inadequate, fleeting or insufficient representations of the 'really real.'" *Id.*

disagreement and discord. Everyone will feel beset on all sides by fundamental challenges to their own beliefs. On the other hand, if we seek agreement on the basis of a scientific method, our opinions will slowly converge. It is this convergence that Peirce defines as truth:

> Different minds may set out with the most antagonistic views, but the progress of [scientific] investigation carries them by a force outside of themselves to one and the same conclusion. This activity of thought by which we are carried, not where we wish, but to a fore-ordained goal, is like the operation of destiny. No modification of the point of view taken, no selection of other facts for study, no natural bent of mind even, can enable a man to escape the predestinate opinion. This great hope is embodied in the conception of truth and reality. The opinion which is fated to be ultimately agreed to by all who investigate, is what we mean by the truth, and the object represented in this opinion is the real. That is the way I would explain reality.[32]

In this way, Peirce reverses the usual order of justification. Generally, we value the scientific method because it produces truth. In Peirce's world, we value truth because it is obtained by the scientific method and will result in stable belief. But this reversal had the following consequence: since Peirce defined truth as the result of a scientific method, he had to shoulder the task of defining the method and explaining its reliability.

To do this, Peirce provided an operational analysis. Science, he believed, was the result of three types of reasoning. The first, deduction, is familiar to all of us as syllogistic reasoning. It is capable of making a prediction based on a major and a minor premise. For example:

MAJOR PREMISE: All heavy objects fall if not supported.
MINOR PREMISE: This is a heavy object.
PREDICTION (CONCLUSION):   This will fall if not supported.

The second type of inference is induction, by which a major premise can be derived from individual cases. This permits an observer to formulate a generalization based upon a finite number of cases. Thus, if every frog we see is green and none is any other color, we infer: "All frogs are green." Our belief in this conclusion may be strong, but it is also subject to revision. One yellow frog will force us to reconsider.

The final form of inference is abduction. In science, an abduction is the action of a scientist in forming a hypothesis that can be tested experimentally. Like induction, it forms a generalization from observed

---

[32] Charles Sanders Peirce, *Collected Papers of Charles Sanders Pierce* 5:407 (Charles Hartshorne and Paul Weiss eds. 1965).

instances. It differs from induction, however, in that it uses a new term to characterize the observations. Thus, for example, in the frog case, we might say that all frogs are green because they are herbivores. We thus posit diet as an explanation for skin color. Obviously, in making this explanation, we are speculating; we have only the slimmest of grounds for thinking it is true. In fact, it is little more than a guess. Peirce argues that we are justified in making such guesses if we hold them tentatively and subject to revision in the light of further experience. If, for example, I see a frog eating an insect or an elephant that is not green, I must abandon this explanation in favor of some other.[33]

For Peirce, these three forms of reasoning were the basis of a scientific methodology. One began with individual observations. These could be generalized by induction. Using abduction, we formulate general hypotheses that introduce new concepts as explanations for observed phenomena. From these "guesses," we use deduction to predict future events. And finally, we must see whether these events come to pass. If they do, we will retain our belief in the hypothesis; if they do not, we must abandon it. This is a method, Peirce tells us, that is self-correcting as each hypothesis is put to the test of future experience.

Peirce believed that this kind of reasoning had important consequences for a theory of meaning. Take, for example, the concept of gravity. The concept arises in a certain scientific context. We see that a number of facts could be explained by supposing that such a force exists. We therefore invent the term "gravity" and use it as an explanation – really as a shorthand expression – for these facts. If someone then asks: "What is gravity?" I can only answer: "It is a name for a force that scientists invented to explain certain practical effects – namely the way in which physical bodies move toward the earth." Thus, "gravity" stands for nothing more than these predictions. It is not a mysterious force; it does not require further description. And this is the basis for what has come to be known as the Pragmatic Maxim. It states:

---

[33] This aspect of Peirce's philosophy has become a central focus of modern philosophy of science. Karl Popper, for example, began his analysis of science with the observation that generalizations could be falsified even if they could not be verified. Thus, he argued, scientists are justified in adopting a generalization so long as they are willing to reject it whenever it is falsified by a nonconforming instance. Karl Popper, *The Logic of Scientific Discovery* 19 (Routledge 1959). Modern students of philosophy often refer to this as the "guess and check" method.

Consider what effects, that might conceivably have practical bearings, we conceive the object of our conception to have. Then, our conception of these effects is the whole of our conception of the object.[34]

With these three moves:

1. Defining truth in terms of the outcome of a scientific method;
2. Identifying the role abduction played in the operation of the method; and
3. Reducing scientific concepts to predictions of physical activity by means of the pragmatic maxim

Peirce ushered in a new era of American philosophy. He would not achieve professional success within his lifetime, but, through James and others, his ideas came to dominate American thought for almost a century.

Peirce's effect on his contemporaries was another matter. Of all his contemporaries, only Bill James would look back and remember Peirce's influence, but James was a generous man who was quick to acknowledge the contributions of others. Holmes, on the other hand, denied the influence: "I think I learned more from Chauncey Wright and St. John Green, as I saw Peirce very little."[35] Holmes also dismissed pragmatism as "an amusing humbug,"[36] and wrote critically about the collection of Peirce's essays published after Peirce's death.[37]

Despite Holmes's disclaimers, the similarity between their accounts is stunning. Holmes began his discussion of legal rights this way:

It starts from my definition of law ... as a statement of the circumstances in which the public force will be brought to bear upon men through the courts: that is the prophecy in general terms. Of course, the prophecy becomes more specific to define a right.[38]

---

[34] Peirce, *supra* n. 32 at 5.402.

[35] Fisch, *supra* n. 20 at 10–11 (quoting Holmes's letter to Hartshorne). But in the same letter Holmes states: "Once in a fertilizing way he challenged some assumption that I made, but alas I forgot what." *Id.*

[36] Howe, *supra* ch. 1, n. 2, 138–139.

[37] Holmes wrote: "I feel Peirce's originality and depth – but he does not move me greatly – I do not sympathize with his pontifical self-satisfaction. He believes that he can, or could if you gave him time, explain the universe. He sees cosmic principles and his reasoning in the direction of religion, etc. seems to me to reflect what he wants to believe – in spite of his devotion to logic." Thomas Goudge, The Thought of C. S. Peirce 325 (1950).

[38] Howe, *supra* ch. 4, n. 2 at 212.

Note that Holmes, like Peirce, reduces the abstract conception of law to its effects on conduct. From there, Holmes makes the analogy of physical force:

So, we prophesy that the earth and sun will act towards each other in a certain way. Then as we pretend to account for that mode of action by the hypothetical cause, the force of gravitation, which is merely the hypostasis of the prophesied fact and an empty phrase.[39]

Again, we see the analysis of gravity as the invented term of an abduction. It is a hypothesis by which we "pretend" to account for concrete facts. Holmes then makes the analogy explicit:

So, we get up the empty substratum, a right, to pretend to account for the fact that the courts will act in a certain way.[40]

Thus, Holmes's definition of a right is entirely pragmatic. To say that someone has a right to do x is to predict that public force will not be used to interfere with that person's performance of x.[41] Thus, like gravity, Holmes thinks that a legal right is the result of an abduction; it is the name of a technical concept that is invented as an explanation – in Holmes's case a "pretend" explanation – for legal decisions in the real world.

If Holmes was not profoundly influenced by Peirce, why do they offer similar explanations? One possibility is that the similarities in their approach are due to a common influence rather than an influence of one upon the other. Peirce was the first to present pragmatism as a coherent philosophy, but it had not sprung fully grown from his head.[42] It was the result of many intellectual tendencies that had shaped the thought of his generation. One particular influence seems clear. As Harvard graduates, both men had taken the required course on logic,[43] learning from

---

[39] *Id.*   [40] *Id.*

[41] For an extended discussion of the similarities between Holmes's elaboration of the nature of a right and Peirce's concept of abduction, *see* Catharine Wells, *Legal Innovation within the Wider Intellectual Tradition: The Pragmatism of Oliver Wendell Holmes, Jr.*, 82 Northwestern U. L. Rev. 541, 564–568 (1988).

[42] In 1877–1878, Peirce published two papers that set out the basics of pragmatism. Charles Sanders Pierce, *How to Make Our Ideas Clear*, 12 Popular Sci. Monthly 286 (1878); Peirce, *supra* n. 28 at 1.

[43] It is unclear whether Holmes took the course at Harvard or at the preparatory school run by Mr. Dixwell. In any case, the text used would have been the one authored by Levi Hedge. If Holmes took the course at Harvard, Francis Bowen would have been his teacher, but Bowen's own text was not published until after the Civil War.

a textbook written by Levi Hedge.[44] Logic, as it was then understood, was not the formal and deductive system we study today. Instead, it taught the student correct principles of investigation. As Hedge wrote in his introduction:

The purpose of Logick is to direct the intellectual powers in the investigation of truth, and in the communication of it to others. Its foundation is laid in the philosophy of the human mind, in as much as it explains many of its powers and operations, and traces the progress of knowledge from the first and most simple perceptions of outward objects, to those remoter truths and discoveries which result from the operations of reasoning.[45]

This was no mere text in cognitive psychology. Instead the book was deeply normative. It prescribed to the Harvard student how he should go about deciding important questions; as a result, it was central to a Harvard education and to New England intellectual life in general.

The structure of Hedge's logic offers a kind of preview of pragmatism. Hedge divided human thinking into two distinct forms. The first is analysis. When we engage in analysis, we break up abstract conceptions into its component parts. We recognize that a generalization will hold true of each individual included within the general term. Synthesis, on the other hand, does just the opposite. It compiles generalizations from individual cases. Today we often capture this distinction by talking about "top-down reasoning" (analysis) and "bottom-up reasoning" (synthesis).

In explaining the difference between analysis and synthesis, Hedge used a mechanical metaphor:

Analysis and synthesis ... denote opposite processes, one beginning where the other terminates; and they reciprocally explain each other. Thus, the mechanism of a complicated machine may be shown by either method. We may do it analytically, by taking the machine in its entire state, and separating its parts in the reverse order of their combination, carefully explaining each part as we proceed, till we arrive at that, with which the mechanical construction commenced. Or we may adopt the synthetic method, and, beginning with the parts, in a state of separation, place them successively in their former order till the combination is restored.[46]

---

[44] Levi Hedge, *Elements of Logick; or A Summary of the General Principles and Different Modes of Reasoning* (1827). Levi Hedge was a Harvard professor of logic and metaphysics.
[45] *Id.* at 172 (quoted in Flower and Murphey, *supra* ch. 1, n. 16 at 373 [1977]).
[46] Hedge, *supra* n. 44 at 151.

This discussion has two important points. The first is that analysis and synthesis are reciprocal – "one beginning where the other terminates." The second is the mechanical analogy. An abstraction is like a Chinese puzzle. A scientist may play with it – pulling it apart and fitting it back together until he achieves the order he seeks. He creates the pieces of the puzzle with certain goals in mind. So he might use the terms "gravity" or "legal right" to account for certain facts. He succeeds when he has fit the pieces into a coherent whole that can be used as a tool to further his inquiry. It is this spirit of play and experimentation that lies at the core of pragmatism. We fiddle with ideas, but we do so with a purpose in mind. And it is this purpose that guides our play. Hedge's logic captures this spirit and, by teaching it to a generation of Harvard students, he may have added a spark to the development of pragmatism. But of course, it makes little difference whether it was Hedge or Peirce who inspired Holmes to analyze legal rights in pragmatic terms. The fact is that he did and his doing so would become the cornerstone of his legal philosophy.

NICHOLAS ST. JOHN GREEN: THE PROTO REALIST

Nicholas St. John Green was the fourth member of the group. He was a childhood friend of Chauncey Wright, and, like Wendell Holmes, he was a Civil War veteran, a lawyer, and a Harvard Law School lecturer.[47] In Club meetings, it was Green who would remind the group to think in terms of Bain's definition of belief as "that upon which a man is prepared to act."[48] This definition became a hallmark of pragmatism, reinforcing the idea that the meaning of any term is a function of its practical consequences. Like the other members of the group, he had learned logic from Hedge, and this had led him to think of reasoning in mechanistic terms. Since he was a decade older than Holmes, he was the first to apply this method to the general problems of legal theory.

In 1870, Holmes had become one of the editors of the *American Law Review*. One of the first things he published was Green's article on proximate cause.[49] It was an insightful piece that was fifty years ahead of its time. In addressing proximate cause, Green saw two choices: either

---

[47] Although he left his post in 1873 and went across the river to teach at Boston University. *See* Bruce A. Kimball, *The Inception of Modern Professional Education: C. C. Langdell, 1826–1906*, at 347–348 (2009).

[48] Max Fisch, *Alexander Bain and the Genealogy of Pragmatism*, 15 J. of Hist. and Ideas 413, 413 (1954).

[49] Nicholas St. John Green, *Proximate and Remote Cause*, 4 Am. L. Rev. 201 (1869).

he could push the causal analysis toward greater abstraction, or he could focus on its practical consequences. The first alternative led to a tangle as it inevitably invoked the philosophical problems that attend causation: Which of Aristotle's four causes was at issue? How could one prove causation if Hume was right that causation could never be proved? Were we interested in "constant conjunction" or something more metaphysical? Green would engage none of these arguments. Instead he appealed to the kind of analysis described by Levi Hedge and Charles Peirce.

He began by attacking the notion of a chain of causation:

The phrase "chain of causation," ... embodies a dangerous metaphor. It raises in the mind an idea of one determinate cause, followed by another determinate cause, created by the first, and that followed by a third, created by the second, and so on, one succeeding another till the effect is reached. ... There is nothing in nature which corresponds to this. Such an idea is a pure fabrication of the mind.

It was this notion, he thought, that created the confusion about proximate cause. Inevitably, the chain metaphor resulted in disputes over the "proper" sequence of events, and which causes were "nearer" to the result than others. To counter this, he articulated an alternative view of causation:

There is but one view of causation which can be of practical service. To every event there are certain antecedents, never a single antecedent, but always a set of antecedents. ... It is not any one of this set of antecedents taken by itself which is the cause. No one by itself would produce the effect. The true cause is the whole set of antecedents taken together.

This is the practical view of causation in which Green says, "there is nothing mysterious. Common people conduct their affairs by it, and die without having found it beyond their comprehension."[50]

From this perspective, the question about proximate cause has nothing to do with the mysterious quality of "nearness." Instead, the issue revolves around the question of selecting the antecedents that are important in a particular context. In law, the issue of proximate cause might be stated this way:

[A] defendant is held liable for the natural and probable consequences of his misconduct. In this class of actions his misconduct is called the proximate cause

---

[50] Nicholas St. John Green, *Proximate and Remote Cause*, 5 Kan. City L. Rev. 114, 126 (1937).

of those results which a prudent foresight might have avoided. It is called the remote cause of other results.[51]

In most cases the line is not hard to draw. If I punch you in the face and your face is injured, the injury is one that "prudent foresight might have avoided." In some cases, however, the question is not so clear. For example, *Palsgraf* v. *Long Island Railroad* has become the paradigmatic proximate cause case.[52] The case arose from an incident on the Fourth of July at a station maintained by the defendant railroad. As a train left the station, one of the defendant's conductors noticed a man rushing to get on and sought to assist him by giving him a push forward. As a result of the push, the passenger dropped his package. Unfortunately, the package contained fireworks that exploded when they hit the platform. Mrs. Palsgraf was injured. She was not related to the rushing man, neither was she standing close enough to be injured by the blast. Instead, she was standing at some distance and was injured by a public scale toppled by the vibration of the blast. Was this an injury that a prudent foresight might have sought to avoid? *Palsgraf* is a paradigmatic case precisely because it presents a close question. Green's approach would have focused on the particular context and on ordinary intuitions about responsibility.[53]

Fifty years after Green's article, the *Palsgraf* case made it to the New York Court of Appeal, where it provoked a sharp division among the justices. Judge Cardozo rendered the majority opinion in which he deployed a number of abstract considerations to show that the requirement of proximate cause had not been met. Judge Andrews, however, dissented, arguing the position taken by Green: proximate cause stands for a number of practical considerations that determine the limit of responsibility in a particular situation. His opinion is a textbook example of legal realism. He asks: in this context how far should we extend the scope of liability? For Andrews, the realist, it is a question of policy and not a question of abstract argumentation.

Holmes is often touted as the originator of legal realism. When we read Green's work, however, we recognize that Holmes is not quite the originator. Holmes's own work, published ten years later, aligns with that of Green. Surely, it is fair to say that it was Green rather than Holmes who first insisted on the use of practical normative decision-making to resolve basic legal questions. Their realism, however, was never a straightforward

[51] *Id.* at 128.   [52] *Palsgraf* v. *Long Island R. Co.*, 248 N.Y. 339 (1928).
[53] He sums up his approach this way: "There is generally no other way of determining [this] than by an appeal to experience." Green, *supra* n. 50 at 129.

proposition, and Green's work – valuable though it was – left plenty of room for Holmes to develop his own theory of legal decision-making – one that would accommodate Green's insight.[54]

CHAUNCEY WRIGHT AND THE DISCIPLINE OF POSITIVISM

Holmes took one more important lesson from his philosophical friends, and this was a lesson he most often acknowledged.[55] Chauncey Wright was a positivist. He followed French philosopher Auguste Comte in recognizing a fundamental distinction between fact and value. Facts were the province of science, but questions about morality and religion were outside of its competency. To an educated person of today, this may seem like an obvious point, but in nineteenth-century New England, it was a truly revolutionary idea. Harvard itself had been founded on the idea that religious orthodoxy provided the appropriate basis for learning about the world, and, even as Harvard had shed its theological commitment to Calvinism, it had not finally let go of the idea that religion is the foundation for human knowledge.

The term "positivism" engenders some confusion. Modern positivists have been emphatic in defining a line between fact and value, the positive and the normative. They have insisted that everything on the fact side of the line can, at least in theory, be conclusively proven either true or false by the methods of science. Everything on the value side, however, cannot be so decided. They therefore declare that value statements are subjective and lack cognitive content. Thus, if I say that it is wrong to kill a man, I am expressing a preference; if, at the same time, you disagree, then that is your preference and there can be no decisive arguments either way. This is not quite, however, the positivism of Chauncey Wright.

Wright's positivism was aimed at a particular target. In his own time, he was best known for an essay in which he dissected the works of Herbert Spencer. Spencer had coined the phrase "survival of the fittest," and, on the basis of this concept, he had articulated a normative vision for human society. Spencer labeled himself an empiricist, and yet his works were studded with moral "observations." Wright was skeptical; he approached Spencer with a magnifying glass and tweezers, dissecting his arguments and exposing the normative assumptions that Spencer had brought into his work. Describing Spencer, Wright wrote:

[54] In Chapters 6 and 7, I question whether Holmes was truly a realist in the modern sense.
[55] Menand, *supra* ch. 2, n. 21 at 212–213.

Constrained by his entire sympathy with modern movements in thought and scientific culture, he is perforce a scientific empiricist though his peculiar genius would have found a more congenial employment in scholastic philosophy. Mr. Spencer believes in developments. All his writings are developments and most of them are about developments. He delights in "evolutions from the homogeneous to the heterogeneous" – in "changes from an indefinite incoherent homogeneity to a definite coherent heterogeneity, through continuous differentiations and integrations." He not only discovers them in all the objects of scientific research, but he rings these changes in all his discourses on them. Analysis is his *forte*, and developments are his foibles.[56]

It was Spencer's fascination with "developments" that led him to carelessly bolster his moral pronouncements with an untrustworthy form of moral argument. He would move from the observation that things were evolving toward X, to the conclusion that X was a higher form of the good; it was this sort of non sequitur that Wright's "positivism" had so firmly targeted. To argue for the value of something based on "developments" in that direction, Wright thought, was to make teleology a universal moral premise.

This line of reasoning left Wright unenthusiastic with respect to certain aspects of pragmatism – especially its views on metaphysics, ethics, and religion. In these areas, pragmatism, itself, was prone to Spencerian non sequiturs. We have seen that Peirce defined truth as the object of final opinion in a community that had indefinitely practiced the scientific method.[57] His argument has a similar structure to those deployed by Spencer:

- Over time scientific opinion moves in a certain direction.
- This is progress. Each development of opinion brings us closer to the truth.
- Therefore, the ultimate opinion is truth.

But there is no particular reason why the ultimate opinion could not be just that – an opinion that, for no reason or for reasons unknown, is apparently stable. But if we insist on calling this opinion "true" in a metaphysical sense, it can only be because we assume that our ideas at the end of inquiry are "truer" than those we held at the outset. Peirce, an able logician, saw the problem, and recognized that his conclusion rested upon a "cheerful hope."[58]

---

[56] Chauncey Wright and Charles Eliot Norton, *Philosophical Discussions* 57–58 (1878).
[57] Peirce, *supra* n. 32 at 5:384.   [58] *Id.* at 5:407.

With respect to moral reasoning, Peirce had a similar problem. He began by affirming that "[e]very man has certain ideals of the general description of conduct that befits a rational animal in his particular station in life, what most accords with his total nature and relations." He continued:

These ideals have in the main been imbibed in childhood. Still they have been shaped to his personal nature and to the ideas of his circle of society rather by a continuous process of growth than by any distinct acts of thought. Reflecting on these ideals, he is led to intend to make his own conduct conform ... to them. Next, he usually formulates, however vaguely, certain rules of conduct. ... Reflection upon these rules, as well as upon the general ideals behind them has a certain effect on his disposition, so that what he naturally inclines to do becomes modified.[59]

Once these rules are internalized, they become active in determining conduct. "Such being his condition," Peirce went on:

He often foresees that a special occasion is going to arise; thereupon a certain gathering of his forces will begin to work and this working of his being will cause him to consider how he will act, and in accordance with his disposition, such as it now is, he is led to form a resolution as to how he will act upon that occasion. ... [N]ow he sits down and goes through a process similar to that of impressing a lesson upon his memory, the result of which is that the resolution is converted into a ... really efficient agency.[60]

For Peirce, the ideals of conduct are not static. They must be revised in the light of personal experience. We review our conduct, asking first whether it conformed to our resolution, second whether it conformed to our rules, and third whether it was in accord with our ideal. At each stage, an affirmative answer is marked by a pleasurable feeling of satisfaction. When we are dissatisfied, it is necessary not only to review the relationships among conduct, resolution, rule, and ideal but also the suitability of our original ideals. Peirce summed it up this way:

The experience of life is continually contributing instances more or less illuminative. These are digested first, not in the man's consciousness, but in the depths of his reasonable being. The results come to consciousness later. But mediation seems to agitate a mass of tendencies and allow them more quickly to settle down so as to be really more conformed to what is fit for man.[61]

And once again we can see the "cheerful hope" at work. Peirce seems to assume that the course of experience will bring us closer to the truth even

---

[59] *Id.* at 1:592.　[60] *Id.*　[61] *Id.* at 1:599.

when we are considering moral questions. It brings us "examples more or less illuminating" that with proper processing lead us to know "what is fit for man." And this kind of forward-looking reasoning fueled not only pragmatists but much of the Progressive Era. For example, in 1906, Roscoe Pound, dean of Harvard Law School, trumpeted exactly these feelings when he argued that society is moving ever upward and that it is up to lawyers to become "conscious factors" who will promote "the course of legal development" and provide the moral leadership for a progressive society.[62]

It is clear, however, that Wright could not join this parade. Wright described social change as like the weather – it is not a case of "onward and upward" but of a dynamic system that moves in accordance with its own unknown imperatives. Holmes agreed; but even so, his skepticism had limits. He may not have believed in universal moral truths, but he did understand the importance of normative argument. The law, for example, could settle disputes even though it was not based upon an objective, external morality. Its power came not just from the force of arms but from the fact that it was deeply interwoven with community norms and expectations. To be a member of a community meant that a person had absorbed these norms so thoroughly that he was not aware of their operation. Silently, they shape one's perceptions, inclinations, and habits. This meant that adherence to these norms was often not a conscious choice – one helped a neighbor because refusing was unthinkable. Thus, even without a priori or teleological arguments, Holmes recognized. that people could not be disconnected from the values that were so deeply entrenched in their perception of the world.

For a modern reader, this view of morality may seem both overbearing and naïve. It is overbearing because it allows others to dictate moral conduct and thereby contradicts some basic notions of individuality, rationality, and autonomy. It is naïve because it seems to assume that all societies are homogeneous and that they will generate a monolithic group of shared values. But this assumption cannot be true. We note, for

---

[62] Roscoe Pound, *The Need of a Sociological Jurisprudence*, 19 Green Bag 607 (1907). Pound decried the old idea that "the so-called legal justice is an absolute and a necessary standard," and argued for a progressive ideal where "lawyers should be conscious factors, not unconscious followers of popular thought, not conscious obstructers of the course of legal development." *See also* Louis Brandeis and Samuel Warren, *The Right to Privacy*, 4 Harv. L. Rev. 193 (1890), where the authors argued for recognition of an expanded right to privacy based upon an analysis of an historical tendency in that direction.

example, that there are moral disagreements among families and other groups intimately bound up in the same social circle. But basic norms exist even if they do not settle every argument. We experience conflict; we rebel; we think we can do better. The point is that a common morality transcends the individual and provides a shared framework within which the community will hold its members accountable.

We must keep in mind that Holmes lived in a time and place different from our own. For two centuries, his ancestors had been part of a tightly regulated New England society. Through that time, there had been controversies and even changes. The stern Puritan values that had been so well adapted to life in the wilderness had given way to a more relaxed regime. Boston had become educated, worldly, and prosperous. To accommodate this, Calvinism had given way to Unitarianism and, for some, Transcendentalism. Nevertheless, their basic worldview persisted. The result was an established moral and religious order that formed the core of Holmes's community. Thus, while we often associate moral positivism with skepticism and amorality, men like Wright and Holmes thought of it in terms of a community that had conditioned them to fulfill the highest aspirations and the most strenuous duties.

ON TO THE LAW

Holmes had spent the decade after the war living up to his high ambitions. His discipline in this regard had been prodigious, but his pursuit of knowledge had been on Emerson's terms. He had read widely in the classics, but he had not allowed them to dictate his approach. He was part of a group of young men who were reinventing American thought. Fundamental to their philosophy was the notion of experience that was not bounded by the narrow definitions of British empiricism. For them, experience was not a passive reception of sensory information. Instead it sprang from their relationship with nature. As they grew, so too did this relationship, bringing them a sense of being at home – or as Emerson might say, "at one" – with the world.

The world ... lies wide around. Its attractions are the keys which unlock my thoughts and make me acquainted with myself. I launch eagerly into this resounding tumult. I grasp the hands of those next [to] me, and take my place in the ring to suffer and to work, taught by an instinct that so shall the dumb abyss be vocal with speech. I pierce its order; I dissipate its fear. ... Any action [I] can partake ... is pearls and rubies to [my] discourse. Drudgery, calamity, exasperation, want, are instructors in eloquence and wisdom.[63]

[63] Ralph Waldo Emerson, *On the American Scholar* (1837).

And so Wendell had climbed in the Alps, hiked through the White Mountains, wandered the shore with George Shattuck, created a garden in Mattapoisett, and gone pigeon hunting in Illinois. And it was through this lens that Holmes was beginning to see the enormous scope of his legal studies. As time went on, he steadily withdrew from his circle of philosophical companions and set out on his own to explore the law. He did not, however, leave behind their influence.

From pragmatism, he took a method for studying law. Pragmatism rejected the imposition of grand theories. Instead it looked to situational theorizing. The point of such theorizing was to detect regularity and formulate predictions. This was useful because it helped to reform and improve one's interactions with the world. In short, theory and practice could not be separated. Theories arose from practice – from doing things in the world. At the same time, participants understood their practices through the lens of theory and it would be theory that would lead them to change, and improve their practice. This was the kind of theorizing that Wendell would bring to the study of law. He would discover no grand theory, no ultimate explanations for the substance of legal duties. He would not deduce ideal law from abstract theories of justice and truth. Instead he would achieve small victories over mountains of detail. As humble as his theories might seem, they would lead to a life of greatness in the law. He would become a great judge, not because he had a grand legal theory, but because he did not. Judging for him was a routine practice always informed by his grasp of legal history and the smaller theories he formulated to interpret it.

From Green, he took a type of realism. It was not a realism that scorned precedent. Rather his realism understood that precedent was not a series of abstract logical statements. It was instead part of an ongoing practice of judging that worked well only because it did two things at once. First, it solved real-world problems in practical ways. Second, it wove its decisions into a coherent framework that enabled practitioners to predict decisions and facilitate future planning. For these reasons, the law could not be studied in an ivory tower. It had to be observed in the context of a community; it had to be treated as an ever-changing response to the needs of society.

From Wright, Holmes took the limitations imposed by positivism. At any given time and place, the law had a purpose. Holmes thought this purpose could be known. What he could not answer were the broader normative questions: What should the law become? What ends should it serve?

Following Emerson, he would always be interested in the ultimate normative questions, but he would have to rest content with considering them solely from his own point of view. His answers would come from lights of his own experience. With law, it would be his job to obtain this experience, and this meant that he had to learn about law throughout its history and to explore it in every intimate detail.

6

The Loneliness of Original Work

But if he is a man of high ambitions he must leave even his fellow adventurers and go forth into a deeper solitude and greater trials. He must start for the pole. In plain words he must face the loneliness of original work. No one can cut out new paths in company. He does that alone.

Commencement Speech, Brown University

In 1869, James Kent was looking for an editor to update his grandfather's classic work, *Commentaries on American Law*. Kent had done for American law what Blackstone had done for English law; he had divided it into logical categories, and for each category, he had provided a general text with footnotes that collected the relevant cases. Since its publication in 1826, it had swiftly become the leading authority for American lawyers. By 1869, there had been eleven editions with regular updates, and it was time, the grandson thought, for a more thorough revision of the notes. Previous editors had not been particularly thoughtful. As Mark DeWolfe Howe described it:

[They] had ... edited the Commentaries "as you edit bricks, by tilting the wagon." Like good and reliable wagoners they had dumped the recent cases in sprawling heaps at the bottom of each page.[1]

Undertaking this project had both pluses and minuses. On one hand, whoever did the work would gain a certain amount of authority and

---

[1] Mark DeWolfe Howe, *Justice Oliver Wendell Holmes, Volume 2: The Proving Years, 1870–1882*, at 11 (1963). The portion in quotation marks is a phrase that Howe noted he had borrowed from Thomas Carlyle.

prestige. On the other, it would be tedious and dull. It would require painstaking research and minute analysis to do a proper job.

The chancellor's grandson first approached James Bradley Thayer, a successful lawyer and a scholar of some renown. The prestige of the project appealed to him, but he had neither the time nor the inclination to engage in the kind of thankless work that the project involved. He therefore hit upon the solution that so often occurs to men in his position – he asked an exceptionally bright and hard-working employee of the firm to assist him on the project. That employee was, of course, Wendell Holmes. After some negotiation Wendell agreed. It was a hard decision, for it was not the kind of job that would further his ambition to do original work. But there were practical considerations in its favor. First, the job would provide needed income. The compensation was ten times the amount he received for teaching his first course at Harvard. Second, there was the prestige of the project. While annotating Kent would not represent creative scholarship, it would certainly advance his reputation as someone who was exceptionally adept in all aspects of the law.

The project took three years. He might have finished it sooner, but he was doing other things as well. These were the years of the Metaphysical Club and his immersion in philosophy. As a sideline, he and Arthur Sedgwick, a fellow member of the Massachusetts Twentieth, assumed the editorship of the *American Law Review*; and since Wendell was still determined to do original work, he wrote a number of articles for its pages. At the same time, he began teaching constitutional law at Harvard. Given all these "outside" activities, it is hardly surprising that the law practice he had begun with his brother, Ned, was not particularly prosperous. In fact, at the age of thirty, he and his new wife, Fanny, were still living on the third floor of his parents' spacious Back Bay home.

One way to do the project was to simply add citations to the existing footnotes, but he considered such an approach inadequate. Instead, he reorganized the notes and added a mini-essay on legal history at the end of each section. His job was made more onerous by the fact that he developed major disagreements with the author. For example, he disputed Chancellor Kent's explanation for the strict liability of common carriers. Kent had suggested that the doctrine derived from Roman law, whereas Holmes believed that it was a product of German and English folk law.[2]

---

[2] The folk law of Germany and England gave a remedy for recovery of personal property to the person in possession and not to the owner. As a result, a bailor could not recover his goods from a third party if they were taken while they were in the bailee's possession.

Wendell, however, restrained himself from "correcting" the chancellor's text. Neither did he feel the freedom to change its basic organization. Toward the end of the project, he complained to a friend:

I have to keep a civil tongue in my head while I am his valet – but his arrangement is chaotic – he has no general ideas except wrong ones – and his treatment of special topics is often confused to the last degree.[3]

The work was further complicated by the fact that he was writing during a period when the common law was rapidly changing and it was frequently necessary to rewrite sections that had been previously finished. Nevertheless, he labored on, taking extreme care about the accuracy of the finished product.

Wendell's edition of Kent was finally published in 1873.[4] It was a success. Lawyers would recognize the thoroughness of his approach. Critics noted its accuracy and depth.[5] The *North American Review* praised it in extravagant terms, noting "the immense size of the field which has been searched for authorities, the discretion with which they have been selected, and the extreme conciseness with which their result is stated." And for the reviewer, even these superlatives did not seem to be enough. He continued:

The diligence which has been used to consider and compare everything that bears on the points discussed ... can be fully appreciated only by those who have occasion to examine with care the same subjects for themselves, or by those who have had the good fortune to see the work as it went on. No such eyewitness can have failed to remark, in the unceasing industry, in the abundant learning, in the patient statement and restatement of propositions till they reached a correct and satisfactory form, in the eagerness to obtain and readiness to consider fairly the views of others.[6]

It was a job well done and Wendell must have been pleased by the recognition it received. Nevertheless, the bottom line remained – no one achieves fame and glory by annotating someone else's work.[7] Thus, Kent

---

Therefore, he had to rely on the bailee to pursue the legal remedy. The effect of strict liability, therefore, was to force the bailee to pursue the remedy that only he could pursue. *See* Holmes, *supra* ch. 3, n. 25 at 131. Howe discusses this example at length and notes that Wendell's copy of Kent had a note next to the passage in question: "This is not so!" Howe, *supra* n. 1 at 206.

[3] *Id.* at 16 (Letter from Oliver Wendell Holmes Jr. to J. N. Pomeroy [May 2, 1872]).

[4] Kent, *supra* ch. 3, n. 22.   [5] Howe, *supra* n. 1 at 19–21.

[6] Kent, *supra* n. 4 *in Art. VI – Critical Notices*, 118 N. Am. Rev. 383, 387 (1874).

[7] Thayer, his nominal supervisor on the project, was not credited as a coauthor, but only profusely thanked in the introduction. Thayer was peeved by this slight, but it is not hard

was only the beginning – it was now time for Holmes to make his own mark on the law. During the next eight years, he would have few companions. Gone were the all-night discussions with Bill James. Gone was the Metaphysical Club and its intellectual camaraderie. And soon, both Chauncey Wright and Nicholas St. John Greene were gone, taken by their sad and lonely deaths. Wendell pushed on, spending most of his evenings in the Social Law Library doing research and finding out all he could about the history and development of the law. Sometimes, he would run into a cousin or John Ropes or Arthur Sedgwick. They might even walk home together, talking about their work. But these conversations lacked the intensity of earlier days. They were more like the radio traffic of ships passing on the open seas. This was his time of "deeper solitude and greater trials."

WRITING *THE COMMON LAW*

To do original work is a complex ambition. It cannot be achieved by simple erudition. No matter how much Wendell knew, it would not be enough. He needed to find his own distinctive voice with respect to the law. Everyone, it seemed, was talking about a "science of law," but what did this phrase mean? Did it mean the kind of logical analysis Dean Langdell was bringing to Harvard Law School? Or did it mean that the law could be analyzed in the same way that physics analyzes movement? Or perhaps it was as Austin's recent book had suggested, a kind of anthropology in which the legal scientist described the operation of law within a specific culture.[8] Any of these seemed plausible. It was even possible, as Wendell was beginning to suspect, that it was a mixture of all three approaches.

Wendell's own views on legal theory are difficult to characterize. Eight years after Kent, he would publish *The Common Law* – a book that represented his own unique perspective. The approach was descriptive. The lectures covered all of the substantive areas of the common law. With respect to each, he presented some historical background and the general principles that governed the area. To a modern reader, the material is dry,

---

to see the matter from Wendell's point of view. The amount of work he did on the project was prodigious. The project occupied most of three years and would go largely unrewarded. The idea that he should share the credit with someone who had done relatively little might well have seemed unfair to him.

[8] John Austin, *The Province of Jurisprudence Determined* (1832).

but his book was no mere treatise. It was not simply a matter of organizing and elaborating on the cases. He was on his own unique journey, and he was offering a different type of analysis. Sometimes the explanations were historical. For example, the first lecture provided some ancient history about the common law. Other times, the lectures were more practical. Law, he argued, has its roots in human instinct. Sometimes – but rarely – he offered his own insights into the nature of law. Thus, we have the famous statement – "The life of the law has not been logic; it has been experience."[9] Mostly, however, he sought to discover fundamental principles. For instance, in the lecture on torts, he sought "a common ground at the bottom of all liability in tort."

The diversity of approaches means that there is no central theme. To be sure, the book has a certain "feel" or "atmosphere," conveying a sense of the law's robust growth and its adaption to human needs. But a mood is not a theory of law; we are left to guess what kind of theory Holmes is proposing. As a result, over the decades, different scholars have placed him in a remarkable number of intellectual camps. For example, Morton White put him in a group that included Dewey, Veblen, Beard, and Robinson and that was marked, White argued, by a rejection of formalism;[10] Robert Gordon linked Holmes's legal views to a logical positivist epistemology;[11] Robert Summers argued that he shared with Dewey, Pound, and others an instrumentalist outlook;[12] and H. L. Pohlman contended that he should be read in the context of a utilitarian philosophy.[13]

As we saw in the previous chapter, Wendell's outlook was the product of several influences. While his philosophy was shaped by Emerson's Transcendentalism, his methodology was pragmatic. Furthermore, his view of law was limited by Wright's positivism. Thus, there is little point in trying to place his theory of law into a preexisting box. Instead, we should recognize that he is searching for an original approach. And, keeping in mind that he characterized this period of his life as a journey, we should think of *The Common Law* as a chronicle of that journey. It is, in effect a travelogue – one that

[9] Holmes, *supra* ch. 3, n. 25 at 1.
[10] Morton White, *The Revolt Against Formalism in American Social Thought of the Twentieth Century*, 8 J. of the Hist. of Ideas 131, 132 (1947).
[11] Robert W. Gordon, *Holmes' Common Law as Legal and Social Science*, 10 Hofstra L. Rev. 719, 723 (1982).
[12] Robert Summers, *Instrumentalism and American Legal Theory* 84 (1982).
[13] H. L. Pohlman, *Justice Oliver Wendell Holmes and Utilitarian Jurisprudence* 5 (1984).

records what he learned during his ten-year period of studying law. Since few of us will undertake a similar journey, his work is informative. Indeed, for those who are interested in a history of the common law, it is an excellent introduction, but there is more here to discover. We want to know not only the details of Wendell's journey but also what he took away from it. What effect did it have on his performance as a judge? What did it teach him about the nature of law? And, remembering Wendell's letter to Emerson, what did he learn about the nature of the Universe?

Treating *The Common Law* as a travelogue, I begin with Holmes's own point of debarkation – the historical context of his departure. Next, I examine his route – a route delineated by his pragmatism. After these preliminaries, I attempt to reconstruct what Holmes thought of his journey and what conclusions he drew about the nature of law. Finally, in the last section, I examine the implication of these conclusions for a theory of judicial decision-making.

POINT OF DEPARTURE

Wendell began his journey in a time of transition. The ancient common law was adapting to the exigencies of nineteenth-century life. Perhaps the most dramatic development of this period was the abolition of the writ system that had dominated Anglo-American law since the Middle Ages. The old system was rigid and extremely technical. Among average citizens, it gave rise to a feeling that the law was mysterious and aloof. Nineteenth-century novels such as Dickens's *Bleak House* and Trollope's *The Warden* capture the fear that many felt of being tangled up in its web.

On its surface, the system itself was simple enough. A plaintiff would begin his lawsuit by obtaining a writ from the appropriate court. The writs were of various kinds – each kind had its own particular requirements for proof and each had its own specific remedy should the plaintiff prevail. A simple example demonstrates how it worked. Suppose that Bates left a chair with Smith for repair and that, at a subsequent time, Smith became furious and threw the chair against a wall. When Bates returned for the chair, he found it in pieces. Seeking to recover his loss, he consulted a lawyer, who procured a writ of trespass for damage to the chair. Unfortunately, this choice would have been wrong and the lawyer's error would have meant that Bates was out of luck. Even though Smith had destroyed the chair, the writ of trespass required more – it required that Bates be in possession of the chair when Smith smashed it. Without possession, the proper writ might have been Trespass on the Case, but that writ too had its own set of requirements.[14] The lawyer had to choose a writ and his choice was made at the client's peril. The system was strict – there were no second chances. Even minor mistakes meant dismissal. Misspellings, trivial inaccuracies, or small variances between the writ and the underlying documentation would all be fatal.[15]

It is not surprising that a growing commercial culture found the writ system cumbersome and impractical. Demands grew for reform. The common story is that a lawyer named Dudley Field persuaded the New York state legislature to abolish the writ system in favor of enacting legislation that would codify the common law.[16] The real story is a little more complex. In Wendell's home state of Massachusetts, reform of the writ system began right after the American Revolution. The first step was to allow plaintiffs to amend their pleadings.[17] This was a meaningful move in the direction of substantive justice – parties were less likely to lose a meritorious claim simply because of a lawyer's misjudgment. Even so, the excessive formalism remained, and this meant that justice was inaccessible except to those who were wealthy enough to afford a lawyer. Thus, legal reform became an issue in Shay's Rebellion of 1786, and, even though the rebellion failed, it stimulated further change.

Over time, the ability to amend pleadings began to undermine the writ system itself. Since amendments were allowed, defendants had little incentive to object to the form of the pleadings, and, if they did not object, the court would proceed to order the requested relief. Thus, for example, one historian reports:

Many actions in which plaintiffs were victorious were given no name – one was labeled merely "a plea of Grievous complaint"; another a "plea for the Recovery" of certain nails; a third, "a Plea for not performing his [the defendant's] promise." Others merely stated the facts upon which the plaintiff relied.[18]

---

[14] A full discussion of Trespass on the Case is available in Frederic William Maitland, *Equity, Also the Forms of Action at Common Law: Two Courses of Lectures* 360–362 (A. H. Chaytor and W. J. Whittaker eds. 1913).

[15] William Nelson, *The Reform of Common Law Pleading in Massachusetts 1760–1830: Adjudication as a Prelude to Legislation,* 122 U. Penn L. Rev. 97, 108 (1973).

[16] The New York experience is described in Mildred Coe and Lewis Morse, *Chronology of the Development of the David Dudley Field Code,* 27 Cornell L. Rev. 238 (1942).

[17] This was done by court rule in 1776 and by the legislature in 1784.

[18] Nelson, *supra* n. 15 at 118, and cases there cited.

Under these circumstances, courts were less likely to insist on the exact letter of the law, and the writ system gradually began to lose its hold on Massachusetts law. Finally, in 1852, the legislature recognized this fact and abolished it entirely.

The Massachusetts approach differed from New York's. There was no civil code. Instead, the Massachusetts legislature opted for a more minimalist course. It simply provided for three types of personal actions – contracts, torts, and replevin – and left the continuing definition of these doctrines to the courts.[19] In addition, it eliminated the technical requirements for pleading and substituted such sensible rules as:

- The action shall be named in conformity with the above-described division (i.e. contracts, torts, and replevin);
- No averment need be made which the law does not require to be proved;
- Only the substantive facts necessary to constitute the cause of action need be stated, without unnecessary verbiage, and with substantial certainty.[20]

The ultimate abandonment of the writ system had consequences for the way in which Massachusetts lawyers thought about law. Once the "unnecessary verbiage" had been cleared from the docket, they began to speak more transparently about the kinds of considerations that were relevant to legal decision-making.

Of course, the ensuing discussion about legal decision-making took place in a particular context. After the Civil War came an explosion of commerce and industry. More activity meant more litigation, and this, in turn, produced a large increase in the number of reported decisions. It also meant that judges were confronting more complicated fact patterns. In torts, there were new kinds of accidents caused by sophisticated machinery. Contract cases too presented many novel issues with new types of financing, new ways of forming contracts at a distance, and new approaches to allocating risk.

This explosion of cases had put the legal profession in a difficult position. Even those who practiced in a narrow specialty had difficulty mastering all the relevant cases. Specialized treatises had become multivolume works. For example, by 1853, Theophilus Parsons was complaining that three large volumes were insufficient to allow for a full discussion of

[19] Mass. Acts, c. 312, § 1 (1852).
[20] *Id.* at §2. Section 2 provided ten rules, all of which could be understood in practical terms.

contract law.[21] But sheer bulk was not the only problem. If lawyers were to earn their fees, they had to be able to tell their clients what the law required and what view the courts might take of their clients' cases. But, with the expansion of possibilities, it was sometimes difficult to tell what a court would do. The law had always operated on the basis of precedent. This meant that courts had made ample use of analogies, deciding in each case whether the facts of the current case were sufficiently similar to those of an earlier case, that the earlier case should be taken as controlling. Thus, judges had to make fine-tuned judgments as to which cases were relevant and what distinctions were salient. These judgments could be subjective and unpredictable, and, as the cases became more complex, this was increasingly true. What was needed was a deeper understanding of legal decision-making, and, for most American legal scholars of the period, this meant paying more attention to legal doctrine.

Lawyers have always used a specialized language to analyze the law. Legal doctrine, as it is called, provides a platform for arguing and deciding legal cases. A lawyer formulates doctrine when (s)he reads a series of cases and attempts to find a principle that will summarize them. But, as the decided cases grew in number and complexity, it became more and more difficult to discern the governing principles. By the mid-nineteenth century, this simple form of legal reasoning was at the breaking point. The old categories had become less useful and the way to form new ones was not obvious. In a nation with multiple jurisdictions, one state court might analyze a problem differently from another. Who was right? What did it mean to be right? How should the new cases be characterized and organized? One way to answer such questions was to look for a comprehensive framework within which an individual case could be analyzed. Since each case presented its own unique facts, courts rarely had time to work out all of the consequences of their rulings. Fortunately, however, law schools were beginning to fill the gap. By hiring full-time faculty, they provided a cadre of men who were ideally situated to devote the time necessary to analyze and organize entire fields. And, in fact, the treatises of the day took on this task. Unlike Blackstone, they did not simply survey court decisions; more and more they were exploring the reasons for decisions and recommending the better course.

The high point of this development was the work of Christopher Columbus Langdell, the dean of Harvard Law School. He took the development of legal doctrine to a new level. As a teacher, he began by

---

[21] Theophilus Parsons, *Preface* to *Parsons on Contracts* (9th edn. 1904).

providing students with copies of selected court opinions. Then, under his careful guidance, they extracted the principles of contract law from the cases. The point of this exercise was to formulate the principles in such a way that they would entail a correct result for a large number of similar cases. In Langdell's mind, this was the science of law: he began with the cases, generalized the principles used to decide them, and checked to see whether these principles were predictive. Then he refined them further by seeking to explain the largest number of cases with the fewest number of principles.[22] Contrary to the common wisdom, he was not engaged in an entirely deductive enterprise. Finding the appropriate principles was a matter of finesse and experimentation. In any case, whatever one thinks about his approach, it is easy to see how this kind of reasoning changed the shape of legal argument. Before Langdell, the law was understood as a collection of precedents; after Langdell, it could be seen as a series of doctrinal principles derived from the cases, and it was these doctrinal principles that formed the basis for legal decisions.[23]

THE ROUTE TO THE POLE

Wendell's route to the Pole would not be the same as Langdell's. He was not interested in converting legal cases into complex doctrines. He had a larger vision. He wanted to understand the role of law in human life, where it had come from, and how it had changed. In answering these questions, he would follow two fundamental principles. The first was the use of the pragmatic method; the second was Wright's positivism.

The pragmatic approach imbued Wendell with a certain attitude. Law was neither mysterious nor exempt from the normal methods of human inquiry. As he would later write, "When we study law we are not studying a mystery but a well-known profession."[24] This meant that the study had to begin with answers to factual questions. How, for example, does the law regulate human conduct? How does it settle disputes? What are the rules? Where do they come from? And these questions had to be answered not just with respect to the present moment, but for centuries past. Law

---

[22] For a more detailed discussion of this process, *see* Catharine Wells, *Langdell and the Invention of Legal Doctrine*, 58 Buffalo L. Rev. 551 (2010).

[23] For clarity I have oversimplified here. It was not so much a case of one or the other – cases or doctrine – it was a matter of emphasis. For example, the practicing lawyer was less likely to think of the "rule in x case" and more likely to think in terms of black letter doctrine.

[24] Holmes, *supra* intro., n. 3 at 457.

was an evolving system continuously shaped by tradition and precedent. One had to know both its history and its tendencies. Thus, Holmes's work was predominantly descriptive. He would detail the facts and then he would interpret them. He was not just interested in the rule but in the rationale for the rule. He did not think that rules stood in isolation. Instead, he recognized that they are generated by human needs and sustained by the role they play in regulating human life. At every stage, Holmes felt, a rule must be considered in this context.

Like the great European philosophers, Holmes was seeking a rationale for law that went beyond doctrinal restatement. The European approach, however, was anything but pragmatic. Kant, for example, had a theory of human experience. So too John Stuart Mill began with a utilitarian theory. In both cases, their arguments moved from theory to substantive legal principles. Wendell, however, would go in the exact opposite direction. Lacking a grand philosophical theory, he sought to give a factual account of the law. From this, he hoped to learn something about human experience and the spiritual world of which it was a part. Remember what he wrote to Emerson: "It seems to me that I have learned ... that the law opens a way to philosophy."[25] The law would be the beginning and not the end of that investigation.

The lecture on possession provides an excellent illustration of this aspect of Holmes's method. In a system of private property, the concept of ownership seems central. From the layperson's perspective, his ownership of certain property means that he can use it however he chooses. In determining ownership, he looks to the facts surrounding the property's acquisition. For example, he knows he owns a book if he bought it or if someone gave it to him, and that he does not own it if he borrowed it from a library. In the latter case, he knows that he has possession rather than ownership.

From a practical point of view, ownership seems like the more important concept. There is a contrast, we think, between the stability of ownership and the transitory nature of possession. But, from a legal point of view, both of these states – owning and possessing – are entitled to protection. Indeed, the concept of possession is central to the law and it is not obvious why this should be so.

Wendell began his analysis of possession with the reasons given by the German philosophers:

---

[25] Letter from Oliver Wendell Holmes Jr. to Ralph Waldo Emerson (Apr. 16, 1876).

Kant and Hegel start from freedom. The freedom of the will, Kant said, is the essence of man. It is an end in itself; it is that which needs no further explanation, which is absolutely to be respected, and which it is the very end and object of all government to realize and affirm. Possession is to be protected because a man by taking possession of an object has brought it within the sphere of his will. He has extended his personality into or over that object.[26]

Thus, Kant began with a moral right, and then translated the moral right into a legal right. Holmes, on the other hand, was skeptical on two counts. First, as a pragmatist, he did not believe in moral rights derived from an a priori system. Second, he had been persuaded by Chauncey Wright that law and morals were distinct. Thus, he would not do as Kant had done, and seek moral justifications of legal rules. Instead, he would answer the question about possession by examining the historical facts. This examination indicated that the Anglo-American tradition had no single rule with respect to possession:

In the Greenland whale-fishery, by the English custom, if the first striker lost his hold on the fish, and it was then killed by another, the first had no claim; but he had the whole if he kept fast to the whale until it was struck by the other, although it then broke from the first harpoon. By the custom in the Gallipagos [*sic*], on the other hand, the first striker had half the whale, although control of the line was lost. Each of these customs has been sustained and acted on by the English courts, and Judge Lowell has decided in accordance with still a third, which gives the whale to the vessel whose iron first remains in it, provided claim be made before cutting in.

He then argued that the courts had good reason for adopting the custom as the rule in these cases:

The ground as put by Lord Mansfield is simply that, were it not for such customs, there must be a sort of warfare perpetually subsisting between the adventurers.[27]

Finally, he generalizes the point by arguing that practical doctrine rather than intellectual theories shapes the law.

If courts adopt different rules on similar facts, according to the point at which men will fight in the several cases, it tends, so far as it goes, to shake an a priori theory of the matter. . . . Law, being a practical thing, must found itself on actual forces. It is quite enough, therefore, for the law, that man, by an instinct which he shares with the domestic dog, . . . will not allow himself to be dispossessed, either by force or fraud, of what he holds, without trying to get it back again. Philosophy may find a hundred reasons to justify the instinct, but it would be totally immaterial if it should condemn it and bid us surrender without a murmur. As long as the instinct

---

[26] Holmes, *supra* ch. 3, n. 25 at 163–164.   [27] *Id.* at 176–178.

remains, it will be more comfortable for the law to satisfy it in an orderly manner, than to leave people to themselves.

In one stroke, Holmes has accomplished two things. First, he has made a powerful case that the rationale for the law of possession does not lie in abstract moral theory. Second, he has made the general point that even the most abstract principles of law are rooted in human need. For Kant and Hegel, human needs are universal and discernible by a priori methods. For Holmes, they are contingent on social realities and can only be understood by observing actual behavior.

This, then, was the route that Wendell would follow to the Pole. Unlike the German theorists, he had chosen a path grounded in empirical reality. He would focus on the historical facts – he would ascertain the rules used at any given point – then he would determine what facts had given rise to the need for court intervention; and finally, he would analyze the relationship between the rule and the facts that spawned it. Looking at the law in this way, he found something most others had missed.

DESTINATION AND DISCOVERY: ARRIVING AT THE POLE

Buried near the end of the first lecture are two paragraphs that describe the discovery Holmes made at the end of his journey. He described it as a paradox existing at the heart of the common law:

The foregoing history . . . well illustrates the paradox of form and substance in the development of law. In form its growth is logical. The official theory is that each new decision follows syllogistically from existing precedents. But . . . precedents survive in the law long after the use they once served is at an end and the reason for them has been forgotten. The result of following them must often be failure and confusion from the merely logical point of view.

On the other hand, in substance the growth of the law is legislative. . . . The very considerations which judges most rarely mention, and always with an apology, are the secret root from which the law draws all the juices of life. I mean, of course, considerations of what is expedient for the community concerned. Every important principle which is developed by litigation is in fact . . . the result of more or less definitely understood views of public policy; . . . the unconscious result of instinctive preferences and inarticulate convictions[28]

It is not hard to understand the paradox. With respect to form, the growth of law is logical – each development must be consistent with the preexisting principles. In this sense, the law may expand but it may not

---

[28] *Id.* at 35.

change. With respect to substance, the law changes to accommodate human needs – not only do judges make law but they make it on the basis of public policy and convenience. Thus, the common law operates on two different tracks. One is logical; the other is practical. Both tracks are essential. A common law system where judges ignore practical realities would not last very long. And a system where each ruling is sui generis would represent mere assertions of power.

In *The Common Law*, Holmes only described the paradox; he did not attempt to resolve it. This should not surprise us. Remember that Holmes sought to give a positive account of law; that is, he meant to set forth the facts about law as it actually operates to settle real-world disputes. In this context, the paradox is not troubling. As we have seen, it amounts to the claim that any theory that will accurately predict legal outcomes must contain elements besides legal doctrine. On the other hand, a true paradox arises when we consider the normative aspect of legal decision-making. How should judges decide cases? Langdell, it seemed, had an easy answer. Judges should study prior cases to ferret out whatever implied principles they contain. Then, they should decide their cases in accordance with these principles. Holmes disagreed. Judges, he thought, must follow two different tracks – a logic track and a policy track. But if the two tracks lead in different directions, how can judges follow both?

The dilemma stems from the assumption that a single legal rule should be the leading edge of any legal decision. Holmes, however, rejected this assumption:

It is the merit of the common law that it decides the case first and determines the principle afterwards. Looking at the forms of logic it might be inferred that when you have a minor premise and a conclusion, there must be a major, which you are also prepared then and there to assert. But in fact, lawyers, like other men, frequently see well enough how they ought to decide on a given state of facts without being very clear as to the *ratio decidendi.*[29]

Thus, he rejected the common understanding about legal decision-making. Langdell labored to find correct legal principles because he believed that these would produce correct outcomes for new legal cases. Holmes, on the other hand, reversed the direction of legal analysis. He thought that deductive reasoning was not the proper method. Logic, he believed, came after the fact; it was supplied by lawyers, by treatise

[29] Oliver Wendell Holmes Jr., *Codes and the Arrangement of Law*, 5 Am. L. Rev. 1, 1 (1870).

writers, and by subsequent legal opinions. Further, he explained why this fact had not been apparent from the outset:

As the law is administered by able and experienced men, who know too much to sacrifice good sense to a syllogism, it will be found that, when ancient rules maintain themselves in the way that has been and will be shown in this book, new reasons more fitted to the time have been found for them, and that they gradually receive a new content, and at last a new form, from the grounds to which they have been transplanted. But hitherto this process has been largely unconscious. It is important, on that account, to bring to mind what the actual course of events has been. If it were only to insist on a more conscious recognition of the legislative function of the courts.[30]

In short, the paradox had not been noticeable because legal change happens very slowly and, for the most part, unconsciously. At any given moment in time the law will appear stable and consistent, but when we step back – as Holmes had done – and consider its development over centuries, the ongoing process of change and accommodation comes into view.

Holmes's recognition of this paradox entails two consequences for his views on law. The first is his skepticism about the work being done by Langdell and the other treatise writers:

What has been said will explain the failure of all theories which consider the law only from its formal side; whether they attempt to deduce the corpus from a priori postulates, or fall into the humbler error of supposing the science of the law to reside in the *elegantia juris*, or logical cohesion of part with part. The truth is, that the law is always approaching, and never reaching, consistency. It is forever adopting new principles from life at one end, and it always retains old ones from history at the other, which have not yet been absorbed or sloughed off. It will become entirely consistent only when it ceases to grow.[31]

The second consequence consists of his doubts about codification:

However much we may codify the law into a series of seemingly self-sufficient propositions, those propositions will be but a phase in a continuous growth. To understand their scope fully, to know how they will be dealt with by judges trained in the past which the law embodies, we must ourselves know something of that past. The history of what the law has been is necessary to the knowledge of what the law is.[32]

For a modern reader, Holmes's doubts are prophetic. Neither formalism nor codification stand in good repute today. Holmes, by contrast, has become the legendary father of a doctrine known as legal realism. Legal

---

[30] Holmes, *supra* ch. 3, n. 25 at 36.   [31] *Id.*   [32] *Id.*

realists are anti-formalists; they reject the idea that law is logic. Realists are of many different stripes. Some argue that judges decide cases by resorting to their own sense of public policy. Others suggest that rulings are based on class prejudice. Still others argue that judges' own personal psychological imperatives are the motivating factor. But, to modern eyes, realism too has its problems. The rejection of formalism has left American law in a quandary. As one American writer famously declared: "We are all realists now." But then he describes the dilemma this has created:

> Yet, if we are all realists, why are some of the insights of the realists so controversial? Why is it still so explosive to claim that law is a form of politics? The answer is that the realists were unable to produce an acceptable alternative to formalism that would enable judges and lawyers to engage in normative argument. Current debates about legal reasoning are best understood as attempts to answer the central question that the realists left unresolved: How can we engage in normative legal argument without either reverting to the formalism of the past or reducing all claims to the raw demands of political interest groups? This is a tough question to answer.[33]

Indeed, it is such a tough question that no one has found a satisfactory answer. Realist legal scholars have not been able to specify what separates a bad legal argument from a good one, and in the practical world this is a substantial problem.

Consider, for example, how the Senate evaluates nominees for the federal bench. In this context, no one claims to be a realist because no one wants to tell a senator that judicial decision-making is unconstrained. Never mind that a formalist approach rarely yields a determinate outcome. The fact that formalism is identified with "following the law" and that realism is identified with "doing justice in some less structured way" is enough to make senators say: "We want judges who follow the law; we want respect for the rule of law." In fact, the perceived illegitimacy of the realist position makes it essentially disqualifying for a judge – a surprising result given that Holmes and dozens of other like-minded men and women have served on the Supreme Court bench with real distinction. The problem with this whole approach is evident. Each side of the realist/formalist debate is subject to its own particular pitfalls. Formalism doesn't give us answers and realism supplies too many. This conundrum has troubled theorists for more than a century.

Holmes's association with realism has become a focal point of contemporary scholarship. It has enhanced his reputation with those who are

---

[33] Joseph Singer, *Legal Realism Now*, 76 Cal. L. Rev. 465, 467 (1988).

sympathetic, and it has made him a target for those who equate realism
with nihilism. Obviously, legal nihilism is a serious charge – especially
against someone who spent fifty years on the bench. I think, however, that
the discussion about realism misses the point. If Holmes was a realist – and
this question really comes down to a matter of semantics – was he the kind
of realist that gets caught in the realist dilemma? This is the issue and it is
an important one. During his lifetime, Holmes was generally regarded as
a first-rate judge. In fact, he was one of the best-known and most popular
judges in American history. It would be shocking indeed if, after all his
study and his years on the bench, his advice to prospective judges would
be: "The law does not constrain you. Do what you like." If law were an
arbitrary exercise, it would be hard to understand the effort he invested in
studying its substance. Indeed, I think that Holmes had a far more sophisticated view of legal decision-making, one that I attempt to clarify in the
next section.

HOLMES AND THE REALIST DILEMMA

Those who think of Holmes as a realist point to statements like the
following:

The life of the law has not been logic: it has been experience. The seed of every new
growth within its sphere has been a felt necessity. The form of continuity has been
kept up by reasonings purporting to reduce everything to a logical sequence; but
that form is nothing but the evening dress which the new-comer puts on to make
itself presentable according to conventional requirements. The important
phenomenon is the man underneath it, not the coat; the justice and
reasonableness of a decision, not its consistency with previously held views.[34]

Like much of Holmes's most memorable writing this statement is
largely metaphorical. The law is portrayed as a living thing – a plant
growing from a seed. Or perhaps it is a garden that "contains new growth
within its sphere." There is also the comparison between legal doctrine
and "the evening dress." These metaphors suggest a duality that gives the
passage its meaning. The contrast is between logic and experience; formal
consistency and substantive justice. From this, the realist interpretation
seems to follow – law is based on intuition and feeling rather than
a consistent logical system. The problem with this reading is that it

---

[34] Oliver Wendell Holmes Jr., *Book Notices*, 14 Am. L. Rev. 233–234 (1880) (reviewing
Christopher Langdell, *A Selection of Cases on the Law of Contracts, with a Summary of
the Topics Covered by the Cases* [1879]).

overlooks Holmes's embrace of the paradox of form and substance. If he had meant that the law was only substance and that formal considerations were simply window dressing, then the paradox of form and substance would not be a paradox. Instead Holmes could have asserted a straightforward denial of the role of logic in legal decision-making.

Furthermore, we can see that Holmes is not a simple realist by paying careful attention to the analogy of the evening dress. We would not necessarily say that a naked man is real while his clothes are an illusion. A naked man is not the same thing as a man who is appropriately dressed. Neither is he a paper doll with one piece of paper representing the man and another representing his clothes. The man and his clothes are intimately connected. He is the man who chose his clothes and who makes a statement about himself by wearing them. So it is with the form and substance of law. We do not get to the "real" nature of law by stripping the form from the substance any more than we get at the "real" man by stripping him of his clothes. The clothes and the man together proclaim: I am the type of man who desires to fit in and I know how to do so.

The point is that we need to reject the simple image of Holmes as a realist. Unlike the modern realists, he is responding specifically to Langdell and to his claims about the logical nature of law. Therefore, the best place to begin is with Langdell and the exact role of logic in his system. Langdell's system was logical in the following sense. He extracted principles from cases and then applied them to new cases using a deductive syllogism such as the following:

1. If there is no notice of acceptance, there is no contract.
2. There is no notice of acceptance in this case.

Conclusion: Therefore, there is no contract in this case.

But this was not the part of the enterprise that was problematic for Holmes. What Holmes objected to was the point at which Langdell assumed that the syllogism compelled a certain outcome in the particular case. In fact, Holmes dismissed this notion as a fallacy:

The fallacy to which I refer is the notion that the only force at work in the development of the law is logic. ... The danger of which I speak is not the admission that the principles governing other phenomena also govern the law, but the notion that a given system, ours, for instance, can be worked out like mathematics from some general axioms of conduct.[35]

[35] Holmes, *supra* intro., n. 3 at 465.

The problem here is not the use of logic but its overuse. Langdell, having found a legal principle, believes that it compels a certain result no matter what.[36] Holmes, on the other hand, views judicial decision-making as a more flexible practice.

To see what this means, we can contrast two different models of decision-making. Each model purports to explain how decisions are made in accordance with a rule. The first is mechanical; it applies the rule syllogistically. There is no discretion, no gray area. This is the model that is generally attributed to Langdell. The second model is pragmatic. It views rule-following as part of a decision-making practice. According to this model, rules are not statements written on a piece of paper. Instead, they represent a routinized way of responding to like cases. A rule may be evidenced by a course of conduct that is understood as being rule governed. Or it may consist of unstated and vague expectations about the nature of future conduct. By contesting the idea that Langdell's syllogism compels the judge to rule in a certain way, Holmes is embracing this second model.

The mechanical model seems to have certain advantages. It is simple because it is based on a syllogism. Furthermore, it avoids the realist dilemma because it does not permit any discretion. If you can establish the premises, the conclusion follows. In fact, the mechanical model is so simple and inflexible that we can easily program a computer to perform this function. We program the computer to print "**There is no contract.**" whenever

> "If there is no notice of acceptance, there is no contract." and
> "There is no notice of acceptance in this case."

are among its inputs.

This is the way computers "think," but do humans think this way as well? Are we like computers? Are we programmed to speak out "**There is no contract.**" whenever we believe the appropriate premises? The obvious answer is no. Suppose someone comes crawling out of the desert. He says: "Socrates is a man," and "All men are mortal." Do I reply "Socrates is

---

[36] This is why Holmes found the following quotation from Langdell so objectionable.

It has been claimed that the purposes of substantial justice and the interests of contracting parties as understood by themselves will be best served by holding &c, . . . and cases have been put to show that the contrary view would produce not only unjust but absurd results. The true answer to this argument is that it is irrelevant. Christopher Columbus Langdell, *A Summary of the Law of Contracts* 20 (2nd edn. 1880)

mortal," or do I get him a drink of water? Maybe his name is Socrates. Maybe this is the only English he knows. Maybe he is delirious. It does not matter; I get him the water. This is not because I am illogical. It is because I recognize that this is not an appropriate occasion for making the inference. Syllogisms are mechanical only because we assume they are situated in an ideal world where logical reasoning is never interrupted by real-world contingencies.

Furthermore, the mechanical model generates conclusions that do not prescribe a specific action. Consider, for example, the syllogism:

If there is no contract the plaintiff loses.
There is no contract.
Conclusion: The plaintiff loses.

Is the conclusion a prediction of what the judge will do or an order that compels the judge to decide against the plaintiff? One would have to say the former. Consider, for example, the syllogism that concludes that Socrates is mortal. The conclusion – Socrates is mortal – does not compel Socrates to die. Neither does it command anyone to kill him. Similarly, the conclusion – The plaintiff loses – is descriptive and not normative. What is needed is not just a prediction but rather a rule that compels ruling against the plaintiff, and this requirement leads the mechanical model to a peculiar paradox.

The paradox was the subject of a Lewis Carroll essay.[37] In the essay, a Tortoise challenges Achilles, claiming to believe in two premises of a syllogism but not to believe in its conclusion. (In describing the paradox, I substitute Langdell's syllogism.)

1. If there is no notice of acceptance, there is no contract.
2. There is no notice of acceptance in this case.
3. **Conclusion:** Therefore, there is no contract in this case.

He then challenges Achilles to "force [him], logically, to accept **The Conclusion** as true." Achilles replies that, obviously, the problem is that the Tortoise does not accept the conditional statement that:

If 1 and 2 are true, then **The Conclusion** must be true.

---

[37] Lewis Carroll, *What the Tortoise Said to Achilles*, 4 MIND 278, 278–279 (1895). There is an extended discussion of this paradox in my article, Catharine Wells, *Improving One's Situation: Some Pragmatic Reflections on the Art of Judging*, 49 Wash. and Lee L. Rev. 323, 327–329 (1992).

When the Tortoise acknowledges this, Achilles writes it down and asks the Tortoise to accept it as a premise. So then there are three premises – 1, 2, and 3 – and when Achilles once again asks the Tortoise to acknowledge the truth of **The Conclusion**, the Tortoise replies that he will do so only if Achilles will add yet another premise to those he has already written. The premise is:

4. If 1 and 2 and 3, then **The Conclusion**.

Achilles adds the premise and the conversation continues:

"And at last we've got to the end of this ideal race-course! Now that you accept 1 and 2 and 3 and 4, of course you accept **The Conclusion**."

"Do I?" said the Tortoise innocently. "Let's make that quite clear. I accept 1 and 2 and 3 and 4. Suppose I still refuse to accept **The Conclusion**?"

"Then logic would take you by the throat and force you to do it!" Achilles triumphantly replied. "Logic would tell you 'You can't help yourself. Now that you've accepted 1 and 2 and 3 and 4, you must accept **The Conclusion**!' So, you've no choice, you see."

"Whatever Logic is good enough to tell me is worth writing down," said the Tortoise. "So, enter it in your book, please. We will call it –

(5) If 1 and 2 and 3 and 4 are true, **The Conclusion** must be true.

Until I've granted that, of course, I needn't grant **The Conclusion**. So, it's quite a necessary step, you see?"

"I see," said Achilles; and there was a touch of sadness in his tone.[38]

Obviously, this line of argument will postpone the inference indefinitely. The Tortoise will not make the inference unless the rule for the inference is included among the premises and, once it is included among the premises, it loses its power to license the inference. To put this in terms of the computer analogy, the Tortoise lacks a program. It is the program that "forces" the computer to print out the conclusion when the two premises are present. It will not do so simply because its input includes a statement of the rule. The Tortoise is in the same position – he has a series of premises but nothing that tells him what to do with them.

Carroll's paradox forces us to think more clearly about the mechanical model. Nothing seems simpler than drawing a syllogistic conclusion. Nevertheless, as the paradox suggests, rules are more than conditional statements written on a piece of paper. They are a part of our programming, and this raises the question: how are we programmed to follow a given rule? It is here that we understand the wisdom of the pragmatic model. We do not learn rules by memorizing a written statement. Rather, the pragmatic model suggests, we learn the rules by engaging in a rule-bound activity. Note, for

---

[38] Carroll, *supra* n. 37 at 279–280.

example, that we teach law by asking students to participate in a process of applying a legal rule to a series of real and hypothetical cases. They learn by doing. At any given point, they may try to formulate a rule by putting down words on a sheet of paper. The mechanical model would take these words and pronounce the job done. But for anyone who truly embraces the pragmatic model, it is the practice and not the written word that determines the rule. This is what Holmes meant when he wrote: "It is the merit of the common law that it decides the case first and determines the principle afterwards." Thus, in a conflict between a written formulation of the rule and the decision of a judge, it is the judge's decision that defines the rule and not the prior formulation.

Inevitably, it seems that the rejection of the mechanical model – justified as it is – contains within it the possibility of lawless judges. Does this mean that Holmes and the pragmatic model are hopelessly stuck in the realist dilemma? I do not think so. There is a structure to legal decision-making even if there are no authoritative formulations. A good-faith decision maker must weigh a whole host of considerations and then come to a decision that best represents the weight of these considerations. In the case of a syllogism, this aspect of deciding is so elementary that it is often overlooked. And this is why Carroll's paradox seems so illogical. In the case of legal practice, however, these complications are commonplace. The rules come from prior cases. They have been interpreted in past decisions. Courts have recognized exceptions; they have employed fictions to circumvent them. As the law has grown more complicated, none of this goes unnoticed. We all understand that a lawless judge can write an opinion that appears well within the rules but violates their spirit and that arguments over whether this has occurred in a given instance can become so complex that there is never a clear winner. Inevitably, it seems that the rejection of the mechanical model – justified as it is – contains within it the possibility of lawless judges.

An example will help us see that this is so. Suppose that you are staying in a strange house. A servant brings you coffee every morning at seven o'clock. He is consistent in this respect for two weeks. You write down the rule: "The servant brings coffee at seven." At the beginning of the third week, the servant comes at eight. Has he broken the rule or was he operating under the rule that he would wake you at seven for the first two weeks and thereafter wake you at eight? Wittgenstein described this aspect of rule-following as yet another paradox: "This was our paradox: no course of action could be determined by a rule, because every course of action can be made to accord with the rule."[39] It is this paradox that is at the heart of the realist dilemma. We are often unable to distinguish between two situations:

The rule is that the servant brings coffee at seven for two weeks and then at the beginning of the third week he comes at eight; and
    The rule is that the servant brings coffee at seven but today he broke the rule because he felt like sleeping late.

The issue here is the good faith of the rule follower. He can disguise his rule-breaking by exploiting Wittgenstein's paradox. To hold him accountable, we must have an authoritative statement of the rule as it applies to the case at hand. But there can be no such statement. No written formulation can describe the infinite number of possible variations on the rule. Furthermore, so long as practice under the rule trumps written versions of the rule, it will be the practice that constructs the rule and not the other way around. Thus, it will be correct in some sense to say that judges can do what they want.

It is this aspect of the common law that creates the realist dilemma. It breaks the mold of formalism while at the same time rendering the realist unaccountable. We can find our way out of the problem only by recognizing that neither formalism nor realism are descriptions of legal decision-making. Instead they are metaphors that describe certain aspects of the process. Formalism is the mechanical metaphor where reasons combine in such a way that we feel the conclusion is the inevitable result. Realism represents the intuitive "all things considered, this is the best result" aspect. Both of these are important constituents of rational decision-making but neither of them can produce a decision by itself. As the Tortoise teaches, formalism cannot decide a case unless it is part of a real-world practice of making decisions in accordance with a rule. Realism, on the other hand, cannot operate without a normative framework that gives substance to the requirement that the decision maker must choose the best result.

Keeping this in mind, we must recognize that legal decision-making is a complex process. Common law judges are not robots who mindlessly follow certain logical forms. Neither are they independent actors who can enforce their own views. They are charged with applying the rules, and, to apply a rule, they must understand it well enough to know a number of things:

---

[39] Ludwig Wittgenstein, *Philosophical Investigations* § 201 (G. E. M. Anscombe trans. 1958).

- Where the rule comes from.
- What activity it regulates.
- The purpose of that activity.
- The purpose of the rule within the context of that activity.
- How it has been interpreted in the past.
- What exceptions have been recognized.
- What role they have with respect to its ongoing interpretation.

It is only by knowing these things that a judge will know what the rule – now taken in its full sense rather than in its written presentation – requires in a particular case. Thus, we see that although judges are not bound by any particular formulation of the rule, they are bound to apply the rule in this pragmatic sense. This is what they do when they are acting in good faith.

The realist dilemma forces us to separate two distinct questions. The first is: what does a good-faith judge do when (s)he follows a rule to make a decision? The second is: how do we recognize the difference between a judge who is following a rule in good faith and a judge who is simply following his or her own desires? Obviously, we cannot answer the second question until we have answered the first. We have seen that Holmes's answer to the first is contained in the paradox of form and substance: judicial decision-making requires a dialectic between formal considerations and practical ones. To understand what this means it is necessary to see how Holmes applies it in particular cases. Therefore, in the next chapter, I review some of Holmes's more notable decisions. Seeing his method at work will help us to assess the value of his approach and to answer the second question about judicial good faith.

7

The Master of Himself

*When ... he has turned misgiving into success, he is master of himself and
knows the secret of achievement. ... He has gained [the] knowledge ... that
one part of the universe yields the same teaching as any other if only it is
mastered. That the difference between the great way of taking things and the
small – between philosophy and gossip – is only the difference between
realizing the part as a part of a whole and looking at it in its isolation as if it
really stood apart.*

Commencement Speech, Brown University

It must have been obvious to all who knew him that Holmes's most
cherished ambition was to become a judge. He had little interest in earning
a large income. He did not find satisfaction in devoting himself to the
business of his clients. Neither was he interested in politics. He had been
mentioned as a candidate for governor but did not pursue it.[1] He was not
a do-gooder, and he did not believe that the world would be better if only
it would follow his advice. He was an intellectual who was interested in
knowledge for its own sake. But he also wanted to be in the thick of things;
he wanted action: "Life is action, the use of one's powers. And to use them
to their height is our joy and duty."[2] Thus in 1882, when Charles Eliot, the
president of Harvard University, offered him a full-time position, Holmes
negotiated an unusual stipulation. It had to be understood, he said, that if
he were offered a judgeship, he would be free to accept it without the usual
notice. Not that there was one in the offing. He had been prominently
considered for a US District Court appointment a few years earlier, but the

---

[1] *Buds, and Blossoms, Milwaukee Daily* J. (Sept. 10, 1883).
[2] John Wigmore, *Holmes and the Law of Torts*, 29 Harv. L. Rev. 601, 604 (1916).

post had gone to another man.[3] Furthermore, Massachusetts had recently elected a Democratic governor, and, since Holmes was a Republican, he was unlikely to receive an appointment in the near future. Nevertheless, the ambition was foremost in his mind and he wanted to make clear he would not stay at Harvard if a judicial appointment was forthcoming.

As it turned out, the offer came sooner than anyone might have expected. Holmes had been at Harvard for only a few months when his lunch was interrupted by his former law partner, George Shattuck. He and Fanny had driven out to Cambridge to tell Holmes of a rapidly unfolding set of events.[4] Justice Otis Lord had decided to retire from the high court, and Governor Long, the outgoing Republican governor, was willing to appoint Holmes to the vacant seat if he would accept immediately. Time was of the essence because the formalities were such that his appointment had to be submitted to the Governor's Council that very afternoon. Holmes did not hesitate. He climbed into the carriage and hurried off to Boston to accept the appointment.

Holmes's hasty departure from Harvard in the middle of the term caused some bad feelings among his colleagues. It is easy to see why. They did not know the details of the arrangement he had made with President Eliot. Neither were they aware of the circumstances that required haste. Given the situation, it is hard to see how Holmes could have behaved otherwise. The judgeship was what he had always wanted. Neither was the offer likely to be repeated. And, of course, he had specifically bargained for the right to accept such an offer if it were made.

Aside from the displeasure of his Harvard colleagues, the public response was enthusiastic. While Holmes was young – forty – he was accomplished. His work on Kent and his authorship of *The Common Law* were ample testimony to his legal knowledge and judgment. Furthermore, it would not have gone unnoticed in the provincial halls of power that he was the grandson of Justice Charles Jackson, who had served the Court with great distinction. The local press was positive. The item in the *Boston Daily Advertiser* was typical:

Governor Long has scored another honor for his administration by the appointment of Oliver Wendell Holmes, Jr., to the bench of the supreme court of the State. . . . He is learned in the history and the philosophy of the law, and has won a place among the first legal scholars of the country.[5]

[3] *See Boston Daily Advertiser* (Dec. 5, 1878).   [4] Baker, *supra* ch. 1, n. 5 at 267.
[5] *Boston Daily Advertiser*, 4 (Dec. 9, 1882).

Reading his press, Holmes must have felt satisfied that at long last his struggle for achievement had been vindicated.

There was perhaps one small fly in the ointment. It is hard to be the son of a distinguished father. There was a second article in the same day's paper. It was headlined: "The Surgeon-Poet's Son Placed on the Supreme Bench."[6] In this article, Holmes's legal achievements were overshadowed by his father's account of searching for his wounded son.[7] The father's notoriety would be a theme of Wendell's life in Boston. For example, in 1894, the *Boston Globe* published an article called "Juniors of Boston: Here Is a List to Delight Hub Fathers." The article begins by noting that some of the sons were more distinguished than their fathers, but that "there are others who never can add to the names they bear any luster or distinction so famous are the previous owners of their names." Holmes, of course, was in the latter class, with the *Globe* writing:

Without any disparagement to his [the son's] own distinguished ability, it is safe to say that he will never make the name which he bears any better known or more generally loved and honored than it is at the present time.[8]

Of course, Holmes could not complain. His father's success had certainly facilitated his own. Nevertheless, the implied competition with his father was ever present and it was not a contest he could win.

In addition, the father could be downright irritating. When Wendell's friends celebrated his appointment by giving a dinner in his honor, they invited Dr. Holmes to be one of the after-dinner speakers. He wrote a poem for the occasion that included the following verses:

> The fearless soldier, who has faced
> The serried bayonets' gleam appalling,
> For nothing save a pin misplaced
> The peaceful nursery has disgraced
> With hours of unheroic bawling.
>
> . . .
>
> The justice, who, in gown and cap,
> Condemns a wretch to strangulation,
> Has scratched his nurse and spilled his pap,
> And sprawled across his mother's lap
> For wholesome law's administration.[9]

---

[6] *Id.* at 8.   [7] The article refers to the story Dr. Holmes told in *My Search for the Captain.*
[8] *Boston Daily Globe* 20 (Apr. 29, 1894).
[9] E. E. Brown, *The Life of Oliver Wendell Holmes* 211 (1884).

This was a typical after-dinner offering by Dr. Holmes – humorous and irreverent. No doubt the son laughed along with the others. Still, it was *his* night and he might have appreciated a prouder and less teasing parent.

On December 15, 1882, Holmes was sworn in. He would spend the next fifty years on the bench. The first twenty would be in Massachusetts, serving at a time when the common law was consolidating the changes necessitated by an increasingly commercial and industrial society. The next thirty would be spent on the Supreme Court of the United States – a period that spanned the years from Theodore to Franklin Roosevelt. As a result of the timing and length of these two postings, Holmes had a unique opportunity to shape the law on all levels – an opportunity greatly enhanced by his ability to express himself in memorable phrases. Indeed, a century later, his opinions are ever present in student casebooks and his theories remain active topics for scholarly debate.

In this chapter, I examine some of Holmes's opinions with a view toward understanding his method for deciding cases and its relation to the wider philosophical issues we have previously explored. So far, I have focused on the interconnections between Holmes's life experience, his philosophy, and his jurisprudence. I now extend these connections to his role as a judge. Since my interest is in his method, I treat a few cases at length rather than provide a wider survey of his substantive legal views.

The chapter is divided in four sections. In the first, I examine two of Holmes's state court decisions as a way of illustrating his approach to common law cases. In the second, I discuss some of his constitutional opinions. Holmes is well known for preaching the doctrine of judicial restraint. I explore the reasons for this as well as its weaknesses as a constitutional philosophy. In the third section, I consider the subjective aspects of his jurisprudence. While Holmes's conception of the judicial role left little room for his private views, it would be wrong to think of them as entirely irrelevant. Once we have abandoned the mechanical model of legal decision-making, we must recognize that every decision maker proceeds from a uniquely personal perspective. As Cardozo put it:

There is in each of us a stream of tendency ... which gives coherence and direction to thought and action. Judges cannot escape that current any more than other mortals. All their lives, forces which they do not recognize and cannot name, have been tugging at them – inherited instincts, traditional beliefs, acquired convictions; ... In this mental background every problem finds its setting. We may try to see things as objectively as we please. None the less, we can never see them with any eyes except our own.[10]

Given this, we cannot understand judicial decision-making without recognizing its subjective dimensions. Finally, in the fourth section, I assess Holmes's judicial legacy.

COMMON LAW DECISION-MAKING

I begin with an examination of two of Holmes's opinions from the Massachusetts bench: *Lamson v. American Axe and Tool*[11] and *Vegelahn v. Guntner*.[12] These are both tort cases that deal with the rights of laborers in a time of rapid industrialization. In them, we see Holmes shepherding the common law in an area where there is sharp dispute about the policies involved and where consensus is rapidly shifting. His opinions are lucid and transparent. Some scholars have suggested that realist judges must dissemble and hide the true nature of their decision-making, pretending to follow the law when in reality they are imposing their own views.[13] But there is little pretense in a Holmes opinion – he tells you exactly why he decided the case in the way he did. Holmes believed in candor – he thought that law should be transparent as a way of ensuring its integrity and accountability.[14]

We saw in the previous chapter that Holmes staked out two positions often associated with realism. The first was a rejection of the mechanical mode of decision-making; the second was his claim that the basis of the common law was substantive policy rather than the preservation of logical form. At the same time, he clearly rejected the idea that judges are free from constraint. Looking carefully at Holmes's opinions, we see that these three positions are fully consistent.

The first case is an easy case, requiring only that Holmes apply established law to the case before him. In *Lamson v. American Axe and Tool*,

---

[10] Benjamin Cardozo, *Nature of the Judicial Process, Lecture I: Introduction: The Method of Philosophy* 1 J. L. 329, 330 (2011).

[11] *Lamson v. Am. Ax & Tool Co.*, 177 Mass. 144 (1900).

[12] *Vegelahn v. Guntner*, 167 Mass. 92 (1896).

[13] *See, e.g.*, Paul Butler, *When Judges Lie (and When They Should)*, Minn. L. Rev. 1785 (2007); Martin Shapiro, *Judges as Liars*, 17 Harv. J. L. & Pub. Pol'y 155 (1994); Scott Altman, *Beyond Candor*, 89 Mich. L. Rev. 296 (1990).

[14] *See Cowley v. Pulsifer*, 137 Mass. 392 (1884) ("It is desirable that the trial of causes should take place under the public eye, not because the controversies of one citizen with another are of public concern, but because it is of the highest moment that those who administer justice should always act under the sense of public responsibility").

the plaintiff worked in a factory where he painted the handles of axes. When he finished an axe, he hung it on an overhead rack to dry. He was injured when one of the axes fell off the rack and struck him. In the subsequent lawsuit, his employer argued that Lamson had assumed the risk. Assumption of risk is a common law defense to personal injury actions. In the nineteenth century, it was one of a number of legal doctrines that shielded employers from liability for workplace accidents. The doctrine had two requirements: the first was that the plaintiff must know of the risk in question; the second was that he must voluntarily act in such a way as to incur the risk. Traditionally, unless both requirements were met, Lamson could not recover.

Holmes's treatment of Lamson's case is very brief. The opinion itself is less than a page long. First, he recited the facts of the accident:

About a year before the accident new racks had been substituted for those previously in use, and it may be assumed that they were less safe and were not proper, but were dangerous on account of the liability of the hatchets to fall from the pegs upon the plaintiff when the racks were jarred by the motion of machinery nearby. The plaintiff complained to the superintendent that the hatchets were more likely to drop off than when the old racks were in use, and that now they might fall upon him, which they could not have done from the old racks. He was answered in substance that he would have to use the racks or leave.[15]

Holmes then made the obvious point that the worker was well aware of the risk: "The plaintiff, on his own evidence, appreciated the danger more than anyone else. He perfectly understood what was likely to happen." Thus, there could be no dispute about the first requirement. The second, however, posed a more serious issue: was Lamson's conduct voluntary if the employer had made confronting the risk a term of his employment? Yes, Holmes answered. "He stayed and took the risk. He did so none the less that the fear of losing his place was one of his motives." He made no argument for this; he only cited a string of cases. This suggests that Holmes regarded this as an open and shut case. Normally we pay little attention to such cases, but if we wish to understand how the law constrains judicial decision-making, this is precisely the kind of issue we must examine. Why, then, is this such an easy case?

The case requires the judge to apply the rule of voluntary action to certain facts. Is an act "voluntary" if the alternative is losing one's job? True, the plaintiff did not have a gun to his head, but it is easy to imagine that he had children at home who would starve if he returned without

[15] *Lamson*, 177 Mass. at 144.

a paycheck. What does the term "voluntary" mean in these circumstances? From whose perspective should we consider the question?
Furthermore, there are policy considerations that would support either
side of the issue. One side would stress worker autonomy and the idea that
workers make their own decisions about what working conditions they
will accept. The other side would argue that there was, in fact, no real
worker autonomy in the industrial workplace. These workers did not have
many options; they knew that bad and dangerous working conditions
were so prevalent that they had no choice but to accept them. Thus, what
some called autonomy others recognized as coercion. Ultimately, the issue
was: who should bear the risk of increasingly complex and dangerous
workplaces – the industrialists who profited from them or the workers for
whom they provided employment?

It is not certain where Holmes stood on these issues. As a member of the
upper class, his sympathies might well have been with the employer. On
the other hand, there is some indication that he favored the expansion of
negligence liability[16] and the merger of assumption of risk with contrib-
utory negligence.[17] This latter move would have changed the criteria for
judging the plaintiff's conduct from "voluntary" (Did the plaintiff voluntarily assume the risk?) to "unreasonable" (Did the plaintiff take a risk
that would not have been taken by the average reasonable person?). By
giving greater weight to the plaintiff's predicament, the latter criterion
would have allowed recoveries in at least some cases. Whatever his personal views, however, Holmes did not hesitate to apply settled law to
Lamson's case.

Obviously, it was the cited cases that made this an easy case, but,
if we look at the cases, what do we learn? Each case involved
a workplace accident. The cases varied with respect to the level of
the defendants' negligence. Some cases involved little negligence on
the part of the employer. For example, in one case, the court found
that: "There was ... no defect in the roadway, the engine or other
appliances nor any negligence in the management of them."[18]
Others, however, involved extremely dangerous conditions. For
example, in one, the employee was working at night in a dimly lit
workplace when he fell into a vat of vitriol that was left uncovered
and unfenced at floor level.[19] In some cases, the plaintiff employee

---

[16] David Rosenberg, *The Hidden Holmes: Holmes' Theory of Torts in History* 132 (1996).
[17] *Id.* at 132–133.   [18] *Leary* v. *Boston and Albany Railroad,* 189 Mass. 580, 584 (1885).
[19] *Carrigan* v. *Washburn and Moen Manuf. Co.* 170 Mass. 79 (1898).

had complained about the conditions; in others, they had testified that they were unaware of the dangers or had not contracted to confront them. Even in this latter group of cases, the court frequently disregarded the testimony and ruled for the employer defendants.[20] After reading the six cases cited and the fifteen additional cases cited therein, two things are clear. First, none of them includes any doctrinal discussion of assumption of risk and several of them do not even mention the doctrine. The second is that in most cases, the plaintiff lost. Indeed, the plaintiff won in only two situations. In one, the plaintiff had permitted his son to work but assumed – as the court said, "justifiably" – that they would not place him in a position of danger.[21] In the other, the plaintiffs were new employees and without the type of experience that would permit them to understand the job site danger.[22] Thus, a fair reading of the cases is that, whatever the grounds, the worker loses unless it is the exceptional case where he can show total ignorance of the risks he faced.

As a result of these considerations, Holmes would have felt himself bound to rule for the employer. The constraints were not formal; there was no underlying doctrine to provide an answer. Rather the constraint was this: the common law had already dictated a policy – worker autonomy – with respect to this particular area of law. A ruling for the plaintiff would therefore change a policy that had been uniformly applied for decades. In effect, Holmes's ruling was based on precedent, but it was not the precedent of formal doctrine. Rather, it was based on the fact that the Massachusetts court had already made a choice between two substantive policies – worker autonomy and employer responsibility – and it would have taken exceptional circumstances to justify a deviation from this course.

What, then, are the exceptional circumstances that might have justified Holmes in coming to a different result? Consider the formal aspect of the problem. While formal considerations may not compel a particular decision, Holmes recognized that they provide a structure for the decision-

---

[20] *Prentiss v. Kent Furniture Mfg. Co.*, 63 Mich. 478 (1886); *Haley v. Case*, 142 Mass. 316 (1886).

[21] *Railroad v. Fort* 84 U.S. 553 (1874) ("The father had the right to presume when he made the contract of service that the company would not expose his son to such a peril").

[22] *Coombs v. New Bedford Cordage Co.*, 102 Mass. 572 (1869) (recognizing "the duty of an employer to take proper precautions for the safety of a person employed in running or tending machinery, especially when such person, through youth, inexperience or want of capacity, may be unable to appreciate or avoid the danger to which he is exposed"). *See also Lalor v. Chicago, B. & Q. R. Co.*, 52 Ill. 401 (1869); *Jones v. Lake S. & M. S. R. Co.*, 49 Mich. 573 (1883).

making process. Thus, a judge who wishes to rule for Lamson has a limited number of choices. He could:

- argue that the case falls into the recognized exception (i.e., that Lamson was totally unaware of the dangers he faced);
- create a new exception; or
- say that the policy is wrong and should be overruled.

Since Lamson had complained to his supervisor, the first alternative is hardly credible. The second would be hard to justify given that the court had previously ruled on situations where the plaintiff had requested abatement of the danger. And the third – changing the policy itself – would require an explanation. Had circumstances changed? Had the court changed its mind?

To reconcile a departure from established principles, courts must produce convincing reasons for the change. In this postmodern, "post-truth" age, it is common to argue that a resourceful person can give reasons for anything, but, despite the arguments of skeptics, this is not actually true. Judicial reasons must be credible; they must resonate with surrounding circumstances. I stress this because it is so contrary to popular wisdom. In the context of legal decision-making, purely formal considerations rarely limit judicial discretion, while a fair reading of precedent often establishes that certain policies cannot be ignored. Because of this, judges have little discretion within a well-developed body of common law. In this context, not every argument is convincing; not every reason commands respect. And respect is essential if the law is to fulfill its function of settling disputes without the need for private violence. This is why good judges do not strain the boundaries of credible argument; this is why they generally defer to established principles.

This point is worth emphasizing because it reconceptualizes the debate between formalism and realism. This debate is generally understood in terms of the power of precedent to constrain judicial discretion. Common wisdom suggests that it is Langdell's formalism rather than Holmes's realism that will bind common law judges to the rule of law. What we see here is something different. The doctrine in this area is negligible, but the judge is still constrained. He is constrained by policy choices firmly adopted in earlier decisions. Thus, as between doctrine and policy, it is policy that mans the laboring oar of precedent. Formal doctrine may assist. It also performs a useful function in rationalizing and organizing judicial decisions, but it does not enforce compliance with precedent.

We can now understand Holmes's real objection to Langdell's theory. The central problem, he thought, was that Langdell's focus on doctrinal rules as the binding force of precedent separated law from the actual cases that had shaped it. This obscured a vital aspect of legal analysis. We create law to solve practical problems. In short, when Langdell detached doctrine from the cases, he detached the law from its "secret root" in social policy. By appealing to policy, Holmes was not saying that courts should ignore precedent. Instead, he was suggesting that a judge who is applying precedent should be bound by the policies it represents rather than by the formal doctrine used to express them.

If *Lamson* was an easy case, the second case, *Vegelahn v. Guntner*, was harder.[23] There was no clear precedent for the court to follow. As a case of first impression, it might seem that it would be ripe for the imposition of a judge's private preferences. Nevertheless, when we contrast the majority opinion of the court with the dissent by Holmes, we can see that it is no simple case of divergent politics. Holmes offers well-thought-out legal arguments to support his view.

In *Vegelahn*, the plaintiff employer sought an injunction against union picketing. Under the applicable procedure, requests for injunctions were first heard by a single justice of the Supreme Judicial Court who would hear evidence and enter an order.[24] It happened that Holmes was sitting on the day in question and so he conducted the hearing and prepared a report that would accompany the case to the full bench. In the report, he divided the defendant's conduct into three different categories. The first set included persuasion and social pressure. These, he felt, were lawful activities and so declined to enjoin them. The second included:

threats of personal injury or unlawful harm [that] were conveyed to persons seeking employment or employed, although no actual violence was used beyond a technical battery, and although the threats were a good deal disguised, and express words were avoided.

This, he thought, was unlawful conduct, and he specifically enjoined it. Third was the patrol itself. The union had two men continuously circling the sidewalk in front of the plaintiff employer's place of business. This, he found lawful.

---

[23] *Vegelahn*, 167 Mass. 92.

[24] Thomas B. Campbell Jr., *The Separate Judicial Opinion and the Growth of the Law: Holmes Dissent in Vegelahn v. Guntner*, 1 Hofstra Labor L. F. 215, 221 at n. 37 (1983).

There were instances, to be sure, when the patrol went over the line that defined peaceful picketing. Sometimes the patrol would block the plaintiff's door. Sometimes it would urge the plaintiff's workers to break existing contracts. These specific activities, Holmes also enjoined. The result of his orders was this: the defendant union could continue to picket so long as it refrained from these particular activities.

The full bench of the Supreme Judicial Court found these orders insufficient and entered a final injunction that banned picketing entirely. Both sides acknowledged that this was an unsettled area of the law. For example, Justice Field noted in a separate dissent that "the practice of issuing injunctions in cases of this kind is of very recent origin" and then pointed out that the first case in this line had come only eight years earlier.[25] Thus, in *Vegelahn*, the court had a relatively free hand in deciding what the policy should be. For this reason, Holmes wanted to make his dissenting views known.

In a case like the present, it seems to me that, whatever the true result may be, it will be of advantage to sound thinking to have the less popular view of the law stated, and therefore, although when I have been unable to bring my brethren to share my convictions my almost invariable practice is to defer to them in silence. I depart from that practice in this case, notwithstanding my unwillingness to do so in support of an already rendered judgment of my own.[26]

The opinion that followed was remarkable for its candor and transparency. Holmes began by setting out the analytical structure that he had previously proposed in an article titled "Privilege, Malice, and Intent."[27] In it, he had argued that courts should analyze tort cases in three steps. First, they should determine whether the defendant's conduct had caused temporal harm. Second, they had to decide whether it was foreseeable that such conduct would cause such harm. Third was the question of whether the defendant's conduct was privileged in some respect. This last factor, Holmes argued, was always a question of policy. Was there a reason, the court should ask, whether the defendant's conduct, though harmful to another, should be allowed? Further, the policy question could not be answered by an appeal to empty phrases:

When the question of policy is faced it will be seen to be one which cannot be answered by generalities, but must be determined by the particular character of the case, even if everybody agrees what the answer should be. I do not try to mention

---

[25] *Vegelahn*, 167 Mass. at 100 (Field, J. Dissenting).
[26] *Id.* at 104 (Holmes, J. Dissenting).
[27] Oliver Wendell Holmes Jr., *Privilege, Malice, and Intent*, 8 Harv. L. Rev. 1 (1894).

or to generalize all the facts which have to be taken into account; but plainly the worth of the result, or the gain from allowing the act to be done, has to be compared with the loss which it inflicts. Therefore, the conclusion will vary, and will depend on different reasons according to the nature of the affair.[28]

Thus, he began his opinion by conceding that the defendant's conduct caused temporal harm and that the harm it caused was foreseeable. In fact, he notes that temporal harm was the very purpose of the defendant's conduct. He then continued by identifying the issue as one of privilege: was there a legally recognized policy that excused this type of harm?

The answer, Holmes asserted, was that the union's picketing fell within the policy of allowing free competition even when it was predictable that these activities would cause harm to another. However, there was a further question: did the privilege extend beyond an individual acting alone to a group of actors acting in concert? He answered it this way:

[I]t is plain from the slightest consideration of practical affairs, or the most superficial reading of industrial history, that free competition means combination, and that the organization of the world, now going on so fast, means an ever-increasing might and scope of combination. It seems to me futile to set our faces against this tendency. Whether beneficial on the whole, as I think it, or detrimental, it is inevitable, unless the fundamental axioms of society, and even the fundamental conditions of life, are to be changed.[29]

Note how similar this argument is to his justification of the whaling cases. In deciding questions of policy, the court should adapt itself to the realities of the external world. It should let the community develop on its own terms, interceding only to maintain consistency and fairness.

Having framed the case in accordance with the method he set out in the article, Holmes proceeded to address the central, precedent-setting question: do the policies governing free competition and permissible group action apply to picketing workers as well as to combinations of capital? Once framed, the answer seemed clear. It was an issue of fairness:

One of the eternal conflicts out of which life is made up is that between the effort of every man to get the most he can for his services, and that of society, disguised under the name of capital, to get his services for the least possible return. Combination on the one side is patent and powerful. Combination on the other is the necessary and desirable counterpart, if the battle is to be carried on in a fair and equal way.[30]

---

[28] *Id.* at 3.   [29] *Vegelahn*, 167 Mass. at 108 (Holmes, J. Dissenting).   [30] *Id.*

This opinion illustrates the way in which form and substance combine to dictate a result. First, Holmes described the case in terms of legal doctrine, setting up what he takes to be the three elements of a tort case – harm, foreseeability, and privilege. Then, quickly disposing of the first two issues, he moves on to the third. To analyze this, he places the instant case with a line of privilege cases that resembled it – namely, the free competition cases. This isolated the policy issue as one of combination in competition. Noting that this privilege is generally allowed to capital, he finally identified the issue as whether the privilege to combine for competitive purposes is available to labor as well.

Looking at the opinion as a whole, we can see how it resembles a conversation between form and substance. At each step, Holmes used formal categories to reframe the issue, narrowing the question for decision. In answering these successive questions, he appealed to substance – defining a policy that furthered the argument. At the more general stages, these policies had already been established by the common law, e.g. there is a privilege for free competition. As the issue narrows, there is a point at which precedent does not contain the answer, i.e., does the privilege of combining apply to labor as well as capital? But, even here, there was an answer – there was another policy, namely, fairness, that required a particular result. Thus, the opinion displays a dialectical process whereby Holmes first used the formal legal categories to formulate the issue and then addressed the issue by invoking well-established policies.

By contrast, the majority opinion never comes to a clear statement of the issue. The judges see the case simply in terms of labor picketing. Thus, they posed the issue in a way that obscured the question of fairness. They focused instead on a different distinction – one that separated agreements to act as a group with a view to changing their own conduct from agreements to act as a group to change the conduct of others:

A combination among persons merely to regulate their own conduct is within allowable competition, and is lawful, although others may be indirectly affected thereby. But a combination to do injurious acts expressly directed to another, by way of intimidation or constraint, either of himself or of persons employed or seeking to be employed by him, is outside of allowable competition, and is unlawful.[31]

Why is this an important distinction? The court does not say. Furthermore, if this had been an established policy of the common law,

[31] *Id.* at 98.

one would expect to see citations, but there are none.[32] Neither are there any arguments that support the court's position. Instead the court seems to rely on the strength of the phrase "intimidation or constraint" to suggest that the conduct is wrongful.

In the majority's world, the labor union never stood a chance. It is evident that the majority disliked labor picketing and thought of it as an act of lawlessness. When they enjoined the activity, they may have felt it was obvious that picketing was undesirable, but, of course, this was probably not a sentiment shared by the workers. On the other hand, Holmes applied a distinctly legal method to the problem. It was a method that was generally applicable to tort cases and one that swiftly identified the particular policy questions at stake. Once identified, the issues had to be addressed not with reference to one's personal views, but with reference to the tide of human events. It was not the job of the court to dictate the direction of future progress. Rather, its job was to intercede only to ensure fair treatment of all parties. In short, the roads would be built by nonlegal forces, but it was common law courts that ensured they could be used by all.

In the years to come, Holmes's opinion won the day. Courts ultimately held that peaceful picketing was allowed under the common law. As one writer described it:

Holmes took issue with the conventional logic of the law as he found it, and argued that the peaceful concerted activity of workers to further their own interests should not be viewed as interference with the right of employers. ... The force of this re-examination of legal analysis by a respected and prominent legal philosopher and historian acting in his official judicial capacity, was too great to be ignored. The attention it gained, and the thought it provoked, eased the profound change brought to the American law of labor relations in the first third of this century.[33]

But it was more than Holmes's reputation that vindicated his views. He had approached the problem carefully. He could see the societal trends and the underlying question of fairness they raised. For Holmes, deciding on the basis of policy was definitely not an invitation to invoke his own

---

[32] The statement is followed by: "Various decided cases fall within the former class," and citation to six American cases. These cases, as the court suggested, established that groups – whether of employers or employees – may combine even if the agreement harms another. Indeed, all these are cases where the agreements only involve actions by those who are members of the group in question, but they do not suggest the principle that such agreements would be unlawful if they affect the conduct of others.

[33] Campbell, *supra* n. 24 at 249.

prejudice. It was an occasion for thoughtful analysis about the interaction of law with surrounding circumstances.

These two opinions illustrate the way in which Holmes's views on legal theory influenced what we might call his "applied jurisprudence." We can see, for example, how the paradox of form and substance, a feature of his general jurisprudence, shaped the way he applied precedent. This paradox highlighted two aspects of legal decision-making. One – the form – was governed by logic, creating the appearance that "each new decision followed syllogistically from existing precedents." The second – the substance – flowed from the "secret root ... of what is expedient for the community concerned." On a descriptive level, we saw that this paradox did not pose a particular problem. Form and substance were simply two ways of describing the same legal developments. The problem arose when the question was normative – how should a judge decide a case? In applying precedent, which set of considerations is controlling? Holmes's answer to this is apparent in his decisions. Both are important, but it is substance that leads the way.

For Holmes, precedent did not consist of formal propositions that had to be followed or distinguished. Instead, he saw it as a series of cases that illustrated a preexisting web of practical policies. Thus, in *Lamson*, precedent had spoken unequivocally, choosing a policy of worker autonomy over one of worker protection. Similarly, in *Vegelahn*, Holmes thought the majority was wrong in its attempt to resolve the case by introducing a new formal distinction. The distinction came from nowhere and had no obvious relevance to the underlying normative question. In Holmes's terms, it missed the "secret root of the law in what is expedient for the community concerned."

When Holmes left Boston, he would sum up his judicial philosophy this way:

I have tried to see the law as an organic whole. I also have tried to see it as a reaction between tradition on the one side and the changing desires and needs of a community on the other. I have studied tradition in order that I might understand how it came to be, what it is, and to estimate its worth with regard to our present needs. ... I have considered the present tendencies and desires of society and have tried to realize that its different portions want different things, and that my business was to express not my personal wish but the resultant as nearly as I could guess of the pressure of the past and the conflicting wills of the present.[34]

---

[34] Speech transcribed in the *Boston Daily Globe* (Dec. 4, 1902).

If Holmes thought that judicial decision-making was a matter of finding the resultant of past and present, what was the role of logic? Certainly, Holmes did not believe that logic is irrelevant. In every case, judges express themselves in terms of recognizable legal principles. The substantive decision wears "the evening clothes" of formal law and thereby becomes intelligible and coherent. But, since the formalities are not decisive, the logical form must be understood as an ex post facto addition meant to generalize the decision and translate it into legal language. In doing this, judges formulate the law in terms of recognizable categories, creating a chart of organization that helps us to file and retrieve legal results.

THE US SUPREME COURT

After twenty years on the Massachusetts Court, Holmes may have been bored. Lawyers appearing before him noticed he was increasingly impatient and cranky.[35] He would often sit on the bench with one ear tuned to oral argument and his mind elsewhere. He spent some of this time writing flirtatious letters to his women friends.[36] But this did not interfere with his work – like many experienced judges, he had the ability to size up a case fairly quickly. All in all, despite the possible boredom, he liked his job on the court. He enjoyed his colleagues, and, after he was promoted to Chief Justice in 1899, he must have felt that he was playing a significant role in shaping the law of Massachusetts.

Not everyone, however, was pleased with his judicial decisions. The business community found him unpredictable and unwilling to stand up for its interest.[37] As it turned out, however, this was no barrier to Holmes's advancement. Holmes was about to obtain his most cherished wish.

---

[35] Baker, *supra* ch. 1, n. 5 at 35 (quoting Senator Hoar, who was quoting a lawyer speaking about Holmes's appointment to the Supreme Court).

[36] Holmes had many women friends whom he had known since he was a young man. It is doubtful whether his flirtation with any of these women represented anything more than a warm friendship. In contrast, however, were the letters to Lady Clare Castletown. Holmes had met her in London in the summer of 1889. While the nature of their relationship is unknown, Holmes's letters to her were passionate, suggesting an affair.

[37] In opposing Holmes's appointment to the Supreme Court, one businessman wrote to Senator Henry Cabot Lodge, "While it would naturally be difficult to get lawyers to express this opinion under all the circumstances they think that [Holmes] is erratic, and that he is not a safe man for such an important position." John Garraty, *Holmes' Appointment to the U.S. Supreme Court*, 22 New England Quarterly 291, 293 (1949).

In 1901, Horace Gray, a Supreme Court justice from Massachusetts, was becoming increasingly ill. Rumors flew about who would replace him. At first, Holmes's prospects did not look good. President William McKinley would make the appointment, and he was likely to appoint someone who was a solid and reliable conservative. Furthermore, George Frisbie Hoar was the senior senator from Massachusetts and his nephew was qualified and interested in the position. But in September, Holmes's chances increased when an anarchist shot and killed President McKinley. This meant that the vice president, Theodore Roosevelt, would become president and make the appointment. Thus, in July 1902, when Gray finally resigned, Holmes was a strong contender.

Roosevelt was not particularly anxious to please the business community, and he wanted to appoint a progressive. He was close friends with Henry Cabot Lodge, and more inclined to listen to him than to Senator Hoar despite the tradition that the appointment "belonged" to the senior senator. Once Gray resigned, Lodge swung into action. He was determined to get the appointment for Holmes. Roosevelt was receptive to the idea; he remembered two of Holmes's speeches and thought well of his militaristic, "do or die" attitude.[38] The negotiations went back and forth – Lodge speaking to Roosevelt, Lodge speaking to Holmes, and at last a meeting between the two at Oyster Bay.

When Holmes arrived, the president was out sailing. A heavy fog had set in and stranded him on an island. As a result, when Holmes walked up from the station, he was greeted only by the Roosevelt children.[39] The children were not shy. They were happy to get to know this tall and lanky stranger and, at dinner, politely pressed him to tell stories about the Civil War. It was not until the next morning that Holmes finally met the president. There was considerable chemistry between the two. Roosevelt reported to Lodge that Holmes was "our kind right through."[40] Holmes wrote that Roosevelt "said just the right things and impressed me more than I expected."[41] Several days later, the matter was settled although the appointment was kept secret until Roosevelt could placate Senator Hoar.

---

[38] The first was "A Soldier's Faith"; the second was "John Marshall, Speech in Commemoration of the One Hundredth Anniversary of the Day on which Marshall Took His Seat as Chief Justice." The speech is reprinted at Holmes, *supra* ch. 3, n. 44 at 266. Apparently, Roosevelt was less enthused by the second speech and its tepid praise of the great Chief Justice. Baker, *supra* ch. 1, n. 5 at 347.

[39] Edmund Morris, *Theodore Rex* 130 (2002).   [40] *Id.*

[41] *Id.* at 612 (quoting White, *supra* n. ch. 1, n. 10 at 312).

Senate confirmation followed on December 4, and Holmes was sworn in on December 8.

During the period from August to December, Wendell and Fanny tended to their affairs and planned their move to Washington. One can only imagine the disruption in their lives. Both of them had spent their entire lives in Boston among an extensive network of friends and relations. They would be leaving their friends, of course, but they were also leaving a way of life. This meant letting go of much of their past. Holmes spent part of the fall burning old papers. Then of course there were his father's two houses. The large house on Beacon Street had to be emptied and sold. He would keep the house in Beverly Farms since the Court's schedule left plenty of time for a summer respite in the quaint little town overlooking the ocean.

At last packed up, the Holmeses were ready to move to Washington. The Boston bar gave a dinner to say goodbye and honor the new justice. In his speech, he expressed his feelings on leaving Boston:

Well gentlemen it is a good deal of a wrench to leave old friends, to leave the memorials of the dead, to leave all the associations of a whole life for an unknown world.[42]

When it came to resettling, Fanny had the primary responsibility. She chose their new house and made it comfortable for her husband. She gave up her reclusive life and entered Washington society. She was determined to help her husband's career, and perhaps a little ambitious to make her mark on the nation's capital. Her name began appearing in the society pages of Washington as patroness of this or that charity event. On New Year's Eve, 1903, she even gave a large housewarming party.[43] All in all, her efforts met with success. Her husband's position entitled her to participation in the social scene, but it was her sharp wit that made her especially welcome. She even became one of the president's favorite dinner companions.

Holmes would spend thirty years on the Supreme Court, retiring in 1932 at the age of ninety-one. During this period, he wrote nearly 900 opinions and seventy-nine dissents. It is a fulsome legacy that left a mark in many substantive areas. His opinions on freedom of speech, for example, are particularly noteworthy and have been the subject of many law review articles and at least two books.[44] As in the previous section,

[42] *Boston Daily Globe* (Dec. 4, 1902).
[43] *Evening Star* (Washington, DC, Dec. 31, 1903).
[44] Thomas Healy, *The Great Dissent* (2013); Jeremy Cohen, *Congress Shall Make No Law, Oliver Wendell Holmes and the First Amendment and Judicial Decision Making* (1989).

however, I have opted not to attempt a comprehensive survey of Holmes's substantive views. Instead, I have selected a few cases that I believe are representative of his practical jurisprudence. Cases on the Supreme Court docket often involve questions that are outside the boundaries of the common law. In the beginning of his tenure, Holmes seemed less sure-footed; although as time went on his confidence increased.

Patterns began to appear in Holmes's approach to these cases. He relied on the common law whenever he could. As a judge, he embraced two central virtues – judicial independence and judicial restraint. But he had vices as well. The most notable of these was his failure to come to terms with the rights defined by the Civil War Amendments on behalf of the country's formerly enslaved citizens.

1 Judicial Independence

Perhaps the strongest message that Holmes sent in his first year on the Court was one of judicial independence. Roosevelt had been clear about wanting a progressive judge. His definition of "progressive" included support for government efforts to restrain the business trusts that were raising prices for American consumers. It did not take long for one of these cases to come before the Court. The case was *Northern Securities*, and it involved some of the richest men in America – James J. Hill and J. Pierpont Morgan were among the defendants.[45] The subject of the transaction was some 9,000 miles of railroad track and two competing lines stretching from Chicago to the Pacific Northwest.[46] The defendants had merged the two railroads by forming a holding company, Northern Securities, and transferring their stock into the new entity. The effect of this transaction was clear: where once there had been two competitors serving a large market, there would now be one. A majority of the Supreme Court (5–4), understanding that this was the type of situation the Sherman Act was meant to address, looked at the transaction and saw a violation of the statute. It therefore granted the government's request to dissolve the holding company and return the two railroads to competitive status.

---

[45] *Northern Securities* v. *U.S.*, 193 U.S. 197 (1904).
[46] A third railroad was involved in the case. The Chicago, Burlington, and Quincy Railroad operated branch lines in the upper Midwest and connected Minnesota to the railroad hub in Chicago. This railroad had been bought out by the other two before the litigation started and its assets were part of the Northern Securities holding company.

Holmes, however, wrote a dissent. In doing so, he was not naïve. He knew how much his action would disappoint and even irritate the president. Nevertheless, he felt that his obligation was clear: a judge must follow the law as he sees it, whatever the personal consequences might be.

The issue, Holmes thought, was one of statutory interpretation. Where the majority had looked broadly at the concerns that motivated the Sherman Act, he looked narrowly at the statutory language. Thus, he argued, it was the words of the Sherman Act that had to be consulted:

Great cases, like hard cases, make bad law. For great cases are called great not by reason of their real importance in shaping the law of the future, but because of some accident of immediate overwhelming interest which appeals to the feelings and distorts the judgment. These immediate interests exercise a kind of hydraulic pressure which makes what previously was clear seem doubtful, and before which even well settled principles of law will bend. What we have to do in this case is to find the meaning of some not very difficult words. We must try, I have tried, to do it with the same freedom of natural and spontaneous interpretation that one would be sure of if the same question arose upon an indictment for a similar act which excited no public attention, and was of importance only to a prisoner before the court.[47]

The Sherman Act prohibited "every contract, combination, in the form of trust, or otherwise or conspiracy in restraint of trade."[48] Thus, the "not very difficult words" that Holmes saw at the center of the controversy was the phrase "agreement in restraint of trade." The argument for the government had been that this phrase expressed two distinct ideas: first, did the parties enter into an agreement; and, second, was the effect of the agreement to restrain trade by lessening competition? The majority answered each of these questions in the affirmative and therefore held that the holding company should be dissolved. Holmes's dissent, on the other hand, treated the phrase as a unitary standard. He noted the phrase "agreements in restraint of trade" was a term of art under the common law that had a precise meaning. He explained it this way:

Contracts in restraint of trade . . . are contracts with a stranger to the contractor's business (although in some cases carrying on a similar one) which wholly or partially restrict the freedom of the contractor in carrying on that business as otherwise he would. . . . Of course, this objection did not apply to [agreements] of substituting a community of interest where there had been competition.[49]

---

[47] *Id.* at 400–401.　　[48] *Id.*

[49] *Id.* at 404. Similarly, Holmes argued that the common law understood "combinations and conspiracies in restraint of trade" in terms of agreements to keep third parties out of the business.

Holmes opted for the common law definition because he felt that the one the majority used was far too broad. It would apply, for example, to all mergers and acquisitions – large or small. Thus, the owner of a small hardware store would be violating the law if all he did was to buy a hardware store in the town next door. Indeed, he could even be indicted under the criminal provisions of the act. It was examples of this kind that convinced Holmes that his narrow reading was correct.

Theodore Roosevelt was not the sort of man to consider whether Holmes had good reasons for his action. The president was outraged, complaining that he "could carve a Justice out of a banana with more backbone than that."[50] Henry Adams described the ensuing scene: "*Theodore went wild* about it, and openly denounced Holmes in the most forcible terms of his sputtering vocabulary."[51] Even the press was in on the dust-up:

The president is angry at Justice Holmes [for his] dissenting opinion in the Northern Securities case, and Mr. Roosevelt is not going to any great trouble to conceal his displeasure. The trouble with Justice Holmes was that he reached his conclusion with his own interpretation of the law, instead of deciding the question as Mr. Roosevelt wanted him to and expected him to. Justice Holmes is to pay for his independence of thought by being practically ostracized from the White House. ... The president's anger has carried him so far that he would remove Mr. Holmes if he could, but as that is impossible he will show his resentment by shutting the White House door in Mr. Holmes' face.[52]

Holmes's response was calm and firm. He wrote to one of his friends:

I have had no communication of any kind with [the president] upon the matter. If he should take my action in anger I shall be disappointed in him. ... But I have such confidence in his great heartedness that I don't expect for a moment that after he has had time to cool down it will affect our relations. If however his seeming personal regard for us was based on the idea that he had a tool the sooner it was ended the better – we shall see.[53]

Fortunately for all, sanity prevailed. Two weeks later the *New York Times* was reporting that the Holmeses were again dining at the White House.[54]

---

[50] Morris, *supra* n. 39 at 316 (citing the diary of John Hays).

[51] Henry Adams, *Letters of Henry Adams*, v. II at 429 (J. C. Levensen ed. 1982).

[52] *The Citizen-Republican* (Scotland, Bon Homme County, SD) 3 (Mar. 24, 1904).

[53] Sheldon Novick, *Honorable Justice: The Life of Oliver Wendell Holmes* 272 (1989) (Letter to Ellen Curtis).

[54] *New York Times* 9 (Apr. 2, 1904) (found on ProQuest Historical Newspaper). Even though the two resumed their friendship, Roosevelt continued to be critical. Two years later he wrote: "From his antecedents, Holmes should have been an ideal man on the

2 Judicial Restraint

Another aspect of Holmes's jurisprudence was a belief in the doctrine of judicial restraint. Many judges hold this position, but they do so with varying levels of intensity. For example, Felix Frankfurter, an admirer and protégé of Holmes, took an extreme position. He believed in the Constitution with all the fervor of a religious convert.[55] For him, this meant strict devotion to the separation of powers and a consequent unwillingness to curtail the powers of the legislative branch. In fact, his belief in judicial restraint was so strong that he hesitated to grant relief in the 1954 school desegregation case.[56] Compared to Frankfurter, Holmes's own commitment to restraint was neither extreme nor ideological. As a practical matter, he believed that a court should be able to decide the case before it without disrupting the society around it. It was for this reason that he emphasized the tendency of the common law to defer to the custom and convenience of everyday life. Judicial restraint on constitutional questions was a consequence of this attitude. But he also recognized that *Marbury* v. *Madison* meant that there would be cases where the Court had no choice but to overrule a public official or nullify a legislative enactment.[57] Thus, his position was a moderate one: while he recognized that the Constitution empowered the Court to overturn specific legislation, he felt that it was a power that should be used sparingly.

Holmes's position in this regard was not unusual. Even in 1903, many judges remembered the bitterness inspired by the *Dred Scott* decision.[58] In *Dred Scott*, the Supreme Court had taken a giant leap in the direction of judicial activism when it used the pretense of constitutional adjudication to impose a proslavery resolution on a wide range of national controversies. Furthermore, its ruling undercut a number of legislative compromises and was one of the factors that led to the Civil War. The episode was clearly a lesson in the value of judicial restraint.

The court's passivity, however, had one notable exception. This was the use of the Fourteenth Amendment to strike down state economic legislation. State legislatures had begun to hear the pleas of industrial

---

bench. As a matter of fact he has been a bitter disappointment." Garraty, *supra* n. 37 at 301.

[55] Noah Feldman, *Scorpions: The Battles and Triumphs of FDR's Great Supreme Court Justices* 253 (2010).

[56] *Id.* at 380.

[57] *Marbury* v. *Madison*, 5 U.S. 137 (1803) (holding that federal courts have the power to invalidate government actions that violate the US Constitution).

[58] *Dred Scott* v. *Sandford*, 60 U.S. (19 How.) 393 (1857).

workers. Some of them had passed wage and hour legislation, workmen's compensation, and other statutes designed to protect workers' interests. These statutes were already making their way through the courts. *Lochner v. New York* was such a case.[59] Joseph Lochner was the owner of a bakery. He had been convicted of a violation of the New York Bakeshop Act that prohibited bakeries from requiring their employees to work more than sixty hours per week. The New York Court of Appeals upheld Lochner's conviction by a narrow margin, and his lawyers appealed to the US Supreme Court. Their argument was that the bakeshop statute interfered with freedom of contract and therefore offended the Fourteenth Amendment and its guarantee of due process. The Supreme Court agreed (5–4) and struck down the law, but Holmes wrote a memorable dissent that stressed the limitations on the judicial role.

This case is decided upon an economic theory which a large part of the country does not entertain. If it were a question whether I agreed with that theory, I should desire to study it further and long before making up my mind. But I do not conceive that to be my duty, because I strongly believe that my agreement or disagreement has nothing to do with the right of a majority to embody their opinions in law.

He then gave examples:

It is settled by various decisions of this court that state constitutions and state laws may regulate life in many ways which we, as legislators, might think as injudicious, or, if you like, as tyrannical.

At stake, he felt, was not only the role of the courts but of the Constitution:

Some of these laws embody convictions or prejudices which judges are likely to share. Some may not. But a constitution is not intended to embody a particular economic theory, whether of paternalism and the organic relation of the citizen to the State or of laissez faire.

To the contrary, he argued, the Constitution was

made for people of fundamentally differing views, and the accident of our finding certain opinions natural and familiar or novel and even shocking ought not to conclude our judgment upon the question whether statutes embodying them conflict with the Constitution of the United States.

Finally, he articulated what he thought should be the test for constitutionality:

---

[59] *Lochner* v. N.Y., 198 U.S. 45 (1905).

I think that the word liberty in the Fourteenth Amendment is perverted when it is held to prevent the natural outcome of a dominant opinion, unless it can be said that a rational and fair man necessarily would admit that the statute proposed would infringe fundamental principles as they have been understood by the traditions of our people and our law.[60]

This dissent, early in Holmes's Supreme Court career, gave rise to his reputation for being a progressive on the Court. He had made, it seemed, the ultimate progressive move by placing workers' rights ahead of property rights. But progressives should have read the opinion more carefully. Holmes had not endorsed workers' rights. For him, the issue was simply one of judicial restraint, and, as subsequent cases would show, judicial restraint could be a two-edged sword. He would step aside for progressive legislation, but he would sometimes do the same when the legislation in question was repressive and imposed upon those who were particularly vulnerable.

Buck v. *Bell* was such a case.[61] In *Buck*, Holmes wrote for the majority. His opinion was similar to the one in *Lochner*. The state of Virginia had passed a law providing for the involuntary sterilization of the mentally "unfit." The procedure for utilizing this law required an evidentiary hearing and an independent judgment as to whether sterilization would be in the best interest of the patient and society. According to the record in the case, the state officials had scrupulously followed all of the safeguards. The record, however, was less than truthful. Subsequent research has shown that the proceedings were a sham. Carrie Buck had not been notified; it was doubtful that she was "feeble minded" or "mentally unfit"; and her illegitimate child had been the product not of license but of a rape.[62] Not knowing this, Holmes found it an easy case – just as the Constitution allowed the state of New York to make its own decisions about the maximum hours for bakers, it permitted the state of Virginia to curtail the ability of Carrie Buck to have children.

A modern reader is struck by the fact that Holmes could not see the significant issues of personal autonomy present in the case. Is it possible that he did not understand the difference between restricting procreation, on one hand, and limiting working hours on the other? Was the right of a woman to have children really no more important than the right of a bakeshop to employ people for sixty hours per week? These questions

---

[60] *Id.* at 75–76.   [61] *Buck v. Bell*, 274 U.S. 200 (1927).

[62] *See* Paul Lombardo, *Three Generations, No Imbeciles: Eugenics, The Supreme Court, and Buck V. Bell* (2008) for a full account of the case and the underlying facts.

are salient, and it is tempting to answer them with considerations of temperament (Holmes was an intellectual and a New Englander to boot), limited personal experience (Holmes himself was childless), intellectual context (it was a time when many considered this kind of social experiment enlightened), and social context (it was also a time when few regarded the rights of women as particularly salient).

No doubt, these considerations were relevant to the outcome of the case. In fact, few judges in 1927 would have ruled differently.[63] What remains unexplained, however, is the immoderate tone in which Holmes concludes the opinion:

We have seen more than once that the public welfare may call upon the best citizens for their lives. It would be strange if it could not call upon those who already sap the strength of the State for these lesser sacrifices, often not felt to be such by those concerned, in order to prevent our being swamped with incompetence. It is better for all the world if, instead of waiting to execute degenerate offspring for crime or to let them starve for their imbecility, society can prevent those who are manifestly unfit from continuing their kind. The principle that sustains compulsory vaccination is broad enough to cover cutting the Fallopian tubes. ... Three generations of imbeciles are enough.

By modern standards, the statement "three generations of imbeciles are enough" is not just insensitive; it is cruel, almost monstrous. So too the argument seems willfully blind in its presentation of the conflicting interests at stake. Holmes showed no regard for the humanity of Carrie Buck. She was not, he thought, one of the "best citizens." She had nothing to contribute. Indeed, she could only "sap the strength of the State" and "swamp [us] with incompetence." He further disparaged her by predicting that her children would be "criminals" and "imbeciles." And finally, the casual comparison between sterilization and vaccination seemed to suggest that pregnancy for such a woman was little better than a disease. The less than judicial tone of this decision is troubling and leaves us with questions that will be addressed later in this chapter when we consider the personal and subjective aspects of Holmes's jurisprudence.

---

[63] This was a time when eugenics was thought to be a compassionate way of limiting the suffering of those who could not easily survive in contemporary circumstances. Indeed, there was only one dissent in the case and that was from a devout Catholic whose religion prohibited any form of birth control.

3 The Civil War Amendments

After the Civil War, three new amendments were added to the Constitution. The Thirteenth Amendment outlawed slavery and all forms of involuntary servitude; the Fourteenth Amendment required the states to afford due process and equal protection to individual citizens; the Fifteenth Amendment protected the voting rights of newly freed black citizens.

By the time of Holmes's appointment to the Court, the Civil War and Reconstruction were decades past. Popular opinion favored a "live and let live" attitude. As a result, the North had little interest in changing conditions in the South. This left the Supreme Court in a delicate position. As one writer explained:

> The commitments to legal equality that the Civil War amendments had made were therefore unsustained by widespread popular conviction. The Supreme Court faced the alternative of enforcing those commitments against the current of popular opinion or of constricting the scope to be given to apparent grants of equality. For some time the Supreme Court mainly chose the latter.[64]

Thus, even if the Supreme Court had insisted on active enforcement, it was unclear what this would produce. Would it produce change in the South or merely a series of unenforceable court orders?

These realities did not prevent Holmes's colleague John Harlan from keeping up a steady stream of dissenting opinions that challenged the Court's timidity. But Holmes did not join him. Indeed, some of his dissents went the other way – disagreeing with the Court when it found a claim meritorious.[65] How was it, then, that the young man who had gone to war to fight for abolition had come to the Court forty years later seemingly uninterested in the project of restoring basic freedoms for those who had been emancipated?

To address this question, I examine two important cases. The first is a majority opinion that denies relief to African American citizens in a voting rights case; the second is Holmes's dissent in a case where the majority had struck down a key element of Alabama's peonage system. Both of these opinions have been soundly criticized by others, and I have no interest in defending them as a matter of substantive justice.[66] Even so,

---

[64] Yosal Rogat, *Mr. Justice Holmes: A Dissenting Opinion*, 15 Stan. L. Rev. 254 (1962) at 254.

[65] *Id.* at 255.

[66] *Id.* This is the second half of Rogat's major work criticizing Holmes's jurisprudence. It is devoted almost entirely to criticism of Holmes's record on civil rights.

I think it is useful to understand Holmes's treatment of these cases and the way in which he integrated them into his more general views on law and jurisprudence.

It is important to begin by noting that Holmes's notion of judicial restraint did not prevent him from striking down statutes that infringed on civil rights. For example, in *Nixon* v. *Herndon*, he wrote for the majority of the Court in striking down a Texas statute that prohibited "negroes" from voting in Democratic primaries.[67] This was an easy case, however, involving a statute that discriminated on its face. Holmes did not find other cases quite so easy. Like the court he sat on, he found many reasons to rule against African American plaintiffs.[68]

In *Giles* v. *Harris*, an African American plaintiff sued on behalf of himself and some 5,000 others who were aggrieved by Alabama's voter registration practices.[69] The basis for these practices was the Alabama State Constitution. It provided two paths for registration. The first could be used prior to January 1, 1903. It permitted registration if the applicant was a veteran, the descendant of a veteran, or a person "of good character" who "understood the duties and obligations of citizenship under a republican form of government." Anyone registered under this section would remain registered for the rest of his life. The second, for use after 1903, was more stringent; it required certain combinations of literacy tests, steady employment, and landownership. On its face, the constitutional provisions were race neutral. Nevertheless, during 1902, most whites who applied for registration were approved, while African American applicants were largely rejected. Holmes summed up the situation this way:

The white men generally are registered for good under the easy test and the black men are likely to be kept out in the future as in the past. This refusal to register the blacks was part of a general scheme to disfranchise them, to which the defendants and the State itself, according to the bill, were parties.[70]

The result of this scheme seemed like an obvious violation of the Fifteenth Amendment, but the Court was unwilling to grant relief. Holmes offered two types of reasons. The first was doctrinal. The plaintiffs, he explained, were seeking injunctive relief – an order to the local board of registration to enroll the black applicants – and this meant that

---

[67] *Nixon* v. *Herndon*, 273 U.S. 536 (1927).

[68] For an extended discussion of Holmes's record on civil rights, *see* Rogat, *supra* n. 66 at 254.

[69] *Giles* v. *Harris*, 189 U.S. 475 (1903).   [70] *Id.* at 482.

their suit was equitable in nature. As such, it ran afoul of the principle that equitable courts will not adjudicate political questions.

Holmes could have stopped there, but he was troubled. Confronted with a wholesale denial of voting rights, it hardly seemed adequate for the Court to decline enforcement because the question was political. By their very nature, voting rights are political rights, and thus a rule that put them outside the equity powers of the Court would mean that Southern states would be able to deny black voters with impunity. So Holmes recognized that the situation was extraordinary and felt obligated to go behind the formal rules to the "final considerations" that were really at play.[71] He then described the second set of reasons – what he took to be the practical problems with the requested relief.[72]

The plaintiff had characterized the state scheme as a fraud on the federal Constitution. If the Court took this as true, Holmes thought, it meant that the Court would be participating in the fraud by adding voters to the county rolls.[73] If, on the other hand, the Court tried to adjust the scheme so that it would no longer be exclusionary and fraudulent, how would the Court enforce its orders? Would a federal judge be needed at each registration board? Should a federal marshal take up a station at every polling place? At the turn of the century, these were real concerns. The Court could deal with explicit discrimination, but, when discriminatory practices were silently adopted under facially neutral rules, the state's

---

[71] "But we cannot forget that we are dealing with a new and extraordinary situation, and we are unwilling to stop short of the final considerations which seem to us to dispose of the case." *Id.* at 486.

[72] Rogat reads this opinion differently than I do. He sees Holmes offering three legal arguments for the conclusion: 1. The idea that equity cannot address political questions; 2. The problem of court participation in a fraudulent scheme; and 3. The problems of enforcement. Rogat, *supra* n. 66 at 261–263. I see one legal argument – the limitations on equity – followed by a discussion of practical circumstances that keep the Court from ruling for the plaintiff.

[73] Rogat was harshly critical of the fraud argument:

[A]t best this argument displays considerable virtuosity, at worst it shows perverse formalism. The abstract provisions were not alleged to be unconstitutional on their face but because of their *raison d'etre*. Equity was being asked to prevent the threatened deprivation of rights in order to keep the scheme from being a "fraud upon the constitution." In essence, it was said, "It's unconstitutional because we can't vote. Make it constitutional by letting us." The Court became a "party to the unlawful scheme," so to speak, only by deciding as it did. *Id.* at 262.

To the contrary, it seems to me that, if the plaintiff is added, the scheme remains fraudulent with respect to other African Americans who wished to vote.

determination to violate constitutional guarantees could far outrun the Court's willingness to insert itself into local affairs.

Holmes was not entirely happy with the decision. He noted that some newspapers had portrayed him as "a second Taney" (Taney was the justice who wrote the divisive *Dred Scott* opinion).[74] *The Colored American,* an African American newspaper, was even harsher: "Judge Oliver Wendell Holmes promptly joins the ranks of the race's enemies."[75]

In a letter to a friend, Holmes wrote:

I think the decision was inevitable, but it was one of those terrible questions over which one would lie awake if he had not strong nerves. The only way is to think only of the problem and nothing else – to be neither egotist nor altruist according to my tiresomely repeated formula.[76]

The "formula" to which Holmes referred is telling. It was part of his analysis of the meaning of life:

The joy of life is to put out one's power in some natural . . . and useful way. There is no other. And the real misery is not to do this. . . . I confess that altruistic and cynically selfish talk seem to me about equally unreal. . . . If you want to hit a bird on the wing you must have all your will in focus, you must not be thinking about yourself, and equally, you must not be thinking about your neighbor; you must be living with your eye on that bird.[77]

And so we see the personal side of Holmes's decision. The decision was a "bird on the wing," and he was "living with [his] eye on that bird." He may not have been happy with the substance of his decision, but his duty – the duty to protect the Court from giving relief that was beyond its power to enforce – had prevailed.

Nevertheless, the decision was distasteful to him, and having to write for the Court only made it harder. He was able to do it by narrowing his focus. He did not see himself as the omnipotent savior of disenfranchised black citizens. Instead, he was a judge, and like a good soldier, he did his job. He wrote the opinion assigned to him as carefully and as candidly as he could.[78] But it had cost him. He was tired:

[74] Letter to Clara Stevens (May 12, 1903), in Oliver Wendell Holmes Papers, Harvard Law School.

[75] The *Colored American* was, as the name suggests, an African American newspaper. The comment appeared in the May 2, 1903, issue.

[76] Letter to Clara Stevens, *supra* n. 74.

[77] Oliver Wendell Holmes Jr., Speech Given to Suffolk Bar Association, Boston M.A. (Mar. 7, 1900).

[78] Holmes often described himself as a "jobbist." For example, "Holmes liked to talk about his imaginary 'Society of Jobbists,' whose members turned their backs on reform and

I have just finished my work for the moment and for the first time since I have been here I have the prospect of the rest of the week to myself. I shall not as before go in search of work from other Judges. I am tired . . . and I fairly hanker after a few days of freedom to read – to <u>flower</u>, to be irresponsible.[79]

The fatigue was the price of his focus. He would not think about what might happen to black citizens if they could not vote. He would not think about the sacrifice made by so many of his comrades to bring about a different result.

Often the need to set aside feelings begins a deadening process. First, we set them aside, then we place them in a secure and private place; sometimes, after a long time, we may even cease to feel them. Thus, even though Holmes remembered his war feelings throughout his life – often, for example, mentioning important anniversaries – it is doubtful that they retained their emotional intensity.

In *Bailey* v. *Alabama*, we can see the result of this kind of numbing process.[80] *Bailey* was a peonage case: the defendant, Bailey, had signed a contract with the Riverside Company to work for a year at the rate of $12 per month. In return, Riverside had advanced him $15. Bailey worked for a little more than a month and then left. When Riverside tracked him down, the state charged him under a statute that defined the failure to perform such contracts as criminal fraud so long as there was "an intent to injure or defraud his employer." The statute further provided that:

the refusal or failure of any person, who enters into such contract, to perform such act or service . . . or refund such money . . . without just cause shall be prima facie evidence of the intent to injure his employer or landlord or defraud him.

Even though this presumption was rebuttable, a court rule limited the evidence available for this purpose. It provided that the defendant could not testify "as to his uncommunicated motives, purpose or intention."[81]

If the statute had simply criminalized the failure to perform such a contract, it would have been a peonage law that ran afoul of the Thirteenth Amendment. The question was whether these three elements:

- the statutory prohibition,
- the presumption of fraudulent intent, and

---

idealism in favor of concentrated and craftsman-like attention to the task at hand. Jobbists believed that in doing 'one's job as well as one can one achieves practical altruism'." Michael Herz, *"Do Justice!": Variations of a Thrice-Told Tale*, 82 VA. L. REV. 111, 130 (1996).

[79] Letter to Clara Stevens, *supra* n. 74.   [80] *Bailey* v. *Alabama*, 219 U.S. 219 (1911).

[81] *Id.* at 228.

- the rule that prevented the defendant from testifying as to his true intent

essentially amounted to the same thing. The majority said it was peonage. They argued as follows:

> Consider the situation of the accused under this statutory presumption. If at the outset nothing took place but the making of the contract and the receipt of the money, he could show nothing else. If there was no legal justification for his leaving his employment, he could show none. If he had not paid the debt there was nothing to be said as to that. The law of the State did not permit him to testify that he did not intend to injure or defraud. Unless he were fortunate enough to be able to command evidence of circumstances affirmatively showing good faith, he was helpless. He stood, stripped by the statute of the presumption of innocence, and exposed to conviction for fraud upon evidence only of breach of contract and failure to pay.[82]

Holmes disagreed; he was not inclined to "consider the situation of the accused." Instead, he focused on his duty to decide in accordance with the law.

Holmes's opinion in *Bailey* was colored by the fact that the case resonated with two of his most deeply felt legal convictions. The first was the idea of an objective standard. With respect to contracts, this meant understanding:

> that the making of a contract depends not on the agreement of two minds in one intention, but on the agreement of two sets of external signs – not on the parties' having *meant* the same thing but on their having *said* the same thing.[83]

Thus, the law need not plumb the internal lives of litigants.[84] Instead, decisions should be based on external facts. What does it matter that I intended to give you five cows if I signed a contract that promised ten? In interpreting a contract, it is what I said rather than what I meant that is important. There are two reasons that support this result. First, objective

---

[82] *Id.* at 236.   [83] Holmes, *supra* intro., n. 3 at 464.

[84] "How is it when you admit evidence of circumstances and read the document in the light of them? Is this trying to discover the particular intent of the individual, to get into his mind and to bend what he said to what he wanted? No one would contend that such a process should be carried very far, but, as it seems to me, we do not take a step in that direction. It is not a question of tact in drawing a line. We are after a different thing. What happens is this. . . . [W]e ask, not what this man meant, but what those words would mean in the mouth of a normal speaker of English, using them in the circumstances in which they were used, and it is to the end of answering this last question that we let in evidence as to what the circumstances were." Oliver Wendell Holmes Jr., *The Theory of Legal Interpretation*, 12 Harv. L. Rev. 417, 417 (1899).

manifestations are what is shared by the parties. And second, after-the-fact testimony about what one's internal state is invariably self-serving and not easily refuted.[85] Thus, we rely on the common understanding of the words used and the context that surrounded their use. Testimony of what someone meant or intended when he signed the contract is irrelevant.

For similar reasons, Holmes was not troubled by the rule that prevented a defendant from testifying as to his true intent. After all, the rule did not prevent the defendant from presenting any facts or circumstances that might convince the jury that fraud was unlikely. Neither was he troubled by the presumption of fraud. If the presumption had been a conclusive one, then the equivalence to peonage would be obvious. But it was not conclusive. It was only prima facie evidence of fraud. The plaintiff could rebut it by presenting "external" circumstances. And even without such evidence, it was still up to the jury to decide, and this evoked the second of Holmes's deeply felt beliefs. Jury adjudication, he felt, was no mere charade. Therefore, he argued:

[P]rima facie evidence is only evidence, and as such may be held by the jury insufficient to make out guilt. ... This being so, I take it that a fair jury would acquit, if the only evidence were a departure after eleven months' work, and if it received no color from some special well-known course of events. But the matter well may be left to a jury, because their experience as men of the world may teach them that in certain conditions it is so common for laborers to remain during a part of the season, receiving advances, and then to depart at the period of need in the hope of greater wages at a neighboring plantation, that when a laborer follows that course there is a fair inference of fact that he intended it from the beginning.[86]

In view of the context – an African American defendant and a white jury in the deep South at the turn of the nineteenth century – Holmes's faith in the reliability of juries seems entirely fanciful. But, while modern readers might think that context was the essence of the case, all of the justices believed it was irrelevant, as this passage from the majority opinion demonstrates:

We at once dismiss from consideration the fact that the plaintiff in error is a black man. While the action of a State through its officers charged with the administration of a law, fair in appearance, may be of such a character as to constitute a denial of the equal protection of the laws (*Yick Wo v. Hopkins*, 118 U.S. 356, 373), such a conclusion is here neither required nor justified. The statute, on its face, makes no racial discrimination, and the record fails to show its

---

[85] *Id.* at 420.   [86] *Bailey*, 219 U.S. at 248.

existence in fact. No question of a sectional character is presented, and we may view the legislation in the same manner as if it had been enacted in New York or in Idaho.[87]

How could the record show that there was discrimination "in fact," if the Court was prepared to ignore what would have been obvious to any observer: those who passed the statute intended to – and did – know that the statute would facilitate peonage in the state of Alabama. This was the predicament of race relations in this time and place. Southern legislatures had learned to implement white supremacy without mentioning race, and the Supreme Court was willing to overlook this form of tacit subordination. Thus Bailey had to show that the statute was defective even if, contrary to fact, it had been enacted with entirely innocent motives. Fortunately for Bailey, the majority was willing to say that he had met this burden.

SUBJECTIVE ASPECTS OF HOLMES'S JURISPRUDENCE

Judges may set out to follow the law as nearly as they can. They may be intelligent, resourceful, and persistent in this regard, but, even so, their personal characteristics will inevitably color their opinions. Neither can we understand this simply by saying, as Cardozo did, that the difference appears in close cases where there are no ready answers. A person's viewpoint is pervasive. Judges do not come to the bench "stripped down like a runner," as Justice Thomas so famously said.[88] They are fully clothed with views about the law, the role of the courts, and the accepted tools of the trade. In addition, they bring their own unique character and attitude toward life. In this section, I turn to the nonlegal aspects of Holmes's persona. He was an impressive historical figure, but he was also an ordinary man with a particular outlook on life. Thus, one cannot fully

---

[87] *Id.* at 231. *Yick Wo* held that a San Francisco ordinance that allowed the city supervisors discretion in banning the use of wooden buildings for laundries was unconstitutional as applied when "the facts shown establish an administration directed so exclusively against a particular class of persons as to warrant and require the conclusion, that, whatever may have been the intent of the ordinances as adopted, they are applied by the public authorities ... with a mind so unequal and oppressive as to amount to a practical denial by the State of that equal protection of the laws which is secured to the petitioners, as to all other persons, by the broad and benign provisions of the Fourteenth Amendment to the Constitution of the United States." *Yick Wo v. Hopkins*, 118 U.S. 356, 373 (1886).

[88] For an extended discussion of this statement and why it is misleading, see Catharine Wells, *Clarence Thomas: The Invisible Man.* 67 S. Cal. L. Rev. 117 (1993).

understand his record as a judge without examining the connection between his life story and his judicial opinions.

In pursuing this, I try to avoid the kind of armchair psychology that has sometimes been applied to Holmes. For example, in 1930, Jerome Frank, himself a legal scholar and a judge, wrote a book called *Law and the Modern Mind.*[89] In it, he decried the myth of certainty that seemed to envelop the law:

> The layman thinks that it would be possible to revise the law books, that they would become something like logarithm tables, that lawyers could, if only they would, contrive some kind of legal slide-rule for finding exact legal answers.[90]

Frank believed that this myth was false and misleading:

> The law always has been, is now, and will ever continue to be, largely vague and variable. And how could this well be otherwise? The law deals with human relations in their most complicated aspects. The whole confused, shifting helter-skelter of life parades before it – more confused than ever in our kaleidoscopic age.[91]

Why, he asked, would the legal profession maintain such a myth when even the most cursory examination of the facts revealed it to be false? To explain this, he turned to psychoanalysis.

Borrowing heavily from Freud, Frank argued that the reason for the continuing pretext of certainty was an ongoing immaturity in the legal profession.[92] The result of this, he thought, was an exaggerated need for the clarity and certainty of an authoritarian father. In this analysis, Wendell Holmes emerged as the hero. In Frank's last chapter – *Mr. Justice Oliver Wendell Holmes: The Completely Adult Jurist* – he praised Holmes's work and summarized his legacy as follows:

> He has himself abandoned, once and for all, the phantasy of a perfect consistent, legal uniformity, and has never tried to perpetuate the pretense that there is or can be one. He has put away childish longings for a father-controlled world and it is for that reason, one suspects, that he has steadfastly urged his fellows to do likewise. As a consequence, whatever clear vision of legal realities we have attained . . . is in large measure due to him.[93]

---

[89] Jerome Frank, *Law and the Modern Mind* (6th edn. 1949).   [90] *Id.* at 5.   [91] *Id.* at 6.
[92] Freud published *The Future of an Illusion* in 1927. In it, he attributed man's continuing faith in dogmatic religion to the same kind of immaturity.
[93] Frank, *supra* n. 89 at 253.

I quote Frank at length because I want to make clear that I am not attempting to follow in his footsteps. Certainly, I am not qualified; in any case, I am skeptical about the value of this kind of speculation. Instead, I merely claim that Holmes had certain individual marks of character that were present in his practical jurisprudence. He had experienced the world under particular circumstances, and in the context of a certain intellectual tradition. This led him to embrace views that are, in some sense, incomprehensible to those of us who were born into a different world. And this reflection is most important in those areas where we find ourselves not just disagreeing with him, but wondering how a civilized man could hold such views. Opinions like *Bailey* and *Buck* are troubling indeed, but while I don't wish to defend them, I think we would do well to understand why they made sense to Holmes.

One place to begin is with the intellectual framework Holmes took from his discussions with the Metaphysical Club. As a pragmatist, he believed that the only guarantee of objectivity was the use of a scientific methodology. At the same time, he recognized that, without objectivity, court rulings would be mere assertions of power. Reconciling these two things was problematic for him because Chauncey Wright had convinced him, years earlier, that moral questions were not susceptible to scientific methodology. Thus, an objective theory of law could not be based upon morality but had to rely upon an empirical study of the legal tradition. For this reason, he was reluctant to base his decisions on moral principles.

A famous exchange with Learned Hand perfectly exemplifies this point.

I remember once I was with [Holmes]; it was a Saturday when the Court was to confer.... When we got down to the Capitol, I wanted to provoke a response, so as he walked off, I said to him: "Well, sir, goodbye. Do justice!" He replied: "That is not my job. My job is to play the game according to the rules."[94]

To be sure, a judge's job was to apply the law with a kind of evenhanded fairness. This was required by his allegiance to the rule of law. Justice, however, was a different matter. Holmes thought of it as an abstract moral ideal that meant different things to different people, and he would not decide cases on the basis of an ideal whose content was so thoroughly encrypted in the eye of the beholder.

---

[94] Learned Hand, *A Personal Confession*, in *The Spirit of Liberty* 302, 306–307 (Irving Dilliard ed., 3rd edn. 1960) (quoted in Herz, *supra* n. 78).

As an alternative, Holmes was most comfortable deferring to the common law. He thought of it as a font of traditional wisdom that transcended the bounds of individual moral belief. On the Supreme Court, however, this alternative was not always available. The common law did not speak to the constitutional limits of state power. Holmes, however, had stated his test for constitutional cases in *Lochner*. He thought that a statute was constitutional

unless it can be said that a rational and fair man necessarily would admit that the statute proposed would infringe fundamental principles as they have been understood by the traditions of our people and our law.[95]

Here we see Holmes deferring to the most general principles of the "common law." These principles embrace not just the decisions of judges but the essential moral fabric of our culture. Thus, once again, Holmes would decide the case by deferring to the wisdom of the community. But the weakness of this view is apparent in Alonzo Bailey's situation. The essence of Bailey's complaint was not that the state's conduct had violated "the traditions of our people," but that the traditional norms violated *his* rights. Indeed, it was the extent of his rights that had to be determined by the Court. Philosophically, this presented a difficult question for Holmes and it is important to see why.

Remember that Holmes embraced a functional definition of a legal right. Saying that someone had a right was to predict that certain things would happen if the "right" were violated:

It starts from my definition of law ... as a statement of the circumstances in which the public force will be brought to bear upon men through the courts: that is the prophecy in general terms. Of course, the prophecy becomes more specific to define a right.[96]

This prophecy, however, did little to aid a judge in setting the boundaries between one person's rights under a state statute and another person's rights under the Constitution. Neither was there a history of precedent to rely on since the latter set of rights were relatively new – they stemmed from the passage of the Civil War Amendments in the 1860s. Each of the amendments was aimed at a well-defined harm, but, as Southern legislatures became more resourceful in obscuring their intent to violate the amendments – as they wrapped their discriminatory motives in seemingly race-neutral language – they raised questions that had no real

[95] *Lochner*, 198 U.S. at 76.   [96] Howe, *supra* ch. 4, n. 2, v. II at 212.

legal answers. Thus, Holmes was in a quandary. How far should he go in striking down statutes that had discriminatory effects but made no overt racial distinctions?

To resolve this dilemma, Holmes reverted to a rule of thumb that seemed implied in the common law tradition. It was a principle similar to the Hippocratic oath: first, do no harm. In the absence of compelling legal reasons, courts should attempt to resolve an individual case in a way that minimizes its impact on society. As sensible as this principle may seem, it is not widely held today. For example, modern torts scholars simply assume that it is desirable that legal judgments should have a widespread regulatory effect. Similarly, the idea of "public interest law" presupposes that courts have an important role in improving society. These attitudes stem from a commonly held idea that the law is a tool for social improvement – a view Holmes emphatically did not share.

There is also a fundamental generational difference between Holmes's vision of the community as a collection of like-minded, well-intentioned citizens and our own notion of the community as the established order that sometimes must be opposed. For example, we believe that those who resisted the Nazis were heroes, and that civil rights protesters and war protesters were well within that same tradition. We do not always view legislatures as "voices of the people"; we are quick to see them as the agents of special interests who are willing to abuse their power by imposing on the powerlessness of others. Indeed, ever since Linda Brown walked into an integrated school, many an idealist has gone to law school precisely for the purpose of improving the world. And, in this mind-set, Holmes's way of approaching cases like *Buck* and *Bailey* seems insensitive and immoral. But, if we want to understand the difference between Holmes and ourselves, we should try not to insist on our own moral superiority. In the light of our own experience, Holmes's notion of a community of like-minded citizens may see seem unrealistic and naïve. But, looking at it from his point of view, there were strong reasons for accepting it. The reasons were both philosophical and historical.

In understanding the philosophical reasons, it is important to remember that the pragmatists thought that the community played a central role in the acquisition of truth. Pragmatists believed that a statement or theory was true if, over a period of time, a consensus could be achieved in its favor. For example, Peirce wrote, "The opinion which is fated to be ultimately agreed to by all who investigate [scientifically] is what we mean by truth."[97] This was why the scientific method was so central to pragmatism. Science relies on experimentation and the replication of observations, leading any given community of scientists to ultimately embrace a common opinion. Holmes, like Peirce, thought that community agreement was the only kind of objectivity there could be.[98] But, for him, this also meant that there was no objective theory of morality. Centuries of argument had failed to deliver a moral theory that was anything more than individual opinion. And, in the absence of objective theory, what should a judge do? How can he decide what is right and just?

To answer this, Holmes relied on a vision of morality that was not derived from a general theory. Ordinary people living ordinary lives are confronted with common problems. As cooperating neighbors, they find shared ways of coping with the world and with each other. These patterns of human activity, Holmes thought, had moral force even if they did not derive from general laws or could not be expressed in an agreed-upon formulation of the values concerned. These norms were real and they played an important role in maximizing cooperation and minimizing disputes. Some of these norms have made their way into the common law. Others remained inarticulate. Thus, when Holmes deferred to the community, he did not think of himself as applying abstract moral principles. Rather he thought of morality as a way of life that gave rise to a shared moral sense. For him, it was this aspect of morality that had to be invoked when all else failed. This meant that absent clear legislative or constitutional instruction, he would interfere with the daily life of the community as little as possible.

---

[97] Peirce, *supra* ch. 5, n. 42. See also the longer discussion of truth in Chapter 5. Holmes had a similar view.

[98] After defining truth in terms of what he can't help believing, Holmes continues:

When I say that a thing is true, I mean that I cannot help believing it. . . . But as there are many things that I cannot help doing which the universe can, I do not venture to assume that my inabilities in the way of thought are inabilities of the universe. I therefore define the truth as the system of my limitations, and leave absolute truth for those who are better equipped." Holmes, *supra* ch. 3, n. 44 at 310.

Holmes's skepticism, however, soon turns into a pragmatic theory of truth emphasizing agreement among fellow inquirers:

[O]ur test of truth is a reference to either a present or an imagined future majority in favor of our view. If . . . the truth may be defined as the system of my (intellectual) limitations, what gives it objectivity is the fact that I find my fellow man to a greater or less extent (never wholly) subject to the same *Can't Helps.*" Holmes, *supra* intro., n. 2 at 40.

The historical reasons for Holmes's trust in the community are also clear. Before the Civil War, Holmes had seen that radicals from the North and the South had polarized their communities by repeatedly forcing divisive issues to the forefront of public debate. This produced change, but that change came at a high price. Given the importance of the slavery issue, it is not surprising that many were willing to pay it. Even Holmes had been eager to enlist. But, having seen the war, Holmes learned two things. First, there was the death and suffering the war had produced. Second, it had become obvious to him as the fight went on that Southern men would go to any lengths to protect their way of life. Even in victory, he did not believe that the subordination of the Negro race would come to an end.[99] And if the Civil War and a ten-year occupation could not do the job, it was doubtful that a few court orders would tip the balance. Given these facts, it would be natural for Holmes to think that court interference in Southern life was not likely to have a good result. From his standpoint, it would be better to trust the ability of Southern society to eventually adapt to the new realities.

One final aspect of Holmes's personal jurisprudence deserves consideration. Reading his opinions, it is easy to see that he is more attune to the operation of large-scale social forces than he is to the plight of individual litigants. A good example of this is an interchange he had with his fellow justice Charles Evans Hughes. In *McCabe* v. *Atchison, T. & S. F. Ry.*, the Oklahoma legislature had required separate but equal railroad facilities for "the white and negro races." It further provided that:

[N]othing contained in the act should be construed to prevent railway companies from hauling sleeping cars, dining or chair cars attached to their trains, to be used exclusively by either white or negro passengers, separately but not jointly.

The issue was whether a statute that permitted the railway companies to provide luxury cars for whites without mandating similar cars for African Americans violated the Equal Protection Clause. The Court did not decide. It dismissed the case because the plaintiffs had not shown harm or injury. Hughes's decision, however, went further and indicated that he and the justices who joined him believed the statute was unconstitutional.

Holmes and two others concurred in the result but not the opinion. Holmes wrote a note to Hughes, arguing that the statute imposed a "logically exact" equality because the railroads could be expected to add luxury cars for negro passengers whenever it was profitable for them

---

[99] See the discussion at the end of Chapter 2.

to do so. Further, it made no sense to him that the railroads should be forced to put on an entire car to carry a single passenger. In response, Hughes refocused the issue on the one detail Holmes had overlooked – the plight of the black passenger. It was not equality, Hughes wrote "to provid[e] sleepers for white men and forc[e] colored men to sit up all night until the railroad could make a black sleeping car pay."[100]

The truth is that Holmes often did not focus on the human dimensions of legal problems. *Buck v. Bell* is perhaps the most glaring example of this problem. Holmes was excited by the dramatic themes he saw running through the case. Science, evolution, eugenics – it was all there. But what he missed was that Carrie Buck was a person with her own life to live. From her, he demanded sacrifice without knowing much about why it was required or what it would cost her. Even in a case like *Giles*, we see a similar blindness. The court, Holmes says, cannot become a party to a fraud, but he does not stop to consider the real cost to the victims of the fraud. The Court kept its hands clean, but where did that leave Giles and the other black plaintiffs?

It is this pattern in Holmes's jurisprudence that has given rise to the idea that he became detached, bitter, and cynical as a result of the Civil War. As I have stated earlier, I believe this analysis is wrong. Holmes must be understood as a product of his New England community. Its moral tradition was inward facing rather than outward facing. The Puritans had not come to the New World as missionaries seeking to benefit others. Their purpose was to seek a deeper relationship with their God, and that was how they understood goodness. They did not credit good works for their own sake, but only as an external sign of the virtue within. Service meant service to the family, to one's neighbors, and to the wider religious community. Empathizing with strangers was not part of the moral equation.

This outlook was deeply engraved in Holmes's character. Holmes admired Emerson and, like Emerson, he sought to live a spiritual life. Indeed, he understood this intention as the highest form of virtue. But we must keep in mind the kind of life Emerson envisioned. In *Self Reliance*, he urges the reader to focus on his own destiny:

Trust thyself: every heart vibrates to that iron string. Accept the place the divine providence has found for you, the society of your contemporaries, the connection

---

[100] Merlo Pusey, *Charles Evans Hughes* v. I at 291 (1951) (quoted in Rogat, *supra* n. 66 at 260). There is a similar interchange between Holmes and Hughes in the *Bailey* opinions. Hughes directs us to look at Bailey's situation, but Holmes never does. For him, the case is not about Bailey; it is about a correct understanding of the common law.

of events. Great men have always done so, and confided themselves childlike to the genius of their age, betraying their perception that the absolutely trustworthy was seated at their heart, working through their hands, predominating in all their being.[101]

Then he specially cautions against charity and compassion:

Friend, client, child, sickness, fear, want, charity, all knock at once at thy closet door, and say, – "Come out unto us." But keep thy state; come not into their confusion. The power men possess to annoy me, I give them by a weak curiosity.[102]

Like their Puritan ancestors, both Emerson and Holmes see duty as something owed to the self and to the impersonal Universe, but not to other human beings.

Nevertheless, Holmes did not isolate himself from other people, other times, and other places. He read voraciously, but the experience of others always became moral lessons that could be applied to himself. For example, when he read the book by Fridjtof Nansen, he was interested in Nansen's exploration of the Arctic. But what he found in the book was an inward lesson – a new metaphor for his own life. He saw his study of law as embodying the same stages that Nansen identified in describing his trip to the Pole. This was not narcissism. He could be kind and compassionate to those he met. Neither was it cynicism. He eagerly pursued what he took to be the highest ideals. Rather it is emblematic of the fact that his culture had taught him to take full responsibility for his own conduct by discerning and discharging the only the duties that attached to his individual life.

The personal aspect of Holmes's jurisprudence has received considerable criticism. Sometime between our entry into World War II and our departure from Vietnam, Americans became impatient with the idea that courts should "play the game according to the rules," rather than do justice. Even if we never discover an ultimate theory of justice, most of us believe that we recognize injustice when we see it. The Nazi genocides, the white supremacy of the Jim Crow South, and the flaming napalm dropped on small Vietnam villages filled many of us with a sense of horror. Surely, we felt, the legal system could and should address these atrocities. But the history of law teaches us that law is not a simple thing. Its legitimacy depends on a complex

---

[101] Ralph Waldo Emerson, *Self-Reliance* 53–54 (1841).   [102] *Id.*

relationship between it and the people it governs. Thus, in the final section of this chapter, I try to put Holmes's legacy in perspective.

THE HOLMESIAN LEGACY

There has been so much controversy over Holmes's contribution to American law that it is hard to have a fresh outlook. But, without stopping to dispute any contrary evaluations, I offer my own. I think that there are three important aspects of Holmes's legacy.

First, he was exemplary when it came to integrity and independence. Of course, there was never a hint of impropriety in the discharge of his public duties. But, more importantly, he let nothing interfere with his honest assessment of the merits of a case. He decided *Vegelahn* in favor of labor, even though he knew that the decision would displease many in his social circle. He decided *Northern Securities* against the government even though he knew it would infuriate President Roosevelt. And finally, he decided *Giles* against the disenfranchised black citizens even though it made him so uneasy that he lost sleep. Whether we agree with these decisions or not, we should admire his determination to decide each case without any type of bias. In this respect, I think he is a good model for contemporary judges, some of whom seem to lose their struggle with the temptations of career advancement and partisanship.

A second aspect of Holmes's legacy is the insight he brought to common law decision-making. Formalism and realism have long been the Scylla and Charybdis of American law. On one shore, the formalists insist that law must be separated from human affairs. They portray law as a form of logic that can be used to calculate the results in individual cases. On the other shore, the realists recognize law's inevitable connection to human life, and argue that this connection makes law indeterminate. A good judge, they argue, is one who makes wise policy decisions. Holmes's study of the common law suggested a middle ground for this dilemma. He agreed with the realist that law is not logic, and that it is shaped by human affairs. On the other hand, he did not agree that this makes law indeterminate. As we saw in *Lamson and Vegelahn*, a commitment to follow precedent is consistent with the idea that law represents practical policy rather than a logical calculus. Holmes teaches us to think of judging as part of an ongoing process that operates under a set of internalized norms. It is a process that combines the need for practical outcomes with a desire for consistency. In this view, the concepts of formalism and realism emerge as metaphors that highlight certain aspects of this process, but cannot be literally applied as methods for decision-making.

The third aspect of Holmes's legacy is his reluctance to embrace a full-throated conception of justice. While I understand the rationale of this position, I think it has certain weaknesses. The conflicts of the twentieth century have taught us the importance of justice as an inspirational ideal, and our increasingly diverse community has suggested the need for a broader empathy. But Holmes never encountered these lessons, and, given his character, it is unlikely that they could have been easily assimilated. This kept him from recognizing that there are times when the Supreme Court must lead rather than follow, or that it must resolve urgent issues that the other branches of government cannot or will not address. Nevertheless, Holmes is a helpful reminder that such leadership is not the main function of the courts.

Holmes was probably the most successful judge in American history. By the end of his lifetime, it was generally agreed that he had been a great judge. Such a consensus will not occur for those now on the Court. Public opinion is currently polarized. For liberals, four of the justices are good, four are bad, and one is regarded as occasionally correct. Conservative views are diametrically opposed: the "good" judges are bad, the "bad" judges are good, and the remaining judge is unreliable. Thus, the public has come to understand "good" judging in terms of political ideology. This is a tragedy. The power of the Supreme Court lies in the respect it commands, and it cannot command respect if it is simply one more place for partisan bickering. Already we hear politicians talking about disregarding Court decisions. With ten more years of ideological struggle, how much legitimacy will the Court retain? And, if we doubt that this is important, we should not forget that it was a Supreme Court decision (*Dred Scott*) that started us on the road to the Civil War.

Holmes reminds us that there are alternatives. The Court has not always functioned well, but there have been times when it performed its duties without bitter controversy. During such times, the public has had faith that the justices are acting impartially, that they are following the rule of law. While it is well to be skeptical – and Holmes certainly was – about the separation of law and politics, we should not conclude that legal decision-making is nothing but politics. Good judging, he taught, was both a matter of integrity and a mature understanding of the legal process. And this may be the most important part of his legacy.

Epilogue

The Consummation

*The consummation ... comes when he applies this knowledge to himself.
[When] he has learned that he cannot set himself over against the universe as
a rival god, to criticize it, or to shake his fist at the skies, but that his meaning
is its meaning, his only worth is as a part of it, as a humble instrument of the
universal power.*

Commencement Speech, Brown University

In the spring of 1929, Fanny and Wendell Holmes had been married for
more than fifty years. The marriage had its challenges, but it was a happy
one.[1] They had been friends since childhood, and they found each other
compatible despite the fact that they were different in many ways. Wendell
was self-confident and charming. He could be the life of any party. Fanny,
on the other hand, was shy and reclusive. Even at home, Fanny and Wendell
had different interests. Wendell pursued a life of the mind, while Fanny was
creative and artistic. In her younger years, she spent much of her time doing
needlework, creating colorful depictions of nature that were so extraordinary they were shown in museums in both Boston and New York.[2]

---

[1] *See generally* Baker, *supra* ch. 1, n. 5 at 218–230.

[2] Reviews of this work suggest its brilliance. For example:

> This is probably the most remarkable needlework ever done. It stands quite alone, and
> there is nothing in the least like it with which to compare it. Mrs. Holmes ... is an artist; but
> instead of using paints and canvas, she makes her pictures with silks and satin. *Boston
> Daily Advertiser* 2, c 3 (April 19, 1880). (quoted in Howe, *supra* ch. 6, n. 1 at 254)

> *See also* Christine W. Laidlaw, *Painting with Silken Threads: Fanny Dixwell Holmes
> and Japanism in Nineteenth-Century Boston*, 10 *Studies in the Decorative Arts* 42–68
> (2003).

On April 29, Fanny died at the age of eighty-nine. When she died, Wendell wrote to his friend Sir Frederick Pollack:

For sixty years she made life poetry for me and at 88 one must be ready for the end. I shall keep at work and interested while it lasts – though not caring much for how long.[3]

As Holmes's letter indicates, Fanny's death brought him thoughts of his own mortality. For her funeral, he chose a sonnet by Spanish poet John Blanco that expressed a somewhat hopeful message about the nature of death.

> MYSTERIOUS Night! when our first parent knew
> Thee from report divine, and heard thy name,
> Did he not tremble for this lovely frame?
> This glorious canopy of light and blue?
> Yet 'neath a curtain of translucent dew,
> Bathed in the rays of the great setting flame,
> Hesperus with the host of heaven came,
> And lo! Creation widened in man's view.
>
> Who could have thought such darkness lay concealed
> Within thy beams, O sun! or who could find,
> Whilst fly and leaf and insect stood revealed,
> That to such countless orbs thou mad'st us blind!
> Why do we then shun death with anxious strife?
> If Light can thus deceive, wherefore not Life?[4]

Without Fanny, Wendell's life continued on as before. He was active on the Court. His clerks took Fanny's place reading to him in the evening or going on afternoon drives. He made frequent trips to her grave. He would bring a single flower – a rose or a poppy – and then would stand for a time, perhaps feeling her presence.[5]

On his ninetieth birthday, his friends arranged a special celebration that was broadcast on the CBS radio network. There were flattering and congratulatory speeches from the Chief Justice, the dean of Yale Law School, and the president of the American Bar Association. Holmes replied to their good wishes from a radio hook-up in his Washington home. While he said it was "too intimate a task to describe his feelings as the end draws near," his brief comment actually said a great deal about his state of mind:

[3] Howe, *supra* ch. 4, n. 2, v. I at 243(May 24, 1929).
[4] Joseph Blanco, *Night and Death* (1828).
[5] *Evening Star* 1 (Washington, DC, Mar. 6, 1935).

The riders in the race do not stop short when they reach the goal. There is a little finishing canter before coming to a standstill. There is time to hear the kind voice of friends and to say to oneself that the work is done. But just as one says that, the answer comes: The race is over, but the work never is done while the power to work remains.

He had always said he would not retire until he felt himself unable to discharge his duties. Eventually that time came. In the summer of 1932, he began to experience difficulty writing. In the fall, he returned to the Court, but it was apparent that he did not have his customary acuity. On January 11, 1933, the Chief Justice paid Holmes a visit at his home and told him it was time to resign. Holmes did not argue; he was not defensive. He wrote out his resignation.[6]

After retirement, there were few changes in his life. He no longer went to the Court, but he kept to his daily schedule, rising at 8:00 AM, breakfast at 8:45 AM, a late supper, and in bed by 10:30 PM. He went out most days for a walk or a ride in a hired car. He spent much of his time reading, and made regular trips to the Congressional Library.[7] He still spent summers in Beverly Farms, where he regularly visited one of his few remaining friends, the man who tended the grade at Pride's Crossing.[8] For the first time in his life, he could do whatever he wanted.

One night, his sister-in-law called to check on him. After the call, she made a note. At the top, it said, "What Wendell said to me 9/6/33," and below she wrote in the shaky hand of a woman in her nineties:

My work is over
    I have no duties or responsibilities and my life is idleness and its confoundedly pleasant
    I really mean it – I enjoy it immensely[9]

Many people who work hard all their lives are impatient and frustrated when they retire. It seems, however, that Holmes was "content with silence."[10]

Six months later Holmes died. He went out for a drive one morning and caught a cold that did not go away. The doctors diagnosed bronchial pneumonia. He remained unpersuaded, making light of the medical measures they had ordered. Nevertheless, those with whom he was closest gathered at his bedside: his nephew, Edward Holmes; his friend and

---

[6] *Id.*   [7] *Id.*   [8] *Id.* at 5.
[9] Handwritten note in Dixwell folder at the Massachusetts Historical Society.
[10] Oliver Wendell Holmes Jr., The Soldier's Faith, an Address Delivered on Memorial Day at a Meeting Called by the Graduating Class of Harvard (May 30, 1895).

executor, George Palfrey; Felix Frankfurter and a number of his former secretaries. He seemed in good spirits. When the doctor insisted upon the installation of an oxygen apparatus, he called it "a lot of damn foolery." He thumbed his nose at one of his former secretaries. Finally, he lapsed into a coma.[11] His doctor said, "It was the most peaceful death I ever saw. Just dropped off into a sleep from which there was no rousing."[12] At 2:00 AM on March 6, Holmes died. Mark DeWolfe Howe made the announcement to the press assembled on the street.

The funeral was held on March 8, 1935, Holmes's ninety-fourth birthday. The church was packed. All of official Washington was there. The minster offered Holmes's own words written many years earlier for the funeral of a fellow judge:

We accept our destiny to work, to fight, to die, for ideal aims. At the grave of a hero who has done these things, we end, not with sorrow at the inevitable loss, but with the contagion of his courage; and with a kind of desperate joy, we go back to the fight![13]

Then the minister read the poem that Wendell had chosen for his wife's funeral. The body was then taken to Arlington National Cemetery for a soldier's burial.

In the end, the man who counseled us not to shake our fist at the Universe did not shake his own at old age and death. When all was said and done, he had realized his ambition to lead a life that was "secretly beautiful."[14] Chief Justice Charles Evans Hughes said it best:

The most beautiful and the rarest thing in the world is a complete human life, unmarred, unified by intelligent purpose and uninterrupted accomplishment, blessed by great talent employed in the worthiest activities, with a deserving fame never dimmed and always growing. Such a rarely beautiful life is that of Mr. Justice Holmes.[15]

---

[11] *Evening Star* 5 (Washington, DC, Mar. 6, 1935).   [12] *Id.* at 1.
[13] *Evening Star* 1 (Washington, DC, Mar. 8, 1935).
[14] The phrase comes from Emerson, *The Young American. See supra* intro., n. 1.
[15] *Obituary, New York Times* (Mar. 6, 1935).

Index